D0893603

BRITAIN IN THE MIDDLE AGES

BRITAIN IN
THE MIDDLE AGES

An Archaeological History

FRANCIS PRYOR

HarperPress
An Imprint of HarperCollinsPublishers

HarperCollins*Publishers*
77–85 Fulham Palace Road,
Hammersmith, London w6 8jb
www.harpercollins.co.uk

Published by HarperCollins*Publishers* 2006

1

A catalogue record for this book is
available from the British Library

ISBN-13 978-0-00-720361-1
ISBN-10 0-00-720361-6

Diagrams by Rex Nicholls

Set in PostScript Linotype Minion with
Photina display by
Rowland Phototypesetting Limited,
Bury St Edmunds, Suffolk

Printed and bound in Great Britain
by Clays Limited, St Ives plc

This book is dedicated to the memory of
DR CHRIS SALISBURY
friend, doctor and archaeologist

CONTENTS

PLATES

Unless otherwise stated, all photographs are © Francis Pryor

Offa's Dyke in Shropshire, built by the Mercian King Offa (757–96) as a
    military defence against the Welsh kingdom of Powys
Part of the Yarnton (Oxfordshire) Anglo-Saxon settlement as it might
    have appeared in the eighth century A D. Painting by Peter Lorimer.
    (© *Oxford Archaeology*)
The magnificent pre-Norman, Saxon tower of All Saints' Church, Earls
    Barton, Northamptonshire
All Saints' Church, Brixworth, Northamptonshire
Three Viking period hogback tombs at St Thomas's Church, Brompton,
    North Yorkshire
Tenth-century carving at St Andrew's Church, Middleton, North
    Yorkshire
The original south-west door of the Church of St Helen, Stillingfleet,
    a few miles south of York
Clifford's Tower, York
Two late-medieval buildings at 28–32 Coppergate, York
Donington-le-Heath Manor House, near Coalville, Leicestershire
Stokesay Castle, Shropshire
Grace Dieu Priory, Leicestershire
Fountains Abbey, North Yorkshire, from the south-west
Fountains Abbey: a view south along the ground floor of the west range
Fountains Abbey: Mill and Abbey Granary

Triangular bridge, Crowland, Lincolnshire
Croyland Abbey's church, St Guthlac's
The ruins of St Guthlac's Church, Crowland
The first of a series of three medieval bridges across the River Trent
    discovered by the late Dr Chris Salisbury in a large gravel pit at

TEXT ILLUSTRATIONS AND MAPS

ACKNOWLEDGEMENTS

I owe a number of specific thanks: to Dr Sam Lucy of Cambridge who helped me come to terms with aspects of Old English spelling and grammar; to Gill Hey for help over her excavations at Yarnton; to David Hall for useful thoughts on Open Field systems; to Professor Mick Aston for information on Shapwick; and to Tom Williamson for his views on Midland and East Anglian landscapes. My wife Maisie Taylor helped me research a number of useful topics to do with medieval woodworking and town life. The excellent illustrations are by Rex Nicholls. As with my other books for HarperCollins I owe special thanks to my publisher, Richard Johnson, my editor, Robert Lacey, and my designer, Vera Brice.

DATES AND PERIODS

Archaeological Period*	Dates (AD)	Defining or transitional events	Notes
Roman	43–410	Withdrawal of last Roman troops from Britain c.409	
'Sub-Roman' or Post-Roman	410–50		This is sometimes included in the Early Saxon period
'Early Medieval'	c. 410–1066		A term generally used to describe pre-Norman times
Early Saxon	450–650		Previously known as Pagan Saxon
Middle Saxon	650–850		
Late Saxon	850–1066	Norman Conquest (Battle of Hastings 1066)	
'Saxo-Norman'	850–1150		A general descriptive term
Middle Ages (or 'Later Medieval')	1066–1550		These may be subdivided thus:
Early Middle Ages	1066–1350	1348–49 first wave of Black Death	

* Terms placed in quotes are used in a general sense. They are not archaeological periods *sensu stricto*.

Archaeological Period	Dates (AD)	Defining or transitional events	Notes
Later Middle Ages	1350–1550	Dissolution of the monasteries 1536–40. The Reformation (Church of England legally established 1559)	Sometimes referred to as the 'Transitional Period'
Post-Medieval	1550–present		

Introduction

Archaeology and the Medieval Period

I found the archaeological exploration involved in the writing of my previous book, *Britain AD*, so fascinating that I decided I had to carry the story forward in time. By comparison with *Britain AD*, I have fewer axes to grind in this book. This is probably because hypothetical mass-migration and invasion are not contentious issues after the three centuries that followed the Roman withdrawal of AD 410.

In this book I want to take an archaeological look at medieval Britain. The word 'medieval' can be taken to mean many things. Here I will use it as a chronological label, which for present purposes begins around AD 650, the end of the period known to archaeologists as the Early Saxon. The finish date is harder to pin down, and later we will see that there are good reasons for this, but here I will follow most archaeological opinion by selecting the mid-sixteenth century, say 1550, and the death of Henry VIII (1547).

This is not a textbook, nor is it a book of social or political history.[1] If you are looking for an authoritative account of the Tudors, the Plantagenets or the Peasants' Revolt, then this is not it. This will be what used to be called a 'narrative history' – except that there is more here about archaeology than about history. I have made greater efforts to explain fields and hedges, waterfronts and trade than the achievements of individual rulers. Another way of describing a narrative account is to see it as a diary or journal of the author's own exploration of a particular subject. That, I think, is closer to what I have attempted to do.

Being a prehistorian of the Neolithic, Bronze and Iron Ages, I am most familiar with the sites and objects of the last four millennia BC, as revealed by excavation. This experience gives me an unusual perspective on medieval times. As we will see shortly, I tend to view the past in the long term. I am more concerned with the processes of social and political change than with a detailed chronicle of the events that marked the progress of those changes. To use a phrase that is currently popular, this book is an attempt to write a sort of 'joined up' archaeology, where the changes seen in the ground can be related to their causes in the ancient world. This approach is perhaps easier for historians, who are good at identifying key events, their causes and consequences. Archaeologists, on the other hand, have found that the techniques available to them make the identification of historical events a problem.

One example will suffice. We know for a fact that Boudica, the rebellious Queen of the Iceni, nearly threw the occupying Roman troops out of Britain during her uprising in AD 60 and 61. In the course of that revolt her forces set fire to parts of towns in eastern England. Accordingly, when archaeologists working in that region find evidence for burning around the middle of the first century AD, they often attribute it to the Boudican revolt. In that way the 'evidence' for large-scale destruction is increasing every year. But in antiquity, just as today, fires are not always started deliberately. Very often they happen by accident, and the archaeologist is presented with the near-impossible task of differentiating between Boudica and, say, the results of a bakery fire. To make matters worse, nowadays the press are always on the prowl for news stories, and fresh evidence for the heroic warrior queen's prowess always makes excellent copy.

This inability to tie down specific historical events has led archaeologists to turn their attention to the longer-term processes that lay behind the development of society in various parts of the world. Today the profession is branching out. There is a proliferation of fresh approaches to the past. Some, the so-called culture-historicists, stay with historical reconstruction. Others (processualists) prefer to work with problems to do with social process; their way of working is heavily influenced by anthropology. But there are many other ways of 'doing' archaeology today, ranging from Marxist to cognitive to neo-structuralists and various strands of post-processualists, who take their ultimate inspiration from post-modern philosophers such as Derrida.[2] Some of their ideas, deconstruction for example, have proved very useful. I believe this diversity of approach gives our discipline strength and resilience. My own approach is a hybrid of at least three of these methods – I think.

The colourfully misnamed Dark Ages mark a return of sorts to prehistory, so far as the archaeologist is concerned. During the half century or so of post-Roman times and the subsequent Early Saxon Period (AD 450–650), reliable written documents are rare, and provide us with far less information than the abundance of new archaeological discoveries, whose sheer quantity today is almost overwhelming. Whether or not you accept the argument of *Britain AD*, that the indigenous population of Britain did not fall victim to Anglo-Saxon 'ethnic cleansing', as the distinguished historian David Starkey suggested in the first episode of his television series *Monarchy* (2004), it is hard to deny that archaeology is revealing a huge amount about Dark Age Britain. But what about the subsequent periods: does archaeology have a role to play in times when documentary evidence becomes more abundant?

There was a rapid increase, indeed 'explosion' would scarcely be an exaggeration, of written documentary sources in the mid-thirteenth century. These documents are mainly about day-to-day transactions, to do with trade, dwellings and land tenure. They are of enormous importance to the study of the way people lived their lives, in both town and country. But do they allow us to paint a full picture of life in the Middle Ages? The archaeologist Paul Stamper thinks not: 'traditionally, few historians exhibited any interest whatsoever in material culture, whether it be the layout of a village's fields, the design of its houses, or the range of their contents. That was especially so with regard to peasant society, which was assumed to be (in every sense) rude, crude and unworthy of scholarly investigation.' He then explains that most historical records are 'terse, factual memoranda'. They throw little light on how or why certain things took place. 'Archaeology's ultimate access to a much larger dataset, and to one with a degree of detail denied to the historian, makes the investigation of explanation far more feasible.'[3]

It is generally believed that day-to-day documents, such as deeds or records arising from other transactions, are by their very nature reliable; but as a farmer who has to deal with the welter of impossibly long forms and other bureaucratic nonsense that has recently sprung up, I have my doubts: this modern documentation can tell a cautionary tale that is relevant to history. Recently the government told farmers that it was illegal to bury dead animals. In future, they announced, all fallen stock was to be disposed of by licensed operators, who would burn the carcasses. This procedure would be accompanied by appropriate and abundant paperwork. But typically of what so often happens today, no practical provision was made for the collection of carcasses. Licensed operators were hard to find, or were miles away. Like other farmers, I tried to follow the new law, but became disgusted by the stench of rotting flesh as a dead animal decomposed for a week in the June heat while it waited for collection. So I buried it. And I may even have buried a few more. The point is that for several months most farmers did what I did – since there was no other option. But my farm paperwork gives no hint that this was happening, because I have no wish to incriminate myself. However, in a hundred years' time an archaeologist digging in my wood could tell from the ear tags on the dead animals that I was breaking the letter of the law. So the documents would say one thing and the archaeology another. And I know which one I would trust.

I do not want to become embroiled in an unconstructive argument between archaeologists and historians, because I believe their two subjects are slowly becoming closer. But wherever possible I will try to make use of those comparatively rare individuals, such as Colin Platt, Tom Williamson, Paul Stamper and Chris Dyer, who seem equally at home in both worlds. I also like the work of historians with a breadth of vision, able to deal effortlessly with great expanses of time and space. For me Jacques Le Goff is just such a historian, and his recent book *The Birth of Europe* has helped me see the wood through the medieval trees.[4] It is also perhaps worth noting that certain historians still seem to be oblivious – sometimes even comfortably oblivious – to the existence of archaeology. I console myself with the thought that as time passes they will have to change.

I have spent over thirty years excavating sites of the last five millennia BC and the first millennium AD, mostly in eastern England. In the course of this work I have taken a long view of the past. This extended perspective partly reflects the imprecision of current dating methods – for example, radiocarbon dates are often accurate only to two or three centuries – but it also results from theoretical approaches that have been adopted by prehistorians since the 1960s. In the last four decades of the twentieth century prehistorians became less interested in one-off events and turned their attention to the gradually evolving processes of social change.

There was also a move away from a straightforward, or functionalist, view of the past. This new approach laid greater emphasis on the roles of symbolism, ritual and structure within the processes of change. Other post-modern approaches have been highly influential. Archaeological evidence, for example, lends itself readily to deconstruction. The result has been a long-term or strategic overview of the past which non-specialists find appealing, because it is often relevant to current issues, such as the development of political authority or the role of religion within society. I think these are positive trends, because archaeology must be relevant to modern life, or it will not survive for long.

It would perhaps be useful if at this stage I gave an indication of my long-term view of the human past. I will take an essentially British perspective. The story begins with Prehistory, which can be subdivided into three: Early Prehistory, being everything from the arrival of the first humans about half a million years ago until the appearance of *Homo sapiens*, around 40,000 years ago; Middle Prehistory ends with the introduction of farming about 5000 BC, or slightly earlier; Late Prehistory extends through the Neolithic and most of the Bronze Age, until the early first millennium BC, after which we are in the Iron Age and the next of my three main periods, Antiquity.

In Britain and France, Early Antiquity ends with the arrival of the Roman Empire, but in north-western Europe outside the Roman Empire there is a seamless transition into Middle Antiquity in the early centuries AD. Late Antiquity starts in the latter part of the Roman period and ends sometime around 600–650, when major social, economic and political changes begin to happen.

The last of my three eras is the Modern Period. Its Early phase starts in Britain around AD 650 with the start of the Middle Saxon period. This was a time of rapidly growing trade networks and the emergence of the first early medieval European states. Soon we have the establishment of the first true post-Roman towns. It ends around 1350 with the Black Death (1348). The Middle Modern or 'Transitional' Period ends around 1550, the date that most archaeologists regard as the close of the Middle Ages; this book will be about the Early and Middle Modern periods, as defined here. The Late Modern Period starts around 1550 and extends until the present. I should also add here that I regard currently fashionable attempts to define a new 'post-industrial' era as being premature. We are far too close in time to view our culture with any clarity at all. Maybe historians in a hundred years' time will have acquired suitable perspective. Maybe.

Period	Start Date	Events
Early Prehistory	500,000 years ago	Humans in north-western Europe
Middle Prehistory	40,000 years ago	First *Homo sapiens*
Late Prehistory	5000 BC	Farming introduced
Early Antiquity	750 BC	Iron and the Iron Age
Middle Antiquity	100 BC	The Roman Empire
Late Antiquity	AD 300	Post-Roman times
Early Modern	AD 600–50	Carolingian Empire Arab Empire. Early Middle Ages
Middle Modern (or 'Transitional Period')	AD 1350	Black Death, Later Middle Ages, Reformation
Late Modern	AD 1550–present	Industrial/agricultural 'revolutions' etc.

I described how I would divide up my 'long view' of the human past because it provides at least partial justification for why I do not regard the Middle Ages as being 'Middle' at all. The term was first used in the Renaissance to describe the period between the Classical world and that of the Renaissance. This was a perspective which viewed that Classical world through modern eyes. That way of looking at the past has little or nothing to do with hard historical or archaeological reality. It has more to do with value judgements about art, literature and knowledge than the development of human culture or society.

Historians generally end the Middle Ages with the Battle of Bosworth (1485), whereas archaeologists, who, Paul Stamper believes, are more attuned to the material world, tend to continue it for another half-century, into the 1540s and the Dissolution of the Monasteries by Henry VIII. Again, some historians and many lay people see the Middle Ages as starting with the Norman Conquest, but I want to extend them back in time to include the earliest kingdoms of Saxon England and the Scandinavian (Viking) presence. I also want to bridge the gap between the world of written history and that historical (but not archaeological) twilight zone the Dark Ages, which had certainly come to an end by AD 650. The Synod of Whitby, which sorted out the direction the Church in Britain would take for the next millennium, took place in 664. It also makes little sense to ignore the early-tenth-century survey and reapportionment of the countryside – one of medieval archaeology's most important contributions to the study of the period. This great survey, which happened in the decades after 900, provided the essential framework for subsequent developments.

The term 'Middle Ages' suggests a time between two other ages which were marked by major social and cultural advances. Being betwixt and between, the Middle Ages are often portrayed as a period when nothing much happened. As I researched this book I realised that this is very far from the truth. I am in no doubt that the centuries of the Middle Ages were the time when the modern world was actually conceived and started the process of development, at first slowly, but latterly with gathering pace. This was when Britain moved from the realms of Late Antiquity into a more familiar world: roads and parishes became fixed; institutions such as the Church and local government came into being and industry became truly industrial, with manufacturing starting to be organised on a national basis. Midway through the period international trade had become routine.

For too long the Middle Ages have been portrayed as a period of slow progress, characterised by feudalism and superstition. Certainly that was the impression I gained at school. Industry was seen as small in scale, farming was held back by the manorial system, and life in town was hidebound by guilds and, of course, the repressive power of the Church. More recently, archaeology has shown that the Middle Ages were far from static. The Church did not exert a dead hand. There was real progress, which happened remarkably swiftly. The latest archaeological evidence shows beyond any doubt that Britain was an integrated part of Europe in the four centuries before the Norman Conquest. This has been a major revelation that I will discuss at some length in the first three chapters of this book. It seems now that the Reformation and the Renaissance were natural processes that had to happen if the progress made in the medieval period was to continue.

I am not alone in bemoaning some current perspectives on the Middle Ages which see the period as somehow irrelevant to the modern world because (it is said) very little actually changed. This view has it that the developments that were to lead to the modern world took place during and after the Renaissance. As I hope this book will show, nothing could be further from the truth. However, despite those reasons to the contrary, I shall continue to use the term 'Middle Ages', because it's a label that has stuck, and besides, my term 'Middle Modern' has too many 'M's and is confusingly similar to the one it tries to replace.

I have mentioned some of the theoretical differences between archaeology and history, but now I want to address a practical issue arising from these contrasts. It concerns the organisation and layout of this book. While our knowledge of the documentary sources relating to Britain before the Norman Conquest remains essentially static, new archaeological discoveries are having a very profound effect on our understanding of the Middle and Late Saxon periods.

The four centuries prior to 1050 are known as the Middle (650–850) and Late (850–1066) Saxon periods, which I will sometimes lump together in the deliberately vague 'Later Saxon'. The term 'Saxo-Norman' is also sometimes used to describe the overlap between Late

Saxon and early Norman in the mid-to-late eleventh century. As I have already suggested, it is now appreciated that the first four hundred years of the medieval period were fundamental to the development of British society in the Middle Ages. It was the time when Britain acquired its county system and its basic administrative geography. It was the time, too, when English became the accepted language in the most populated areas. It was, of course, also the period of the Vikings, who we must now see as far more than the rapists and pillagers in horned helmets beloved of movie-makers. For me the story of Later Saxon and Saxo-Norman Britain is as exciting as archaeology gets, because it is currently going through a period of major reappraisal. Turmoil might be a better term. Nothing seems beyond dispute, whether it be the role of the Vikings or Britain's place within Charlemagne's Europe. The more we understand about Viking Britain and the earliest England, the more we realise that their inhabitants did not dwell in Little Britain. They were part of a far larger world.

These are the reasons why I have decided that this book will depart from the usual convention of dismissing Saxon Britain in a chapter, before devoting the rest of the text to the high Middle Ages. Instead I have divided the medieval period into two Parts (I and II) of four and five centuries each. Part I will mainly be about Britons, Scots, Saxons and Vikings; Part II will be about aspects of town and country in the Middle Ages which are separated from the Saxon period by the Norman Conquest of 1066. I have attempted to be fair in the way I have apportioned chapters. But when it came to writing the book I was forcibly struck by the fact that there was far more interesting new material emerging about the pre-Norman, or Saxon, periods than about the Middle Ages. Furthermore, as much of this new work is taking place in southern Britain the book will, I am sorry to say, be biased towards the south and east in its geographical coverage. I regret this, but as I shall reiterate from time to time, this is not a textbook. I want it to reflect the way ideas are changing. The new information about Later Saxon England is having a profound effect on the way we view what happened later. So it cannot be ignored. As a result, the first four chapters are slightly longer than the following four.

While I was writing I became increasingly aware that the archaeology of buildings was a major new field in its own right. Today it involves detailed drawings, but also techniques of remote sensing that range from digital photography to enhanced forms of computer-aided design. I would very much have liked to discuss this in the pages that follow, and I must confess that I tried to put something on paper, but sadly none of it worked. I simply lacked the necessary hands-on experience to write with any conviction. So rather than fake it, I decided to leave it out.

Another important development has been the study of medieval woodworking and carpentry. I was introduced to this subject by my wife Maisie Taylor, who had begun to research the development of Bronze Age carpentry joints we encountered at Flag Fen. So she invited the leading expert on medieval carpentry, Cecil Hewitt, to come and see them. At the time he was recovering from a stroke, but even with slightly impaired speech he managed to give us one of the most exciting and rewarding days of our professional lives. Cecil's excitement knew no limits, and was instantly transferred to both of us. The great man made us both look at our Bronze Age timbers through fresh eyes. What I didn't know then was that Hewitt's work was just one aspect of a rapidly growing new field of study which I will briefly touch on in Chapter 7.

I acquired an enormous respect for medieval archaeologists when I was a student in the mid-1960s. In fact I nearly forsook the True Path of prehistory to follow them. One of my teachers at Cambridge was Brian Hope-Taylor, who today is rightly regarded as an extraordinarily innovative pioneer. We all liked Brian. He was down to earth and never gave himself airs or graces. He was also a perfectionist, and refused to compromise on quality. His reports were beautifully illustrated, because earlier in his life he had been a professional artist and illustrator. He was particularly famous for the cover he had drawn for the Ordnance Survey *Map of Britain in the Iron Age* (sadly out of print).

While I was a student Brian was in the final throes of writing his most famous work, a huge report on his excavations at Yeavering, in Northumberland. Yeavering, or Ad Gefrin, to give it its Saxon name, was an Anglo-British palace complex beside a major pre-Roman hillfort, known as Yeavering Bell. The area was also stiff with prehistoric remains, which was why I was sitting at Brian's feet. I had no intention of staying for more than the first lecture of his course, because then he would start on the post-Roman material. In the event I attended the entire course, and I even bought his great report shortly after it appeared in print in 1977, for the then huge sum of £33.[5] It is still one of the most treasured books in my library. At the time Brian was one of a small group of medieval archaeologists who believed in 'open area' excavation. This was a new style of excavation that has now become commonplace: it involves the exposing of huge areas of land to get a clear impression of the totality of a site.

Brian didn't just expose single buildings. Instead he looked at the spaces between and around the various structures, and in the process was able to build up a picture of a developing royal centre. His excavations took place over several seasons, mainly between 1953 and 1962, and seemed to touch on all aspects of life, from graves to humble dwellings, halls both great and small, and even a huge timber grand-stand-like theatre. This was a vision of the seventh century AD that I desperately wanted to paint for earlier periods. It was quite simply inspiring, and it fundamentally affected my own style of archaeology.

Brian was a pioneer in the developing study of (in his case early) medieval archaeology. Medieval archaeology is still a very young discipline. The national learned society devoted to the subject, the Society for Medieval Archaeology, was founded in 1957, four years into the Yeavering project. This can be compared, for example, with my own field, where the Prehistoric Society came into being in 1935, as a development from the earlier Prehistoric Society of East Anglia (1908–35). There are many reasons for this relatively late academic acceptance of subjects like medieval and post-medieval archaeology (1967). In part one can blame simple academic snobbery along the lines of: 'If it's earlier it's got to be better and more important.' I also once detected (thankfully I think it has largely vanished) an attitude to these more recent subjects, among certain colleagues, which implied that the archaeology of recent times is somehow easier to do, and makes fewer intellectual demands on its practitioners. Nothing, *but nothing*, could be further from the truth.

But I must return to my own early exposure to medieval archaeology. Like every archaeological student in Britain, I had heard of the Wharram Percy deserted medieval village project in Yorkshire. The project was one of the longest-running research programmes in England

(1950–90), and reports on various aspects of the work are still appearing in print. The results from Wharram continue to surprise. For example, recent work by Dr Simon Mays on the bones from the village churchyard has produced some unexpected results: babies were breast-fed until they were eighteen months old.[6] During this period they thrived, but then began to fall behind when compared to modern infants. Comparisons between the rural population at Wharram and the nearby city of York show that although life in the country was generally healthier, women in the city did less demanding physical work. The urban population was exposed to a greater risk of infection, which also resulted in greater disease resistance. The rural population did not escape all the urban ailments. One would expect them to suffer from the 'bovine' form of tuberculosis, which they would have caught from animals, whereas they were actually infected by the 'human' form, which they probably contracted from regular visits to York, where the disease was relatively common. Only four of the 687 skeletons from Wharram showed signs of violent death, which was in stark contrast with the smaller Fishergate cemetery in York, where no fewer than nineteen people – mostly men – had met untimely ends.

Simon Mays' work shows vividly how archaeology can illuminate history. What documents could possibly have differentiated between the two forms of tuberculosis and thereby have told us something new about town–country relations in the Middle Ages? Wharram Percy has been a most remarkable project, and I will return to it in some detail later, but medieval archaeology is now such a diverse subject that we cannot confine our attention to field projects, such as Wharram, alone. In these respects I think medieval and post-medieval archaeologists are facing considerable challenges of synthesis and comprehension. It would be so easy to lose oneself in detail. But somehow the best of them, people like Professor Richard Hodges at the University of East Anglia, can cope with the mountain of information and make it tell a fascinating story.

I'm aware that terms like 'mountain of information' are emotive and do not actually tell us very much, but in truth that 'mountain' has been produced by a quantum leap in archaeological activity. In this instance it is almost impossible to avoid superlatives, because the changes brought about by better advice to local planning authorities have transformed the way archaeology is practised in Britain. I will try to explain what has happened, and I apologise in advance for the acronyms, which are as unavoidable as the hyperbole.

In 1989 government in Whitehall issued a document called Planning Policy Guidance No. 16, known universally in archaeology as PPG-16. Despite its dreary title, PPG-16 has revolutionised the way archaeologists work – and think. PPG-16 established the principle that the 'polluter pays'. In other words, if a developer is going to make a huge profit from building houses on top of, say, a deserted medieval village, he must first pay to have the site properly excavated and recorded. If a discovery made in the commercial excavation warrants it, he must also be prepared to accommodate what the archaeologists have revealed – perhaps in a museum or beneath an open space within the housing estate.

PPG-16 has now 'bedded in', and similar schemes exist across Europe. Many archaeologists have reservations about the competitive tendering that takes place between contracting archaeological companies for the big development contracts, but at least something is being done, and something is much better than wholesale destruction. Some of the discoveries have been spectacular. In *Britain BC* I described at least three PPG-16 commercial projects (in Cambridgeshire, Oxfordshire and the Thames Valley), and in *Britain AD* I could not possibly have ignored the astounding Anglo-Saxon 'royal' grave at Prittlewell on the outskirts of Southend. All of these sites were found by commercial excavations in advance of development schemes such as new roads, gravel quarries and housing estates. To give some idea of the scale of modern commercial archaeology, the total spend on British archaeology in the years just before the introduction of PPG-16 was in the order of £3–4 million. In 2004 it was £40–50 million.

This more than tenfold increase in excavation has brought with it a huge number of finds. There are millions and millions of them. Museum stores have ceased to cope, and many contractors are leasing warehouses, or simply dump what they cannot store after a few years. As someone who occasionally looks at prehistoric flint and pottery produced from commercial projects, I always find it much harder to persuade a contractor to take the finds back when I've done with them than I do to get them delivered in the first place.

A modern excavation, if it's properly undertaken, will produce a representative sample of the range of pottery types, for example, that were being used on the site. So a small Anglo-Saxon farm would produce a relatively restricted range of kitchen and household wares, whereas finds from a major trading site would also include household vessels, plus finer table wares and a few exotic traded items. Assuming that the pottery found on the site does indeed represent what was being used in the past, the range and origin of the finds will tell us much about the status, tastes and preferences of the people who lived there. Although at first glance one might suppose that pottery can tell us less about life in the past than coins, which usually have known mints, dates and values, the statistical analysis of pottery (which computers now allow us routinely to perform) is having a huge effect on our understanding of the Middle Saxon period. We will see shortly that this was the first time since the Roman period that pottery began to be produced and distributed on an industrial scale. Richard Hodges considers this period to have been the first industrial revolution.

The huge increase in commercial archaeology has brought with it problems. New data is being produced daily,* but nobody is in a position to grapple with what it all means. As a result it simply remains dead data, and never makes that all-important step to become something of interest, which one might label 'information'. A digest of the raw data is included in reports that archaeological contractors produce for their clients and which are housed in the various Sites and Monuments Records (SMRs) of the counties and self-governing cities of Britain. These client-reports form what is known in archaeology as the 'grey literature'. Unlike 'proper' reports, submitted to established journals or monograph series, they are not peer-reviewed, and sometimes – I put it as mildly as I can – they are not very good. The good ones, usually of large-scale projects, can be excellent, but even the worst sometimes contain the basic information that someone who understands what he or she is doing can subsequently extract.

The basic information contained in the 'grey literature' reports is extracted to the records in the SMR, which today is computerised and

* I am aware that *data* is the plural form of *datum*, the Latin for a thing or object, but in its English form it is singular, just as the plural of stadium is stadiums, not *stadia*.

linked to a map-based Geographical Information System, or GIS. Again I apologise for the sleep-inducing acronyms, but I shall use them all together just once: the combination of new data from PPG-16 projects, combined with the rapidly growing picture of ancient settlement patterns revealed by GIS in the county SMRs, has made it vastly simpler to place individual sites in their landscape contexts. And this has had a crucially important influence on the way we now think about early towns and the hinterland around them. At last, as we will shortly discover, our analyses of past landscapes can truly be considered 'joined up'.

Many country Sites and Monuments Records also include information taken from aerial photography. This is a field which grew by leaps and bounds in the later twentieth century. In the best county SMRs the information on air photos is accurately transposed straight into the GIS, using sophisticated computer rectification software. Most air photos are not taken by flying directly above the site or landscape being surveyed. If the pictures are taken from an oblique angle, which may be necessary if slight humps and bumps on the ground are to show up in low sunlight, the images must be 'rectified' – i.e. straightened out – before they can be traced onto a map. Hence the need for the clever software.

The results of these processes can be little short of astonishing. Again I make no apologies for the language, because there really has been an information 'explosion' in aerial archaeology and its sister sub-discipline, Remote Sensing. Remote Sensing is a way of mapping ancient landscapes from the air, using radar and other techniques aside from photography. It's still relatively young, but is already producing exciting results. Conventional aerial photography, on the other hand, is probably in its heyday.

Aerial photography has had a profound effect on archaeology since its first widespread use as a tool of reconnaissance during the Great War. In lowland England years and years of ploughing have removed most of the humps and bumps from the actual surface of the ground, but long-vanished features such as trackways, field ditches, even house foundations, can be seen as dark marks in growing crops. In a dry year, and only in a dry year, the roots of growing crops such as wheat and barley need to dive deep to find moisture. Directly above buried

and long-filled-in ditches, wells or rubbish pits, the roots find damp-
ness and the crops grow thick, lush and luxuriant. This darker growth,
known as a cropmark, shows up clearly from the air.

The summer of 1976 was one of the driest on record, and it produced fabulous cropmarks. Subsequently we have had about a dozen
good years for aerial photography, and much of this new material is
slowly finding its way into local SMRs and the three National Monuments Records.[7] It would seem that global warming does have a few
beneficial side-effects. Cropmarks are particularly important in rural
areas that have been subjected to intensive arable agriculture. They
reveal the remains of farms, fields, roadways and settlements, some of
which may already have been destroyed by farming and only survive
as differences in soil texture. After some practice one can begin to
'read' a map of cropmarks and separate Bronze Age barrows and
livestock fields from Iron Age farms and arable fields; one can also
follow the extent of early medieval fields and the development of the
ridge-and-furrow fields that have been so seriously denuded in the last
two decades of the twentieth century. It is fair to say that this book
could not have been written without the new information provided
by commercial archaeology and aerial photography. It has affected not
just the quantity of what we now know about the past, but its quality
too. By learning more about them, modern archaeologists have gained
huge respect for the humanity and achievements of the people they
are privileged to study.

If my correspondence is anything to go by, there is a growing
interest amongst the public at large in 'real' history and archaeology. A
recent piece in the authoritative popular journal *BBC History Magazine*
suggests that teachers are being told by their pupils that they have too
much of Hitler and the twentieth century, and want to learn more
medieval history.[8] If their elders fail to grasp the point, brighter
younger people now realise that the roots of the modern world lie in
the Middle Ages. It is a period which demands reassessment from the
bottom up: for too long it has been viewed from the perspective of
the Normans, the Plantagenets and the Wars of the Roses. Certainly
these were important dynasties and political events, but they were no
more crucial to the development of the modern world than were
the activities of millions of anonymous builders, merchants, farmers,

mariners and miners. These people, and the inspired artists, architects and managers who supervised their work, were the true ancestors of today's Britain.

Walk beneath the magnificent lantern above the transept of Ely Cathedral atop its 'island' of drier ground in the East Anglian Fens. Look up into the soaring space at the eight massive shaped oak trees that appear like so many distant gilded matchsticks, and you will be convinced that this is a modern building in every sense of the word. It was built by modern people who just happened to be living in an age of faith. Does that make them fundamentally different from us? I think not.

Religion and piety are foreign to many in the increasingly secular West. Speaking personally, I find the power exerted by religion over rational people quite inexplicable. But that simply reflects the fact that I do not believe in God. Today many people in Britain share my views, or rather lack of them, but my atheism does not make me somehow more modern than a person who has faith. Besides, faith and religion were never exclusively confined to the Middle Ages. The works of that great eighteenth-century genius J.S. Bach are suffused with faith. In Victorian times Charles Darwin encountered fierce public opposition, led by the Church of England, when he published *On the Origin of Species* in 1859. Even today, biblical creation and 'directed evolution' or 'intelligent design' are increasingly hot topics of debate. Many people in numerous countries across the modern world are perfectly content to live their lives within social and political contexts that are structured around faith. A strong belief in the power of God and the Church does not place the medieval world somehow outside our own times.

But to return to Ely, I find the achievements of those medieval master craftsmen still speak directly to me in a way that surpasses simple reason and logic. The construction of that soaring octagon high above the transept, apart from being one of the greatest achievements of medieval carpentry, required modern technical expertise, combined with modern thought and vision. I just cannot see the people with the minds to imagine, build, rebuild, maintain and support Ely as being significantly different from us today. I am aware, of course, that I am reading too much into one building, but it was the octagon at Ely that set me thinking. So I have reason to be thankful for that afternoon in the Fens. I looked upwards at the right time and in the right place. It was that single transporting moment that provided me with the motivation to write this book. Now it is time to start the story.

PART I

On Britons, Saxons and Vikings (650–1066)

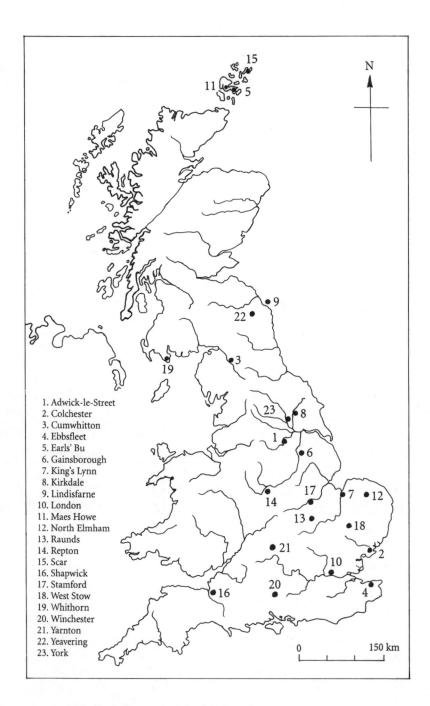

1. Adwick-le-Street
2. Colchester
3. Cumwhitton
4. Ebbsfleet
5. Earls' Bu
6. Gainsborough
7. King's Lynn
8. Kirkdale
9. Lindisfarne
10. London
11. Maes Howe
12. North Elmham
13. Raunds
14. Repton
15. Scar
16. Shapwick
17. Stamford
18. West Stow
19. Whithorn
20. Winchester
21. Yarnton
22. Yeavering
23. York

0   150 km

FIG 1   *Principal places mentioned in Part I.*

CHAPTER ONE

The North/South Divide
of the Middle Saxon Period

THIS CHAPTER will mainly be about the emergence of England. First, however, I must say a few words about the state of the countryside in general in the three centuries or so after the departure of the last Roman troops in AD 410, the generally accepted date for the end of the Roman presence in Britain. To summarise briefly, in the years prior to about 1960 it was believed that the British countryside reverted to a state of near wilderness when everything collapsed after the Roman withdrawal. The term often used to describe the situation was a 'waste' or 'wasteland', in which forests covered the land and the sun was excluded from the ground. Then waves of new settlers from across the North Sea arrived in Britain, felled the forests and pushed the few inadequate natives west towards Wales. The new people brought with them an entirely new way of life.

In *Britain AD* I discussed how archaeology and environmental science have shown that there was in fact very little forest regeneration, and that if anything the post-Roman landscape became more open, and the styles of farming more diverse. All the evidence points to continuity in the landscape: there was no wholesale disruption, such as one might expect if the entire population of what was shortly to become south and east England had in fact changed. Most towns and cities were indeed abandoned, but this was a process that had begun long before, in a remarkably sudden and coordinated fashion shortly after AD 300 – a full century prior to the Roman departure. The distinguished scholar of Roman Britain Richard Reece has suggested that this was because towns in Roman Britain were an idea ahead of their time, and that their grip on the population was at best tenuous – and soon slipped. Whatever the explanation, and I find Reece very convincing, Romano-British town life effectively ceased in the early fourth century and there was a (consequent?) rise in rural prosperity, which included the construction or enlargement of many elaborate country houses, known to everyone today as Roman villas.

To the north and far west the British population at large was less affected by the Roman presence, and many aspects of Iron Age life continued right through to post-Roman times. This is not to say that rural settlements here were grubby hovels, because the pre-Roman inhabitants of these areas had developed their own ways of living in what was sometimes quite a wet and windy environment. As we will see when we look at life in the Bernician royal centre at Yeavering in Northumberland, these people were perfectly capable of achieving a remarkably sophisticated style of life.

Plague may have played a role in keeping the population of Britain down in Early Saxon times. Bede mentions it on several occasions with reference to the seventh century.[1] The problem I have with this is that the seventh century was a time when town life in Britain was pretty much non-existent, and it was in the crowded towns of the fourteenth century that the Black Death reaped its most devastating harvest. It affected rural areas too, but not as much. As we will see when we come to discuss that particular outbreak, plague tends to recur again and again, and it seems odd to me that it should die out at more or less the precise time that towns, in the form of the Middle Saxon *wics*, begin to come into their own.

It is also worth noting that the impact of the Black Death in 1348 was so devastating that the southern British population could not have retained any vestiges of immunity from earlier infections. In other words they must have been completely free from it – and for several generations. It seems to me that the plagues Bede writes about are unlikely to have wiped out whole swathes of the British population, thereby releasing land for huge numbers of people from across the North Sea to settle on. It is, however, entirely possible that plague in the seventh century could have played a role in freeing the survivors from restrictive ties and obligations.[2] Just as we will see in the four-

teenth century, the greater availability of land ultimately led to prosperity – which was such a feature of southern Britain in the Middle
Saxon period.

For these and other reasons I suggested in *Britain AD* that the
Anglo-Saxon invasion was more a spread of ideas than of actual people,
as there is no convincing archaeological evidence for war cemeteries
or for David Starkey's 'ethnic cleansing'. In a few decades I feel sure
that genetics will be able to sort the problem out, one way or another.
If it is indeed found that wholesale population replacement did take
place, the challenge to archaeologists will be to work out how this
could have happened. What was the social mechanism that enabled
such a huge ethnic transformation to occur without, it would seem,
major social disruption and conflict?

Maybe we can learn something here from the story of the Vikings,
who were successful invaders, but who also seemed hell-bent not so
much on rape and pillage (which certainly happened) but on settling
down and becoming English peasant farmers. The Viking army, however, left clear and unambiguous documentary and archaeological
evidence for warfare – something which is still lacking in the archaeological record of the Dark Ages. Perhaps some other, more subtle and
archaeologically undetectable, process was at work in Early Saxon
times. Maybe strict new codes of marriage introduced by the arriving
Anglo-Saxons prevented native British women from having children;
maybe too there was some other form of eugenic apartheid. As yet we
simply don't know, but one day we might find out. Either way, it will
require some creative thought.

In *Britain AD* I also discussed the events that led up to the Synod
of Whitby (AD 664), at which it was decided that the future of England
lay with the Roman rather than the Celtic Church. From a very long-
term perspective this was a most important decision, because it ensured
that thenceforward British intellectual and spiritual attention would
be directed towards Europe. The medieval period was also a time when
the authority of the Church played a central role in most aspects of
the life of the nation. Before Whitby the Church was altogether more
fragmented, and its growth more organic. After Whitby it became both
more centralising and more institutional, and soon became a significant power in the land. The increasing importance of the Church also

promoted literacy and gave rise to a greater and more widespread use of written documents.

By the early seventh century the Anglo-Saxon kingdoms of what was later to be England were beginning to emerge, and we know of a series of very rich or 'royal' burials at places such as Sutton Hoo, Taplow and Prittlewell. I described these graves in *Britain AD*, and I will not repeat myself here, other than to say that these lavish finds show that society was clearly becoming increasingly hierarchical, and that powerful ruling elites had begun to emerge.[3] By the end of the Early Saxon period Christianity was of growing importance, as is well illustrated at Prittlewell (AD 650), where an otherwise pagan chamber burial, with roots that can be traced back to the pre-Roman Iron Age, had been 'Christianised' by the addition of two gold foil crosses.

The documentary evidence for Middle Saxon England is much better than that for Early Saxon times. Among the sources available to us, two stand out. The first has to be the work of that great genius of northern Britain, the Venerable Bede, who wrote his *Ecclesiastical History of the English People* in 731. But there is also a most remarkable eleventh-century source, a tax assessment known as the Tribal Hidage. This document gives us an important glimpse into the earliest geography of England, and I will consider it further in Chapter 3, when we come to discuss the development of administrative units such as the shires.

I mentioned Brian Hope-Taylor in my Introduction. His remarkable excavations at Yeavering in Northumberland transformed our knowledge of Earlier Saxon high-status architecture. His work has given us a vivid picture of life within a royal household in northern Britain prior to the onset of Viking raids. Strictly speaking, Yeavering was in use in the decades just before 650, the notional start of the Middle Saxon period, but dates such as these are for convenience only – and it is convenient for me to ignore them now. First I want briefly to discuss life in Britain north of, say, Yorkshire. Then we will turn our attention further south. The contrast between the two regions will help explain the phenomenon that has come to be known as the Vikings.

It is strange how certain bits and pieces of what you learned at school or university stay with you in later life. Sometimes these half-remembered fragments are of little consequence: does it really matter, for example, that one could have walked across the North Sea 12,000 years ago? Although I was quite interested in the archaeology of early medieval Britain, I never really got to grips with what was happening in the north of the island, except to marvel over the illuminated pages of that superb masterpiece in the British Museum, the Lindisfarne Gospels. This came to the museum in 1753 as part of its 'Foundation collections', which also included the only copy of that remarkable Anglo-Saxon epic poem, *Beowulf*.[4]

Before Brian Hope-Taylor's excavations and the great growth in Scottish and northern archaeology that has happened since, the main sources of information on early medieval Britain were carved stone crosses, inscriptions, and of course those superb illuminated manuscripts. Their rich decoration owed much to various influences from within Britain, and the style has come to be known as the 'insular tradition'. Here the term 'insular' is not meant to be pejorative; it simply signifies that the manuscripts produced on the island of Britain were quite distinct from those being produced elsewhere in Europe. They were also just as good as, or even better than, anything on the Continent. Besides the Lindisfarne Gospels there are two other famous examples, the Books of Durrow and of Kells (both in the Library of Trinity College, Dublin).[5] All three are Gospels and are particularly renowned for their intricate 'carpet pages' of elaborate interlaced design whose vivid 3-D effects would actually make them lethal if woven into floor coverings. The spirit behind the restless movement of this work recalls, for me at least, the unquiet world of pre-Roman, so-called 'Celtic' Art. There is little here of the Roman Church, or indeed of Roman culture.

The suggestion of 'Celtic' influences summons up images of Ireland, but one should not be misled into thinking that the insular tradition was about Ireland, or those Irish settlers in Scotland, the *Scotti*, alone. English, or rather Anglo-Saxon, influences were also very important contributors to this rather heady graphic cocktail. We saw in *Britain AD* how there is growing evidence for mobility in Anglo-Saxon England, and the same can be said for the lands around the western seaways.[6] The art of the insular tradition is clearly a fusion of both English (Anglo-Saxon) and British traditions, but its great flowering was sometime after the Synod of Whitby. The Book of Durrow and the Lindisfarne Gospels are probably mid-seventh century, and Kells is slightly later (late eighth). It may have been the stability provided by the new post-Whitby political and ecclesiastical regime that provided the environment for the new style to emerge and flower. One is tempted to reflect that it is far easier to alter the outward form of religious rituals than the feelings and emotions that lie behind them.

At college we learned in some detail about the glories of these three great works. I also remember seeing the Book of Kells as a small boy when I was taken by one of my Irish uncles, Esmonde, to the library of Trinity College, Dublin, where he himself had been a student. Esmonde was to become a historian of Hitler's pre-war policy at London University, but at that stage his life in Dublin was rather wild and included some very colourful friends, like the playwright Brendan Behan. Esmonde taught me by example that the past was far too important to be taken too seriously. In the drab days of the 1950s those huge, colourful pages, glinting with gold, made a lasting impression on me. The Book of Kells features large animals, strange beasts and the huge-eyed faces of biblical characters such as the Gospel writers. It has always been among my favourite works of art.[7]

One might suppose that such great art was produced in a well-endowed culture where people had the time and resources to lavish upon such things. Indeed, that was how life in northern Britain was seen when I first learned about the Celtic Church. Brian Hope-Taylor's excavations at Yeavering, if anything, reinforced this view of a heroic age that could still find the time to encourage the contemplative life of men such as Bede, or the masters who created the great illuminated manuscripts. That term 'heroic age' says it all. But what does it really mean?

The best answer I have come across has been provided by the greatest scholar of northern Britain in early medieval times, Professor Leslie Alcock, who has just published a magisterial review of his subject.[8] Alcock makes it clear that this was indeed a heroic age in which great feats of valour on the battlefield were celebrated in verse and song; but there was more to it than just fighting. Many sources refer to scenes from the life of Christ, and it is apparent that the essentially pagan ideals of the heroic age were transferred to Christian beliefs. The ideals of a warrior elite were tempered by the humanity of those who, like Bede, opted for the quieter life of the soul.

The political situation in what is now northern England in the seventh–ninth centuries was extremely unstable. This is remarkable, because the eighth century saw what has been called a Northumbrian Renaissance, epitomised by scholars such as Bede and religious houses such as Lindisfarne. To the north and east, occupying the land in England and Scotland around the Cheviot Hills, was the kingdom of Bernicia, with Deira to the south, centred around the fertile Vale of York. Deira was taken over by Bernicia in the mid-seventh century, and both were then subsumed within the large kingdom of Northumbria, whose borders fluctuated quite widely, especially when campaigns against its northern neighbours took a turn for the worse. Southwestern Scotland was occupied by the Scots (or *Scotti* in Latin), who were in fact settlers from Ireland. North of the Firth of Tay were the Picts. During the heroic age much of the warfare took place between Angles from Bernicia and the Picts or the Scots further north.

Yeavering is about as far north in what is now England as it is possible to go. It is located in the Cheviot Hills, at the heart of Bernicia, just below a prehistoric hillfort known as Yeavering Bell. If you struggle over the ramparts of this hillfort in late winter, when the rough grass is low, you can clearly see the circular outline of collapsed Iron Age roundhouses. The settlement is on gently sloping ground at the foot of Yeavering Bell, whose commanding presence is everywhere, and which must have been the principal reason why the site was selected as a royal centre. The inhabitants of Yeavering could claim descent and protection from the ancestral figures who constructed the great hillfort.

This Bernician royal settlement – and I use that loaded word advisedly – went through a number of different phases. Great timber halls appear, are modified and replaced. Cemeteries even grow, come and go. But throughout its development the site shows the clearest signs of organisation and thought. Alignments matter, and symbolism is significant. Sometimes as I read Brian Hope-Taylor's report – which I still consider the finest excavation report produced by a field archaeologist working in Britain – I feel I am in the Bronze Age, where sites like Stonehenge were about alignments almost more than anything

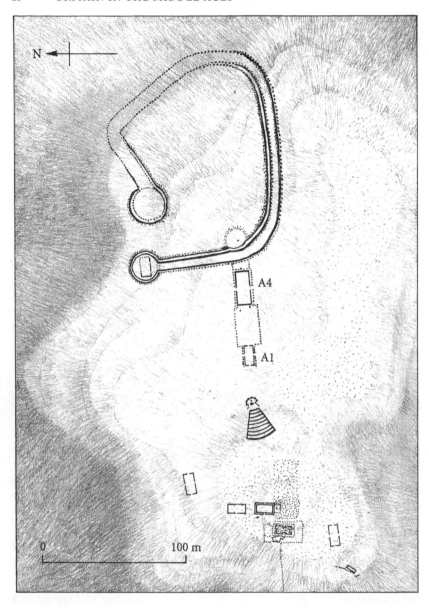

FIG 2   *The Bernician royal settlement at Yeavering, Northumberland, at its climax in Phase III, in the 620s. Six timber halls and a kitchen building lie to the east of the Great Enclosure, an elaborately defended meeting place, with two circular entranceworks, one of which contained a timber hall. At the centre of the settlement is a tiered timber grandstand or viewing platform where public ceremonies would have taken place. The large hall A4 and the smaller building A1 were joined together by a post-built yard or enclosure.*

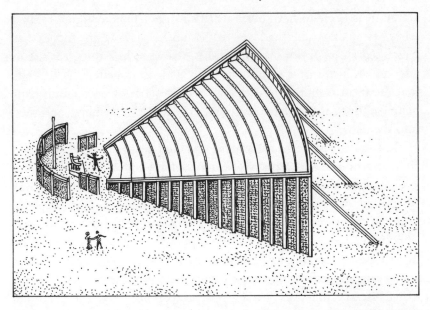

FIG 3   *Reconstruction drawing of the tiered viewing platform or grandstand at Yeavering, Northumberland. This grandstand may well have been built as a place where royal announcements were made. Alternatively it could have been the scene of other ceremonies or activities, such as executions. It was burnt down, possibly deliberately, some time in the later 620s or early 630s.*

else. Just as the presence of the nearby hillfort had a political message, alignment on celestial phenomena such as solsticial sunrise (or sunset) was a way of linking the world of the living to the power and authority of another world. These things mattered in the Bronze Age, as in Saxon times – as indeed they do today. Ceremony and ritual are methods that society uses to confer special authority on those selected (by whatever means) to rule.

Hope-Taylor was able to distinguish five phases of post-Roman occupation at Yeavering, of which the most elaborate was Phase III. This phase ended with a catastrophic fire which the excavator attributed to hostile action. I'm not certain that the evidence he cites is absolutely convincing, because timber and thatched buildings can burn like tinder in exposed situations. All it takes is a spark on a dry roof on a breezy day – or night. But if the fire was indeed caused by hostile action, it is likely to have been a British rather than a Viking raiding party, as Viking raids had yet to get under way. Leslie Alcock has reassessed Hope-Taylor's dating and is unable to link the great fire to any known historical event. Taking the evidence together, he suggests that the most elaborate and extensive phase (III) of occupation happened in the 620s. The later two phases (IV and V) may have continued into the 640s.[9]

Just to the east of the settlement was the Great Enclosure, with two circular entranceworks, one of which contained a hall. The enclosure is a massive affair, perhaps resembling a lowland hillfort, and was surrounded by two ditches and two sets of triple palisades of posts. This has to be seen as a fortification of some sort, but at the same time it does seem strange that the largest halls were positioned outside it. I think we are looking here at some form of gathering place that was meant to instil confidence in those who met there. Maybe it was a marketplace that was given royal protection – and the elaborate defences were also a way of reminding people that they were only able to trade there safely thanks to a powerful ruler.

In post-Roman Phase III the settlement consisted of at least six rectangular timber halls, one of which, Hall A4, was truly huge: 80 x 37 feet (24.4 x 11.3 metres); this gives a floor area of 3,000 square feet (275 square metres) – the largest known hall of the Saxon period. The settlement also included a cemetery and a unique timber grandstand or viewing platform. Hope-Taylor suggests that the shape of this structure would fit with the focus being on some sort of throne. The curved wall to the rear of the possible throne would have helped to project the voice of anyone addressing the audience from it. Perhaps a single post behind the throne carried some sort of royal standard or emblem.

The buildings at Yeavering were grand in the extreme, but the finds from the site were strangely unexciting, comprising perhaps two or three boxes of locally made pottery, a handful of coins, clay loom-weights, some metalwork and a quite a few iron nails. Compared to the 'productive' sites of Middle Saxon southern Britain, which I will discuss shortly, this is a less than lavish collection of material. The underlying concept of what constitutes royal pomp, or panoply, at Yeavering contrasts hugely with what we know about contemporary sites in the south, at places like Sutton Hoo in Suffolk, where the ship-grave of King Raedwald of Essex (who died in AD 625) contained treasures from all over Europe and the Mediterranean world. Yeavering seems to be more introspective, to be about impressing people with grand buildings and awe-inspiring structures rather than with wealth pure and simple. It also suggests that the royal house of Bernicia was probably more concerned with local relationships and hostilities than with long-distance trade. Again, this attitude to political life is markedly at variance with what was happening further south – and indeed with what was happening, and was about to happen, in monasteries in the north, at places like Lindisfarne, Jarrow and Monkwearmouth, where those masterpiece manuscripts of the 'insular school' were to be created.

Yeavering was not unique in its large timber halls. Other early examples have been found across Northumbria (there are a dozen at Thirlings) and in southern Britain, at sites like South Cadbury in Somerset and West Stow in Suffolk, which I will discuss further shortly.[10] We know from sources such as Bede that these great halls were spaces where feasting and general carousing took place under the approving eye of the lord. But they were also about more than simple pleasure. They were places where justice was dispensed, and their arrangement was intended to show – display would perhaps be a better word – the lord and his family to good advantage. The guests were either the lord's subjects or neighbouring nobility who attended his table as part of the continuing business of regional diplomatic relations. The great halls played an important part in the development of early medieval society in Britain.

The rarity of finds at Yeavering tends to be a feature of early medieval sites in northern and western Britain. Coins too tend to be rare, and it would seem that the economy was mainly based around barter. In situations such as this we should be careful of simply assuming that somehow coins = trade. In actual fact exotic coins can be collected as beautiful objects in their own right, they can be used as a way of storing wealth, and of course the royal name and portrait carried on many of them is a political statement in itself – and one which would only be seen by members of the upper echelons of society.

Throughout northern and western Britain there is evidence for trade with the Mediterranean region and Gaul. Usually this comes in the form of amphora fragments. Amphorae were large, robust vessels in which wine and oil were exported from the Mediterranean. Fine table wares were often made in north Africa. Coins do not appear to have been used in these transactions, and it is usually assumed that other items were exchanged, such as tin (in Cornwall) or copper, lead, silver or gold (elsewhere). Other items produced in north-western Britain probably included hides, fur and slaves. Wool and cloth do not seem to have been produced in exportable quantities.

Many sites, such as forts and rural settlements, echo Yeavering in revealing fine buildings but a rather small inventory of finds. One exception is the early Christian community at Whithorn Priory in south-west Scotland. This remarkable site has produced many fine buildings, which were accompanied by a large collection of pottery, glass and other objects.[11] Many of these were imports. The site developed into a very significant settlement that has been described as proto-urban – not quite a town, but almost. The large numbers of finds might in part reflect the high quality of the excavation, but then Yeavering, to name just one example, was dug to equally high standards and produced little. One key to what might be special circumstances at Whithorn was provided by the distribution of the sixty-five coins, which mainly occurred around the church doorway. This could possibly suggest that there had been a church collection point of some sort here, and that the coins around it were mislaid offerings. However, it doesn't explain how the people who made the offerings obtained their coins in the first place.

So if the coins at Whithorn cannot be linked *directly* to trade, what about the many imported Mediterranean, Gaulish and Continental objects? Surely these indicate extensive trade? In fact a close study of the various types of exotic pottery shows that they were actually imported rather sporadically and over quite a long period, from the late fifth to the eighth century. What was the nature of the trade between north-western Britain and elsewhere? Some would have taken place through Anglo-Saxon middlemen at places such as York, where we know that a coin mint had been established in the late seventh century. Some took place under the *aegis* and protection of the Church, as at Whithorn. But was there regular to-ing and fro-ing; was there continuous and active communication? On the whole I think not.

Contacts had been established and could be called upon when needed, which is another way of saying that this was essentially a command economy.

Professor Charles Thomas has suggested that the trade between the Mediterranean region and his site at Tintagel Castle in north Cornwall would have involved ships which loaded up at various Mediterranean ports and then headed towards Britain, probably via the Spanish and Portuguese coast.[12] Maybe this happened every few years, we cannot tell, but it was never the constant and increasingly active, coin-based trading network that we now realise existed around the southern North Sea basin from at least the later seventh century. That was something altogether different, and both north-western Britain and Ireland lay outside it.

In 1970 I briefly flirted with the idea of transferring my academic allegiance from prehistory to the Saxon period. There were several reasons for this. First and foremost, I suddenly felt daunted by the prospect of directing my first major excavation at Fengate, in Peterborough. This was already one of the best-known prehistoric sites in Britain, and its sheer complexity was very challenging. I also knew that the following spring I would have to turn talk into action, and like many young men I had been quite free in voicing my criticisms of the previous generation. Now I would have to prove whether or not I could dig as well as them – and secretly I knew that many of them had been very good indeed. Prehistory was also going through a rather complacent period; by contrast the archaeology of the Saxon period seemed very exciting. New discoveries were being made on an almost daily basis. It wasn't just a matter of finding new sites and artefacts, but people were coming to grips with what seemed to be a wholly new world. In the 1950s the post-Roman centuries were seen as retrogressive, a return to barbarism and incompetence, but in the sixties and seventies this was reversed. It was realised that the Saxon landscape was not cloaked in forests of neglect. People did not live in muddy holes – so-called *Grübenhaus* 'pit-dwellings' – in the ground. Instead, new buildings, settlements and landscapes of great sophistication were being revealed. Vitally important excavations at places like York, Lincoln, London, Thetford and Southampton were radically transforming our knowledge of Saxon and Viking towns.

I watched all this and I freely admit I wavered, but I then decided to stay a prehistorian. Now I'm quite sure it was the right decision. But I recall one lunchtime on the first excavation at Fengate that I directed, back in 1971. In those less Health and Safety conscious days we would go to the pub for beer and sandwiches, and then – I'm now ashamed to admit this – sometimes I'd drive heavy machinery in the afternoon. Anyhow, I was standing at the bar listening to our Inspector from the Inspectorate of Ancient Monuments at the Department of the Environment, Brian Davison. He was telling us how his dig a few years previously at Thetford had thrown light on the way Saxon townspeople organised their rubbish collection.[13] I almost choked on my beer. That was precisely the sort of detail I wanted to reveal about the Bronze Age. But where was I to find the evidence? For that brief moment I bitterly regretted my earlier decision. Then, as happens, the feeling wore off when I returned to site.

Archaeology often seems to advance in fits and starts. First there will be a period of major reassessment brought about by new discoveries, then things will calm down while people consider the implications of what has just happened. Sometimes there is then a long period of stability – some would call it complacency – when every new discovery is seen to support the *status quo*. Finally the first hints begin to appear that all might not be as it seems – and the whole cycle starts again. These major changes in outlook and interpretation (theorists refer to them as 'paradigm shifts') tend to happen one by one in the different sub-disciplines of the subject. Thus prehistory today is just recovering from a major change of direction when straightforward functional interpretations, often based around economics, gave way to so-called 'post-modern' approaches, which placed symbolism and ceremony at the heart of ancient culture.

A big change in direction has just happened in the world of early medieval studies, and we now find ourselves at the second stage, when the implications of what has happened are being considered. As often occurs in archaeology, the shift in thought appears at first to have been triggered by new discoveries – in this instance thousands of metal finds, many of them coins – but the new information has come at the right time to support a radical new view of Europe in earliest medieval times.

The principal exponent of the new approach is Michael McCormick, Professor of History at Harvard University, whose huge new book will take most people some time to assimilate.[14] I won't attempt a summary of its 1,101 pages, but some of his conclusions are directly relevant to our story. We will shortly be discussing trade in greater detail, but to understand what was going on we have to look at the bigger picture, because trade cannot take place in a vacuum. People trade with each other not just because they need what others can supply, but because they have the means to do so and have established reliable lines of communication. Trade and communication are inextricably linked. Professor McCormick has shown that sometimes the communication can take place over very long distances indeed.

McCormick's reconstruction of trade in the fourth to the ninth centuries is based on a number of sources, but especially on an exhaustive study of Mediterranean travellers' records, findspots of Arab and Byzantine coins, and ship movements in the Mediterranean Sea, which in turn are based on contemporary records such as customs registers. These sources have provided a huge amount of information on the way that people and ships moved around Europe, and McCormick fully acknowledges that many Arabic records have yet to be tapped.

Europeans have a tendency to regard Europe as the wellhead from which all culture springs, following the flowering of Classical Greece in the fifth and sixth centuries BC. The modern concept of 'the West' is of a culture which is entirely European and essentially self-generated. The one or two acknowledged non-European influences, such as Christianity, are the exceptions that prove the rule. This Europe-centred world view is dangerously flawed, one-sided and misleading. Currently the Muslim world is seen by some as being in direct opposition to the West. It is viewed as having different attitudes to democracy, women's rights and the relationship of Church and state. Laying aside the validity or otherwise of these modern perceptions, it might be helpful to show how the early flowering of culture and science in the rapidly expanding Muslim world played a significant role in fostering the development of early medieval Europe. The cultural traffic has by no means been in one direction only. But first, some essential dates and facts.

The Prophet Mohammed (the name means 'praised' in Arabic) was born sometime around 570 and died in 632. The Muslim or Arab

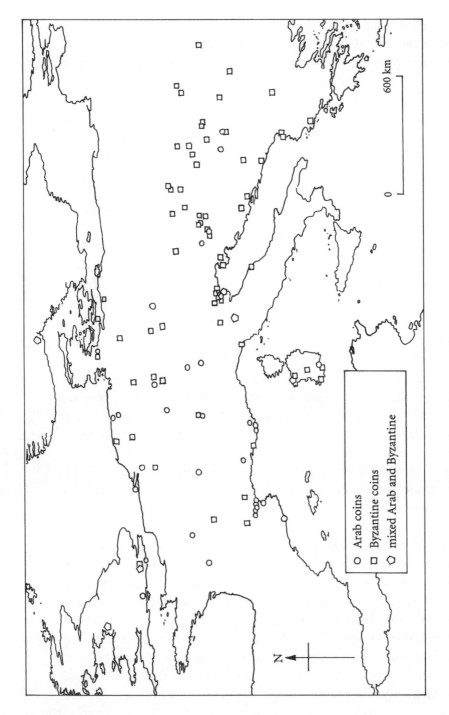

FIG 4   *Distribution of Arab and Byzantine coins in Carolingian (750–900) Europe. Some of the findspots contained more than one coin. The findspot in north-west England is the Viking hoard from Cuerdale, Lancashire, which included many Arab and Byzantine coins.*

○ Arab coins
□ Byzantine coins
⬠ mixed Arab and Byzantine

0   600 km

N

Empire expanded rapidly between the year of the Prophet's death and 650.[15] From the mid-seventh to the mid-eighth century this vast empire was ruled by the Umayyad dynasty from their capital in Damascus, Syria. They were considered impious and tyrannical by many – especially in Iraq – and were replaced in 750 by the Abbasids, whose capital was in Baghdad. The Abbasids claimed direct descent from the Prophet, via his uncle Abbas. The Shi'ites disputed this claim, holding that true direct descent could only be via the Prophet's daughter Fatima and her husband Ali.

The sheer scale of the cities of the early Islamic Empire dwarfs anything in contemporary Europe. We still do not know the precise size of Baghdad under the Abbasids, because no accurate survey exists, but it was probably in the order of seventy square kilometres.[16] Their royal city at Samarra, 125 kilometres north of Baghdad, has been described by Alastair Northedge as the largest archaeological site in the world. It was built and occupied for less than a century, yet its streets and houses covered a staggering fifty-eight square kilometres after only twenty years. Although now entirely deserted, it is still visible from the air, where mile after mile of carefully-laid-out gridiron streets can clearly be seen. Within the city were hunting reserves, racecourses and gardens. There were also numerous palaces, one of which was approached by a massive processional way, perhaps resembling The Mall in London.

The rulers of the Muslim world were known as caliphs (from the Arabic *khalifa*: 'deputy of God'), and the caliphate of the great Abbasid, Harun al-Rashid, who ruled from 786 to 809, and who features in the *Arabian Nights*, was truly vast. It extended from modern Tunisia through Egypt, Syria, Iraq, Iran and what was once Soviet Central Asia. Oman, Yemen and much of Pakistan were also within his power. This great empire was no flash in the pan. Harun's capital Baghdad was the largest city in the known world, and spread for miles on either bank of the Tigris. By this time the early internal conflicts within the Muslim Empire had been resolved. We know that Harun was in contact with Charlemagne, because he gave him, among other things, a superb and highly decorated enamel water jug on the latter's coronation by the Pope in Rome in the year 800. During this time the Caliphate and Byzantium were in almost permanent conflict. Harun's son, al-Ma'mun, who eventually succeeded him and ruled from 813 to 833, was an enlightened ruler, a great builder and supporter of science and the arts. But following Harun's death, Baghdad and the Caliphate began to be plagued by civil war. Baghdad itself eventually fell to Shi'ite attacks in the mid-tenth century.

McCormick (following the work of earlier Belgian historians) has shown that trading contacts with the thriving economic, cultural and scientific world of the Caliphate played an important part in the development of Europe, most of which was under the control of Charlemagne's Carolingian Empire (about 750–900). It was contact with the Caliphate and Byzantium (once the eastern Roman Empire) that helped to kick-start early medieval Europe following the disruption caused by the collapse of the western Roman Empire. Westerners tend to think of the Carolingian Empire as huge and magnificent, but it would have appeared less significant and perhaps somewhat peripheral to someone like Caliph Harun. It was the Carolingian Empire which ultimately fuelled the growing trade around the southern North Sea.

Slaves, many of them from Britain and mostly captured on military campaigns, were the principal 'commodity' exported to the Arab Empire. The trade had been very brisk between 650 and 750, but received a boost when sometime around 750 the Caliphate suffered an attack of bubonic plague. European traders from Venice, Byzantium and the Carolingian Empire filled the gap in the Arab labour market. The scale of this trade was truly remarkable:

> The last five decades of the eighth century were also the era when the Carolingian conquests could well have flooded the market . . . through the capture of large numbers of war slaves . . . As the slaves flowed out in these final decades of the eighth century, Arab coins, eastern silks, new Arab drugs, and old eastern spices surged into Italy. The slave market fuelled the expansion of commerce between Europe and the Muslim world.[17]

The new vision of early medieval Europe differs profoundly from the existing 'conventional wisdom'. As McCormick puts it, this is a Europe

> which is not the impoverished, inward-looking, and economically stagnant place many of us learned about in our student days. On

the contrary, in its origins, Europe's small worlds came to be linked to the greater world of Muslim economies ... These links were perhaps more modest compared with what had once existed [in Roman times] and with what would develop ... but they were real and, in economic terms, they counted, especially given Europe's small scale.[18]

He goes on to point out that trade brings with it cultural contact, and that at the time Arab science was far ahead of anything happening in Europe. The trading contacts were also with Byzantium, which was not then the sealed-off world within the walls of Constantinople that it was later to become. McCormick sees early medieval Europe as more culturally open than at any other time in its history, before and in all probability since. We know that Charlemagne would have been acquainted with Franks, Anglo-Saxons, Danes, Lombards and Visigoths, but McCormick points out that he would also have had Venetians, Arabs, Jews, Byzantines and Slavs among his many contacts. It is thus surely not completely absurd to imagine an Arab or Venetian merchant walking through the streets of Lundenwic, as London was then known.

How did this flowering of early medieval trade affect life in Middle Saxon England? To find the answer we have to consider the origins of the first towns, because these were the safe places in which trade could take place. I will discuss the flourishing of Later Saxon towns in Chapter 4. Here I am concerned with the origins and roots of urbanism. Put simply: how and why did towns develop? What was the wider economic picture that encouraged their growth? Had I been asked those questions twenty years ago, I would probably have replied with a stock anthropological answer – as befits a prehistorian. I would have said that elites in various communities were competing with one another to control certain key natural resources such as salt, water, ores or productive land. But in the last two decades simple ideas such as this have been blown out of the water by a mass of new information. What sparked, and continues to fuel, controversy within the profession is that this new information was produced by hobby metal detectorists. These people are non-academics, and almost every archaeologist's Aunt Sally. But are they wholly evil? I think not. Far from it, in fact.

Even so, I have to admit I am not happy about metal detecting. In archaeological terms it is fundamentally wrong to wrest objects out of their contexts for personal gain. Responsible metal detectorists might reply, with justification, that often they donate their best objects to museums, and that in any case the 'context' from which they removed their finds had usually been eradicated by intensive modern agriculture. That may be true, but for every responsible metal detectorist there are others who prefer to conduct their hobby less openly. I was president of a local detectorists' club in the 1980s, and I well recall that our weekly meetings were attended by two or three dealers in antiquities who often had extended 'conversations' with club members in the car park.

In the 1980s metal detecting grew rapidly in popularity. Even if they had wanted to – and many did – archaeologists would never have been able to make the hobby vanish. It was clear that it could never be banned, because the law could not possibly be enforced: detectorists would be driven underground, and if that happened, any chances of monitoring what they were finding would disappear. As it is, it's hard enough to prevent dedicated illegal 'nighthawks' from detecting over legally Scheduled Ancient Monuments (sites of national importance granted statutory protection).

While the attitude of most archaeologists in the early 1980s was hardening, one exceptional and farsighted individual, Tony Gregory, began to work with detectorist clubs in Norfolk. Pretty well single-handed he started to change archaeological attitudes. He was a close friend of mine (sadly he died in 1991 of cancer), and I spent several smoky evenings upstairs in Norfolk pubs while club members showed him their latest finds and he made notes of where they had been found. As he pointed out, it was bad enough that the finds were being removed in the first place, but it was an archaeological catastrophe that their findspots were being lost too. Those findspots are archaeologically every bit as important as the objects themselves.

Eventually the government bowed to archaeological pressure to regulate what was going on. In 1997 it sponsored the Portable Antiquities Scheme, which exists to ensure that findspots are recorded and major new finds are saved for the nation.[19] This work is carried out by regional FLOs, or Finds Liaison Officers, who have the tricky task of retaining the trust of both archaeologists and detectorists. Even despite the Portable Antiquities Scheme, I still find the haphazard removal of finds from their contexts a very difficult moral dilemma, and one made no simpler to resolve by the outstandingly important new information that has recently begun to emerge.

This new information is transforming our understanding of trade and exchange in northern Europe between the seventh and tenth centuries, and it is doing this by means of so-called 'productive' sites. The term was coined (pun unintended) by numismatists, and would never have been chosen by archaeologists, who might have dubbed them 'rich' or 'significant' sites. To me, 'productive' is a word one might attach to an oil well. That quibble aside, 'productive' sites have turned the world of Middle Saxon archaeology upside down – with more than a little help from some distinguished specialists in ancient coinage.[20]

The four hundred years between 600 and 1000 (the seventh to eleventh centuries) are now seen to have been a period of economic renewal following two centuries when northern Europe was searching for new identities and direction, following the demise of the official Roman Empire in the west. I say 'official' because some form of Romanised authority did continue, but it had now been devolved to local and regional government. The Church, which had become the favoured religion of the Roman Empire under Constantine from AD 324, also played an important role in maintaining such government during a period which archaeologists and historians now refer to as Late Antiquity.

The new economic order seems to have been arranged around a series of major commercial centres, known as *emporia* in Latin and *wics* in Anglo-Saxon or Early English. Finds from the *emporia* in Britain and on the Continent are characterised by their richness and range. Most importantly they provide clear and unambiguous evidence for long-distance trade. These sites sprang up quite rapidly around the coasts of northern Europe, and their arrival coincided with the appearance of a widely adopted silver coinage which became the common currency for the emerging states around the shores of the North Sea. The importance of the *emporia* has been recognised for some time, and it was believed that they came into existence in the earlier seventh century as seasonally occupied trading centres, operated by independent merchants who worked outside aristocratic or elite control.[21] It was believed that from about the 670s they began to come under such control. But following discoveries such as the magnificent burial at Prittlewell (AD 650) at the *emporium* or *wic* of Ipswich, we now realise that these places were probably under royal or elite control from the outset. That is not to say, however, that they were not also well integrated into the local economy, or that specialist traders were not also involved. They almost certainly were.

The *emporium* system was essentially elite-driven: it was all about power, prestige and display in the highest echelons of society. We now understand that while such motives were undoubtedly significant, many more people were involved, and it has become possible to see the whole process in far broader terms. It is becoming clear that the *emporia* formed the pinnacles of an integrated trading system that was united not just by ships and the sea, but by the network of good roads that had been established by the Romans, and had never been completely abandoned.

The true significance of 'productive' sites has only slowly filtered into the academic literature, largely because the realms of academia and metal detecting rarely come into contact. Archaeologists and numismatists are rather better at making such contacts, so the new discoveries have gradually been surfacing in journals and websites devoted to those particular interests. As the information is largely derived from metal detectors it is biased in favour of non-ferrous finds, because most of the machines used today have a discriminator function which allows iron to be screened out. The reason is that the modern ploughsoil is richly scattered with millions of old nails, many of them derived from the ash of scrap timbers burnt on farmyard muckheaps to add potash to the manure. Signals from these nails tended to drown out other signals in the metal detectorist's headphones. Iron nails, it must also be said, are of no commercial value. So all iron finds, and usually non-metal finds too, such as pottery, tend to be ignored, thereby biasing the information enormously. Were archaeologists to excavate and metal detect 'productive' sites, they would plot and keep everything.

This mass of new information is appearing not just in England, but in Europe too. Places like Holland and Denmark have decided to cooperate with the detectorists, and as a result information is flooding in. Elsewhere, however, in Germany, France and Italy, for example, the hobby is still illegal, so new discoveries in these countries are happening very much more slowly, and through traditional means, such as official excavation. We know that illegal finds from these countries are entering the black market. We also know that some are being given false provenances in countries where detecting is less frowned upon.

It is becoming clear to numismatists working with this new material that there was something approaching an explosion of coin-making around AD 700. To give some idea of its scale, the volume of money then in circulation in southern England was not to be paralleled until the thirteenth and fourteenth centuries. The situation in Britain was mirrored on the Continent, and it is now quite clear that the 'explosion' in currency production represents a sudden increase in trade across large parts of northern Europe.

There is good evidence to suggest that the coins from 'productive' sites were still more or less *in situ* when the detectorists found them. This would suggest that at such sites coin-loss equates with coin-use. In other words, we can safely assume that the coins were mislaid during trade, and were not placed in the ground as offerings, or concealed in hoards for safekeeping in times of strife. This assumption is based on the distribution of finds from 'productive' sites, which are spread across the landscape and do not occur in small, tight clusters. Numismatists have shown, moreover, that the coins found on one site reflect those from others. Changes in currency tended to happen across regions, which again suggests trade rather than hoarding and burial (often hoards contain antique or outdated coins kept purely for the value of the gold or silver they contain).

Analysis of the coin finds from 'productive' sites and other smaller 'hot spots' is still at an early stage, and so far no new mints have been identified, but we can be reasonably sure that the patterns revealed in these new and very early distributions are 'real' – in the sense that they reflect ancient trade. One example will suffice. Detectorists have discovered an isolated 'hot spot' of late-seventh-century Early Saxon coins, known as 'primary porcupine *sceattas*',* in the upper Thames

---

* *Sceattas* (pronounced 'shatters') were small Early Saxon silver coins minted in Britain and Frisia (along the southern North Sea coast and inland) between about 690 and 790. They occur in two series, a primary and a secondary. The secondary was more widely distributed than the primary.

Valley. We know from other evidence, including coinage, that this was to be an important area for the production of wool, starting in the mid-eighth century. The new 'hot spot' suggests not only that the wool trade in the chalklands of this region was under way much earlier, but that it began less gradually than was previously supposed.

It would be a mistake to view trade in early medieval Europe as being part of a free market economy, any more than it was in the Bronze Age. In the past, just as in certain parts of the world today, trade was controlled or encouraged by influences other than purely market forces. Usually these non-market forces represented figures or centres of power within the structure of the state, such as kings, landowning nobles, military leaders and, increasingly, the Church. Protectionism – in the sense of the protection of vested interests – is not just a modern phenomenon. Having said that, the evidence provided by *emporia* and 'productive' sites does strongly indicate that genuine trade did take place within the contexts of a rapidly developing political structure. The question that has to be asked is, to what extent did these power politics affect the growth and development of early medieval commerce?

Two recent studies have suggested that royal power was used both in the Baltic area and in Rouen to influence the arrangement and location of the trading quarters in major *emporia*.[22] In the Baltic example the Danish King Godfred relocated all the merchants from the original settlement to one over 130 kilometres distant in the early ninth century. In the French example an essentially organic trading landscape of ports and trading posts, many of them owned and run by monasteries, was centralised by royal authority, reacting to increasing Viking raids, around Rouen, which then became an important urban centre, but one very much under royal control. In neither instance was trade discouraged by these changes.

Studies of eighth-century coin distributions suggest that trade within the various regions of northern Europe was tightly-knit and integrated. There were consistent patterns that developed over time and space. There does not seem to be evidence (yet) for currency stopping short at national boundaries. Although we know that the process of state formation was under way at this time, there is as yet no evidence that this was impeding or adversely affecting the development of wider patterns of trade.

The relatively recent recognition of 'productive' sites, 'hot spots' and other smaller centres within the hinterland of the major *emporia* does raise the question of the extent to which non-royal patronage and influence could affect the day-to-day business of trade in such places. It seems inherently unlikely that the hand of royalty extended to these more remote and distant places. So did these places develop as a result of simple private enterprise? The general consensus, while acknowledging that individuals and individual motives undoubtedly played a significant role, prefers to see the Church as the engine or inspiration for these smaller centres of trade. Some of the English 'productive' sites in Suffolk, Norfolk and the Isle of Wight were located at or near former ecclesiastical sites, and for others in, for example, East Anglia, the change was the other way around, with seventh- and eighth-century 'productive' sites acquiring a religious dimension by the eleventh century. There is other evidence too that the Church played an important part in the growing economies of southern Britain in the eighth and ninth centuries.

What were these 'productive' sites like? Were they towns, administrative centres, trading posts, religious houses, settlements – or what? Here we are confronted with the biggest problem of all: none in Britain has yet been thoroughly or totally excavated. So the short answer is that we don't know. But some work on the setting of these sites has been done, and of course we do have the non-ferrous metal finds themselves to guide us. As we will see shortly, most are located on rivers or at spots where roads are readily accessible. It's possible that some 'productive' sites were temporary fairs, but so far this has not been demonstrated for certain. Many of the finds – which we must remember are a highly biased selection – compare well with what one might expect to find at a settlement. So it does seem likely that people were actually living at these places.

It is possible to view the growth and development of individual British 'productive' sites in two ways. They might have sprung up as trading centres because of their location close to rivers and roads. Prehistorians have found that a safe or 'neutral' position at some distance from a large centre of population might help in the establishment of such a place, where trade and exchange could happen with some assurance of security. After a while the trading post would grow as a settlement and soon it would acquire other facilities, such as the provision of justice, administration and financial services – a mint, for example.

But there is another way of looking at the situation. J.D. Richards, basing his remarks on fieldwork he carried out at Cottam, a 'productive' site in East Yorkshire, wonders whether we are placing the cart before the horse by putting so much stress on the productiveness of 'productive' sites.[23] He asks whether, if they had been found by more conventional archaeological techniques, they would simply have been seen as important regional communal centres – rich settlements, in other words. Although he seems at first glance to be taking a less dramatic, and rather more conventional, view of the period, I find his ideas ring archaeologically true. His suggestion is persuasive because it helps to demystify the concept of 'productive' sites, which otherwise seem to lack a rationale.

It is not often that I come across an academic paper that excites me so much that its implications keep me awake at night, but it happened recently when I read Ben Palmer's thoughts on *emporia* and 'productive' sites in southern England.[24] It happened to be the first chapter I read in Tim Pestell and Katharina Ulmschneider's *Markets in Early Medieval Europe: Trading and 'Productive' Sites, 650–850*, a collection of essays that I have already drawn upon quite heavily and that will undoubtedly have a profound effect on the way we think about the archaeology of early medieval Europe for years to come. Palmer's paper is original because it focuses on what used to be called *inter*-site (as opposed to *intra*-site) archaeology. Most archaeologists spend their time wondering how people led their lives or conducted ceremonies on one specific site. This inevitably follows the process of excavation, which is intensely focused and usually has the archaeologist 'by the throat' – I speak from personal experience. Plainly one looks at other sites for comparisons and parallels, but that tends to happen very late in the post-excavation period.

Such short-sighted introspection is discouraged if the information is coming from a number of separate places, and when detailed excavation and survey are usually not involved. The result is what the prehistorian Robert Foley termed 'off-site archaeology', where one studies what was happening *between* rather than *on* sites. This approach helps one to understand both what it was that held the network of sites together, and why the system appeared on the landscape in the first place.[25] Ben Palmer's paper is an excellent example of the genre. He confines his attention to south-eastern England, the main region of rapid economic growth in the Middle Saxon period.

The first impression I had when I read Ben Palmer's paper was of geographical 'connectedness'. This paper could never have been written about prehistoric Britain, and it certainly did not resemble anything I knew on the archaeology of the post-Roman 'Dark Ages'. These periods were simply too remote, and lacked the necessary information. It took just two centuries for that to change. The world he was discussing was a working, functioning trading system. We don't know whether they had such things, but it would have been possible to compile road maps showing places where one could stay the night, get a meal and find fresh horses. It seems to me that the false emphasis on loot – on coins and 'productive' sites – tends to obscure the fact that Middle Saxon southern England was about more than just trade in objects from foreign parts: these networks were also about people living their daily lives – selling their wool, making their clothes and growing their food. We can now discern coherent trading landscapes where we can observe the relationship of the town to the countryside – and how each supported the other. To my eyes this paper showed the first signs of a geography that was recognisably modern.

There has been some debate as to whether the three major centres (*emporia* or *wics*) at Ipswich, Lundenwic (London) and Hamwic (Southampton) were 'true' towns, in the sense that they supported a large population and were self-governed. Pre-Viking York (Eoforwic) is another likely contender for *wic* status. Personally I'm in little doubt that these settlements were fully urban, as we would understand the term today, because I cannot see how places with such a density of settlement could survive and prosper in any other way. Further, a significant proportion of the population must have spent all their time being merchants or artisans. They would have had little or nothing to do with the production of food from the land.

But I will leave that particular discussion aside, because I'm not sure it's either relevant or interesting. What matters is that these places are something altogether different from anything that had gone before:

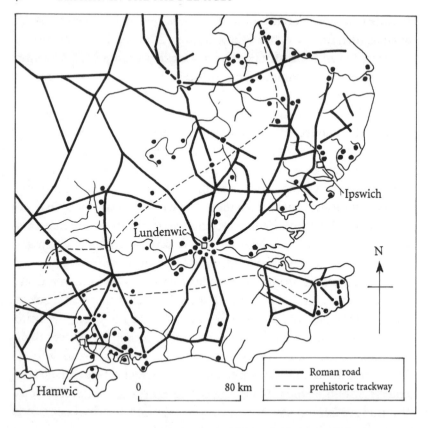

FIG 5 *South-eastern England in the Middle Saxon period, showing the location of the three major centres (emporia or wics) at Ipswich, Lundenwic (London) and Hamwic (Southampton). 'Productive' sites and other significant settlements or trading centres are shown by dots.*

not only are they larger and richer, but they are positioned at key points in a much larger network of settlement, trade and communication. It cannot be a coincidence that they are all more or less the same distance apart, and straddle the south-eastern approaches, like the open mouth of a vast trawler net being slowly towed towards the North Sea. The traditional view of *wics* and *emporia* is that they were one-offs, isolated and before their time. Ben Palmer describes the old view of them as a failed experiment in kingdom-building. They owed their existence to the fact that they were 'gateway communities' that stood on the periphery of the developed core of western Europe, represented by Francia, the Empire of the Franks.

Here I must briefly break off to say a few words about Charlemagne and the Franks. Charlemagne is often seen as the father of modern Europe, and his empire the true ancestor of the European Community. Jacques Le Goff takes a more sceptical view. For him, Charlemagne produced an abortive Europe that nevertheless left behind a legacy.[26] This is a view with which most archaeologists would probably agree.

The Franks were a Germanic people who expanded west across the Rhine in the late fifth and sixth centuries, under the command of their remarkable king Clovis (died *c.*511), to occupy most of central and eastern Gaul (France). This expansion was continued by their greatest emperor, Charles the Great, or Charlemagne (771–814). Under his leadership the Carolingian Empire was to occupy most of western Europe, excepting Spain and southern Italy. Charlemagne, who was barely literate himself, reformed and expanded the power of the Church and encouraged the development of art and letters. While he was in sole charge his empire was stable and very prosperous. The tradition of scholarship was continued by his successors Louis the Pious and Charles the Bald, but the old flair had gone, and Europe now entered a less stable period when political allegiances were shifting. By the mid-tenth century the driving force of the Carolingian Empire shifted towards Germany, with the accession of Otto I in 936.

The traditional view is that the *wics* and *emporia* stood at the boundary of the developed core (Francia) and the underdeveloped periphery, represented by Britain and Scandinavia. In today's politically correct world we would doubtless refer to the latter as 'developing' – which the new archaeological evidence would suggest was factually correct too. As in subsequent core/periphery relations between an imperial centre and outlying regions, it was held that the *wics* and *emporia* were the places where raw materials were exchanged for luxury goods from Europe. Put cynically, the periphery produced the things that mattered, and received showy trinkets in exchange.

This view of the setting up and operation of *wics* and *emporia* was given added weight by scholars such as Richard Hodges, who analysed these processes in the contexts of European macro-economics. He reasoned that trade and exchange only make sense if you look at the whole picture. His approach was anthropological, and rings sort-of true to a prehistorian like myself. I say 'sort-of' because there are no such things as permanent, static laws in anthropology, and Hodges's seminal study of the subject, which appeared in 1989, now seems to me at least somewhat dated and mechanistic, although at the time it deservedly had a huge impact.[27] His views on the social and economic forces behind the growth of *wics* and *emporia* in the seventh and eighth centuries are still very influential, and are essentially based on the competitive relationship between the governing elites in the various emerging states and kingdoms.

Anthropologists love relationships. They believe that the way humans react to each other is governed by forces other than instinctive or emotional likes or dislikes. So anthropologists hold that a married man will tend to have strained relations with his mother-in-law because she resents the loss of her daughter, and he feels that his wife is reluctant to leave her original family because her mother wants her back. Such competitive relationships have also been found in the world of tribal politics, where family considerations also complicate matters. The competitive nature of the relations between ruling elites was first discussed in detail by the great anthropologist Bronislaw Malinowski in *The Argonauts of the Western Pacific* (1922). He studied the exchange of gifts between the inhabitants of the Trobriand Islands, and realised that the exchange formed part of a complex system of social obligation known as the Kula cycle. This cycle was based on what anthropologists refer to as 'Malinowski's principle of reciprocity' – a sonorous phrase which suggests that no gift-giving is without some form of motive. As the words imply, each 'gift' was actually nothing of the sort, because it carried with it the prospect of something in return: either another gift later, or some form of social obligation. Malinowski also realised that these exchanges encouraged competition between the elites on different islands. So a particularly lavish gift was less a generous donation than an expression of power on the donor's part.

Malinowski was an extraordinary man who also established the ground rules of anthropological fieldwork. Among other achievements he pioneered the process of structured interviews, which allowed him to compare the responses he received from different people right across the huge island archipelago he studied. Today his approach is seen as 'functionalist'. In other words he based much of what he observed on common-sense observation and a rather masculine (dare I say it, simplistic) view of human relationships, perhaps summed up by: 'one good turn deserves another'. Subsequent workers, most famously Margaret Mead in her wonderful book *Coming of Age in Samoa* (1928), showed that there was a great deal more to human relationships in the Pacific – and of course elsewhere – than could readily be defined by laws of reciprocity alone. Returning to ancient trade and exchange, more recent studies such as *The Gift* by Marcel Mauss (1950) and *Stone Age Economics* (1974) by Marshall Sahlins have been far less functionalist than Malinowski; but even so, his fundamental principle still seems to apply.[28] Reciprocity and exchange are now seen as organising structures that are about more than the giving of gifts: they underlie most social, economic and administrative processes in both ancient and modern societies.

Archaeologically speaking it is very hard to distinguish between the exchange of gifts and trade, pure and simple, because each involves reciprocity of one form or another. Moreover, where exchange at an elite level happens, it is not unusual to find other, smaller transactions also taking place further down the social ladder. Transactions of this sort do resemble trade, when seen in the archaeological record, because a large variety of objects – even coinage – may be involved.

One useful rule of thumb that can help us define what was going on concerns the nature of the places where transactions took place. Traditionally the *emporia* and *wics* have been seen as rather isolated phenomena that contrasted markedly with the not-so-very-prosperous rural settlements that surrounded them. There are signs too that they were laid out by a central authority: for example, streets were arranged on a grid pattern, and many buildings seem to have been erected simultaneously. The finds include exotic items such as wine containers and pottery imported from the area around the Rhine. Taken together, these clues suggest that the *wics* and *emporia* were set up by powerful elites to control trade to and from the territories they ruled. The reason they wanted to control the trade was simply to establish a royal monopoly on prestige goods, which they could then use to grease the wheels of power both externally, as regards foreign policy, and internally, by rewarding the loyalty of key families and individuals. In a command economy which was based on the exchange of prestige goods, the control of commerce led naturally to the control of people.

It was believed that the establishment of the *wics* and *emporia* by royal patronage did not protect them forever, which is why they began to decline. They lost their central role by, and just after, the end of the eighth century. There was then a gap of about a century, during which time there was effectively no substantial urban presence in Britain. This apparent hiatus coincided with the first period of Viking raids and settlement (we will see that their first raid, on the monastery at Lindisfarne, took place in 793). The next set of major urban foundations were the fortified *burhs*, which we know for a fact were established by royal command, first as a defensive measure against raids and then as protection from Viking forces present in Britain. I will return to the *burhs* in the next two chapters, but the important point to make here is that the bulk of them were established in the late eighth and early ninth centuries.

The conventional wisdom on early towns and the separation of the earlier *wics* and *emporia* from the later *burhs* only really makes sense if we can detect good evidence for discontinuity – which in archaeology must always be proved, and never assumed. The idea of discontinuity also subsumes that of abandonment. In other words, one system replaces another after a period when people either moved elsewhere or the system itself collapsed in some way. Notions of discontinuity were more fashionable in the past, when there was far less data to play with. Archaeology was constructed with a textbook or a historical account in one hand – to provide some form of context – and site notebooks and photographs in the other. You concentrated on the details of the site you had just excavated, and only towards the end of the operation did you attempt to place it all in context. Nowadays all of that has changed, because context is being provided by new archaeological finds, as well as by documents.

I have touched on metal detecting, but a far more significant factor in shaping the way we view the past has been the explosion of new information from commercial archaeology, which I discussed in the Introduction. Thanks to computers and Geographical Information Systems (GIS) this store of new information is now available to archaeologists and others. To be more specific, this means that we now have the information to re-examine the way that *wics* and *emporia* have traditionally been interpreted.

Two questions spring immediately to mind. The first is perhaps the most obvious: were they isolated, one-off royal foundations that existed to promote and exploit a royal monopoly of imported prestige goods? The answer to that is relatively simple: yes they were, and no they were not. They were, inasmuch as they show all the signs of royal involvement, but they were not isolated, nor did they monopolise all trade – or even most of the trade that was taking place in and around them. There was simply too much going on to attribute everything to some form of royal prerogative. One glance at the map of southern England (see page 47) showing the three *wics* at Ipswich, London and Southampton reveals that the hinterland of these three places was liberally peppered with subsidiary, but still very significant, settlements and 'productive' sites which are positioned close to either Roman roads, ancient routes or navigable rivers. It is most noticeable that none is positioned on the more remote hills of the southern Midlands, in East Anglia or the South Downs. Good access and easy communication were clearly essential. These must be seen as trading places, but that of course does not mean they could not have been settlements or small towns in their own right. It does suggest, however, that royal power was not employed to confine all trade and exchange to the major *wics* and *emporia*. The evidence suggests that Middle Saxon trade was indeed organised around the *wics* and *emporia*, but that these formed just one part of an integrated system in which many people played an active part.

The second question that we can re-examine with the benefit of so much new information concerns the demise of the *wics* and *emporia*. Can we still confidently assert that the best part of a century of abandonment separated the appearance of the first *burhs* from the last feeble gasps of the declining *wics*? This suggestion becomes increasingly hard to support if the *wics* were indeed part of an integrated system, because if they declined and vanished, then surely the system as a whole must also have collapsed. But there is no evidence to suggest that anything of the sort happened. Yes, the *wics* and *emporia* declined in the late eighth and early ninth centuries, but certainly Lundenwic never disappears off the map. Nor do 'productive' sites simply vanish.

Trade within Britain has slowed down by, say, 850, and the Late Saxon successors to the widely traded pottery known as Ipswich Ware (Thetford Ware, Stamford Ware, etc.) were never as widely distributed as their Middle Saxon precursor. This winding down can be attributed in part to political turmoil within the Carolingian Empire across the Channel, and to increasing Viking raids and conflict within Britain. But trade within Britain certainly didn't cease. There was no hiatus; the Late Saxon economy never hit the buffers.

The emphasis on coins and metalwork from both the *wics* and the smaller 'productive' sites has tended to obscure the true nature of much of the trading that was taking place. I've already mentioned that Richard Hodges considers that something of an 'industrial revolution' was happening in the eighth century, and the best evidence for this comes in the form of Ipswich Ware.

I remember when I first came across this starkly functional, unglazed, dark grey pottery. I was with my friend and colleague Keith Wade, who had been the deputy director of the Saxon and medieval dig, which I had co-supervised in 1970, at North Elmham Park in central north Norfolk. In the late summer, when digging ended, I went with Keith in search of Ipswich Ware, which he rightly felt was very important because it represented the beginnings of a major Saxon industry. I don't think either of us realised back then just how important Ipswich Ware was to become. I recall looking at my first sherds and noticing that they were lightly dimpled on the outside, and Keith explaining that this was an example of the slow-wheel technique of manufacture, where the vessel being formed was on an unpowered turntable that was revolved by a sideways flick of the thumb on the vessel itself, which left the distinctive 'girth grooves'. Thanks to the Ipswich Ware Project we now realise that this pottery was produced in very large quantities and was distributed widely across southern England, presumably along the same roads and rivers that linked the various *wics* and 'productive' sites. If we are not looking at actual batch-based mass production, then we must be getting very close to it. Whatever the true situation, we have now moved well beyond a simple craft-based rural manufacturing tradition to something more standardised and, indeed, industrial.

I have to admit that I was only slightly aware of its importance at the time, but when I was working at North Elmham one of us found a sherd – actually it was a handle – of fine dark pottery which somehow seemed to have acquired a diamond-shaped piece of tinfoil which had stuck to its outside – as if it had accidentally stuck there when the Christmas turkey was being cooked.[29] The digger who found it had the good sense not to scrape the foil off with his finger – as I fear I might have done in my naïveté – and he showed it to Keith, who stared at it with eyes like saucers. 'Good grief,' he said (actually he used a stronger term), 'it's Tating Ware!' And off he hurried to the director, Peter Wade-Martins, in the site hut. Peter was absolutely delighted, because Tating (pronounced 'Tarting') Ware mostly came from the Rhineland, and was the finest and most skilfully produced pottery in late-eighth- or ninth-century Europe.[30] It was very high-status stuff indeed, and the best evidence possible for trade.

As I have already mentioned, Keith and I went in search of pottery and pottery kilns when we had finished at North Elmham. In the autumn I visited him on a dig behind a farmyard at the beautiful Essex village of Wicken Bonhunt. The first find he showed me when I got there was another sherd of Tating Ware.

In the early 1970s the gradually increasing quantities of exotic early imported pottery were causing something of a stir. What did it all mean? Today, because we have the coins and metalwork provided by the detectorists, we can see that it was part of a larger pattern of trade. At the time we put the presence of this exotic material down to the Church. There was good evidence that the ruined church at North Elmham, known locally as the Old Minster, which stood just outside the excavations, might in its early stages have been the minster church* of the Saxon see (or seat of the bishop) of the diocese of Elmham, which incorporated most of the northern part of the kingdom of East Anglia (i.e. most of Norfolk). When the dig had finished and all the finds were assessed, it became clear that North Elmham had produced about 30 per cent of all the imported sherds of pottery known from Norfolk. I had chosen the right dig to take part in.

It would now appear that we may not have been wrong in assuming

---

* The role of Saxon 'minster' churches is a matter of current debate, but most would agree that the word refers either to a 'mother church' – one which was important to evangelical work and pastoral care – or to a monastic church.

a link with the Church. Other important places and 'productive' sites, such as Barking Abbey (Essex), Burgh Castle and Caister-on-Sea (Norfolk), have produced exotic imports and are known to have had links to the Church. So, rather like the links to the ruling elites, it would appear that the Church also wanted its slice of the action, and probably took an active part in encouraging trade: God and Mammon shared the same interests.

So far, evidence for the vigorous trade in Middle Saxon southern Britain comes from coins and other metal objects, from Ipswich Ware and from imported pottery such as Tating Ware; but what were the other products being traded? I have already mentioned wool in the Thames Valley, and there are good indications that wool and indeed finished cloth were important commodities produced and manufactured in rural British sites. In modern terms the farmers of Middle Saxon England were 'adding value' in a significant fashion to their basic product, wool. The evidence for this comes from several sites, including Shakenoak in the Upper Thames, where *sceattas* (those early silver Saxon coins) were found associated with loomweights. Clear evidence that the trade was not always just for money, and involved the exchange of imported goods as well, comes from the Anglo-Saxon village at West Stow in the sandy Breckland of north Suffolk.[31] What makes West Stow so interesting is its early date. Middle Saxon Ipswich Ware only makes its appearance in the village's final phase, and it declines in importance during the seventh century. During this time families moved off the sandy knoll where the original settlement was positioned, probably towards the church of the existing village of West Stow nearby.

West Stow was a pioneering excavation by Stanley West, who successfully achieved what we are trying to do at Flag Fen in Peterborough. He excavated the village in 1965–72 and then set about reconstructing it, using authentic techniques. It became a major visitor attraction, and is growing in popularity year on year. Somehow he managed to obtain support from the local authorities, and this has made all the difference to the operation. I go there regularly in the springtime, and having lived with sticky, wet Fenland clay all winter, it makes a wonderful change to stand on warm, dry sand and listen to the wind in the Scots pines, or watch siskins feed on alder cones in the damp valley at the bottom of the knoll. It can be a magical spot.[32]

The excavations at West Stow produced a large number of finds, many of which were metal, and although this is a site where coins are rare because of its early date, it is hard not to imagine that had it been systematically worked over by competent detectorists, it would have proved very 'productive' – to reuse that slightly distasteful term. So was it a trading centre of some sort? A quick glance through the list of finds might suggest that it was. No fewer than thirteen buildings produced fragments of querns made from a volcanic lava which occurs in central Europe. There was abundant evidence for weaving, not just the familiar fired-clay loomweights, but an iron 'weaving batten' – a tool used to beat down and compact the threads. Trade was well under way by the late sixth century, when pottery made by an important group of regional workshops based around Lackford appears at West Stow. Other objects, such as the fine bronze brooches, together with glass and amber beads, found on bodies in the cemetery, suggest that many of the inhabitants could afford exotic finery. In the late phases trade with the outside world was expanding. We see this not just in the quantities of Ipswich Ware being brought to the site, but in very upmarket and unusual things, such as a cowrie shell and two silver miniature shields, probably worn around the neck as pendants.

There is nothing at West Stow to suggest that the inhabitants had access to, or controlled, any unusual resource such as salt or ore. Stanley West is convinced that this prosperous community earned its wealth by farming and by selling the surpluses it produced, such as wool (cloth), hides, meat and so forth. It's quite possible that they sold slaves as well – an unpleasant trade for which there is good archaeological and documentary evidence in Saxon times. It's hard not to conclude that it was this pattern of trading essentially rural products that was taken forward into the eighth and ninth centuries. In other words, by the mid-seventh century exchange and commerce were an integral part of rural life, and provided the goods that were traded from the *emporia* and 'productive' sites – many of which would have housed people who were also making and producing things.

If the economy at West Stow seems to have been mainly centred around wool, cloth and hides, other later sites show signs of greater specialisation. Sometimes the specialised production was encouraged by a local church; in other instances it seems to have been private enterprise by landowners and farmers. I've already mentioned Keith Wade's site at Wicken Bonhunt in Essex, which produced many pig bones, suggesting that it specialised in the production of pork. Very close to where I am currently writing, a group of Fenland sites on the silty banks of tidal creeks surrounding the Wash were most probably cattle farms specialising in beef.

These cattle stations, as they might be called in Australia, were first revealed by Bob Sylvester and his colleagues of the Fenland Survey around 1984 when they spotted scatters of Ipswich Ware lying on the surface (being dark, it shows up quite well in dry weather, when the silty soil turns pale).[33] Contrary to popular opinion, the Fens are not all boggy areas, and the so-called 'Marshland' soils around the Wash are naturally well-drained; they mainly consist of Iron Age tidal silts, which are actually quite porous because the individual particles of silt are halfway in size between sand and clay, so there are spaces for the water to pass through. This silty soil is very fertile – my vegetable garden grows sprouting broccoli the size of small trees – and it also makes excellent cattle pasture, being sufficiently dry on the surface to prevent foot problems in most animals.

Bob's work was particularly important because it shows how archaeology can be used to extend and amplify the historical record. It has long been known from documentary sources that the silty marshland west of King's Lynn was a very wealthy area. This wealth derived mainly from livestock, especially sheep, but salt was also extracted from the creeks around the Wash, and the proximity of the prosperous and growing port of King's Lynn certainly aided this process. If we rely on documentary sources alone, it would seem that the wealth of the region began to increase from the time of Domesday (1086) until the thirteenth century, by when it was a very prosperous area indeed. There were, however, no reasons to suppose that Marshland was particularly important in Saxon times until Bob Sylvester and Andrew Rogerson started methodically to survey the Norfolk parish of Terrington St Clement.

I first met Andrew when I was working at North Elmham in 1970, and I knew him to be an imaginative but essentially hard-nosed specialist in early medieval archaeology. He was never one to jump onto bandwagons, and he scrupulously avoided exaggerated claims, which is why I well remember his huge enthusiasm about discoveries at a site named Hay Green, just outside the village. It was the scale that was so extraordinary. Andrew and Bob revealed a vast scatter of about a thousand Ipswich Ware sherds along the banks of an extinct tidal creek, or roddon. From the air you can see a network of pale, silt-filled roddons snaking their way across the landscape. At ground level they show up as low silty mounds which would have been where Middle Saxon communities placed their homes, their farms and their stockyards. This was the land that rarely flooded, even after the heaviest rains.

Bob and Andrew found Ipswich Ware across thirteen fields, covering about seven hectares (over seventeen acres) and extending along the roddon for a distance of 1.5 kilometres. This was a truly massive spread, but what was even more interesting was that Hay Green was almost entirely Middle Saxon – there was only very little later material, probably because by then Late Saxon and Norman settlement had moved to Terrington, just north of the fine medieval church. On the face of it, this might suggest that the life of the Middle Saxon farming settlement was short and sharp. The scatter was large, but it was difficult to say any more about it without digging some selective holes. This happened a few years later, when some of the most important sites revealed in the Fenland Survey were given a closer look.[34]

It would now seem that Hay Green was not alone. The Fenland Survey revealed six other comparable sites that were evenly spaced out across the Marshland silts. This arrangement strongly suggested that these farms or settlements were part of a Middle Saxon planned development. It was also suggested, in line with what we know happened somewhat later, that the individual farms or settlements could have been linked to upland estates on the higher ground of 'mainland' Norfolk, to the east.

Like all good surveys, the 'field-walking' was more than just a pot-pick-up.* Metal detectors were also used, but to everyone's surprise they failed to find significant quantities of coins (*sceattas*) or any other metalwork. This was most peculiar, given the huge quantities of quite

---

* 'Field-walking' is a way of methodically searching a bare field for fragments of pottery, flint tools etc., that may have been brought to the surface by the plough. It is usually done in the winter months.

high-quality pottery. The surface survey also revealed a number of animal bones, many of which had been burnt. It was all rather mysterious. Everyone was agreed: trenches must be dug.

They decided to excavate at Hay Green and two other sites of the remaining six. All three sites produced a number of archaeological features, which was a relief to the excavators, who had feared that most would have been destroyed by modern farming. Big ditches had been dug along the roddon, and at Hay Green these ended in a series of large pits which were filled with quantities of animal bone and debris. Much of the animal bone showed obvious signs of butchery (butchery marks are now well-studied in archaeology), and it was clear that this had happened *in situ*. It therefore appears that meat was being exported from the site as joints or sides, rather than 'on the hoof'.

So far no clear evidence for settlement has been found, but this probably reflects the fact that larger, 'open area' excavation was not possible. The excavators believe it is likely that the six sites were only occupied in the summer months, when the grazing was at its best and the risk of flooding was minimal. So this livestock enterprise represents the planned exploitation of an underused natural resource at a time when conventional history might have us believe that the economy was still largely underdeveloped. It shows not only that these farmers had the wealth to buy in quantities of pottery, but that their products could be distributed efficiently to markets that were sufficiently rich to justify such a large-scale enterprise. The more we look at the Middle Saxon period in southern Britain, the more we realise that it was about far, far more than mere subsistence farming.

Ben Palmer is of the opinion that some rural sites may have had access to traded goods because of their location close to one or more roads or rivers. Laying aside the fact that the same can be said for most settlements, he points to rural sites such as Lake End Road near Maidenhead which do not seem to have anything special to offer, but which contain traded goods. This site lies close to the Thames, and has produced imported pottery, lava quernstones and Ipswich Ware from filled-in pits. So far, and despite extensive excavation, there is no clear evidence for metalwork or for permanent settlement. Whoever frequented this rather enigmatic site could also 'tap in' to passing trade. That is the theory. Palmer also suggests a nearby Thames-side site at Yarnton in Oxfordshire as a place that benefited from the passing trade along the river. But in this particular case I think it was rather more than that.

I first came across Gill Hey's complex multi-period project at Yarnton when I found my wife Maisie, a specialist in ancient wood-working, standing at the kitchen sink examining a waterlogged Bronze Age notched-log ladder. She had collected it the week before from the store at the Oxford Archaeological Unit, and was working indoors because it was bitterly cold in our barn, where she normally did such things. The ladder had been excavated by Gill Hey at Yarnton, which had also revealed a large Iron Age community, Roman settlement, Early Saxon and now Middle and Late Saxon occupation. Most of these important sites were later destroyed, either by gravel quarries or road schemes.

Maisie had known Gill as a student when Gill was doing research into Peruvian pottery, of all things. Subsequently she quit South America for the Thames Valley and began her remarkable project at Yarnton, which I first mentioned in *Seahenge*, my autobiographical book on Bronze Age religion.[35] Yarnton is that rare thing, a large-scale excavation which also happens to be a thoroughgoing landscape project.

Gill recently published her report on the Saxon period at Yarnton.[36] Yarnton lies on the very edge of the gravel terrace, on land that would have been just outside the limit of the river's winter floodplain. This location 'at the edge', as it were, was deliberately chosen both in the Bronze and Iron Ages, as in Saxon and medieval times. The Thames floodplain is dressed with a thin layer of flood clay, known as alluvium, every time the river is in spate. This material is very fine, and is rich in natural fertilisers. As a result the grass gets away to a very good start in the spring, and gives young lambs and calves what farmers refer to as 'a good bite'. In the past, before we learned how to ignore traditional ways of doing things, this land was never ploughed. Today it is, and surprise, surprise, the soil washes away and clogs up streams and drainage dykes.

Good arable land was to be found on the light, well-drained gravel soils around the villages that clustered at the edge of the floodplain, and up the gentle slopes of the valley sides to the north of them. Beyond this arable belt was another landscape of rough pasture, woodland and scrub. This was where most of the building material for houses and fences was grown. It was also a good 'emergency reserve' of fodder in wintertime and in very dry summers. Most grazing animals are quite happy to browse (in other words to eat the leaves of trees and shrubs) if grazing is running short – in fact my sheep prefer browsing the young shoots of hawthorn hedges around the fields to the rich Fenland grass at their feet. So Yarnton and the villages around were carefully positioned not just to be safe from flooding, but to exploit their natural surroundings as efficiently as possible.

Yarnton has produced huge quantities of Iron Age and Roman pottery. I can remember being in the finds shed surrounded by trays and trays of pottery stacked up to dry. This is what one would expect of an Iron Age site in the Thames Valley. But archaeology isn't always predictable. As a general rule of thumb, in areas where pottery is common in the Iron Age, it remains popular in post-Roman times. The converse also applies, so in places like the west Midlands around Cirencester, the Iron Age is almost aceramic – presumably people used basketry and wooden bowls instead – then the usual types of semi-mass-produced Romano-British pottery appear in the Roman period. At the close of the Roman period people revert to their old ways and pottery vanishes from the scene. But at Yarnton, despite the richness of its Iron Age pottery, post-Roman sherds are rare. This is particularly odd given the size and seeming prosperity of the Saxon settlements. These were not pokey, subsistence-style farmsteads clinging onto a blasted hillside somewhere in the mountains, but a thriving and vigorous set of expanding communities in the heart of the pastoral lushness that is the Thames Valley. So what was going on?

Yarnton and other sites around it revealed Early Middle and Late Saxon settlements, yet the total number of pottery fragments found there was just 117, weighing a fraction more than two packets of sugar (actually 2.192 kg). I would have expected something more like a quarter of a tonne, comprising anything from 10–50,000 sherds. We must assume that there isn't a simple physical reason for the rarity of potsherds, like very acid ground water, which can dissolve shell and other calcareous components of the pottery. So the answer has to be cultural. For some reason the people living in Saxon Yarnton didn't make or use much pottery. To an archaeologist, and probably only to an archaeologist, that might seem odd. But it isn't. In fact the decision not to use pottery is perfectly rational, if unusual, because good containers can be made from wood or basketry, and of course birch bark, which we happen to know was used in the Thames Valley in prehistoric times. These organic containers will only survive in waterlogged conditions, where the air needed for fungi and bacteria to break down organic materials is absent. Such containers are durable, they don't shatter when dropped, and they don't require complicated technology to make. In fact it's interesting to note that two probable Iron Age pottery kilns are known from Yarnton. But in Saxon times they wanted none of it, and preferred instead to use local materials such as willow and birch bark that would have grown plentifully nearby. To me, this seems a perfectly reasonable choice.

The pottery that did manage to survive was very interesting, and Gill's pottery specialist, Paul Blinkhorn, made the most of what little he had to work on.[37] Perhaps the most remarkable result actually took very little analysis: the features of the Saxon settlement contained more Iron Age and Roman pottery (3.5 kg) than Saxon. This was material that was lying around on the surface when the Saxon houses were built, ditches were dug and so forth, a strange inversion of what one might normally expect. During the life of the settlement this earlier debris slipped into the various ditches, pits, wells and post-holes, along with fragments of the few contemporary Saxon pots.

The Saxon pottery included nine sherds of Ipswich Ware, and Yarnton is so far the most westerly site to have revealed this early form of mass-produced pottery. Paul Blinkhorn has pioneered a sophisticated form of chemical analysis, known as ICP-AES (or Inductively-Coupled Plasma Atomic Emission Spectroscopy), which has shown that all the Ipswich Ware we currently know about was made from clays occurring in Ipswich. It can therefore be considered a very reliable indicator of Middle Saxon trade. Ipswich Ware was made between about 720 and 850, but was not traded outside East Anglia until about 730. At the height of its popularity it was traded as far north as York and as far south as Kent. Huge quantities have been found in the *emporium* at London, and it is assumed that Yarnton would have been within its trading area. Recently other sites in the Thames Valley have

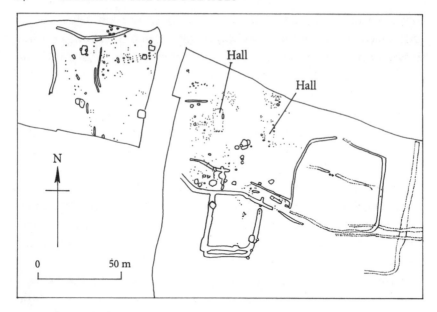

FIG 6   *The Middle Saxon settlement in the Thames Valley at Yarnton, Oxfordshire (AD 700–900).*

revealed Ipswich Ware, so it would seem reasonable to suggest that Yarnton was part of this trading network. As at other non-East Anglian sites, the Ipswich Ware from Yarnton included just a few vessels (around seven), the majority of which were large jars that probably originally contained some traded commodity such as salt or oil. It is always a problem, when it comes to pottery, to determine whether the vessels were bought for themselves, or for what they may once have contained.

There have been relatively few recent excavations of Middle Saxon settlements, so Gill Hey's work at Yarnton is most important. A series of radiocarbon dates has indicated that occupation began in the late seventh century and lasted through the ninth (say 700–900). There was occupation in and around Yarnton in the Early Saxon period, but Gill is keen to emphasise the contrast between that and what followed: 'The contrast between the Early and Middle Saxon settlements at Yarnton is strong. There are radical differences in the size of the settlement area, in the degree of organisation within it, in building type and in the variety of structural remains and other features . . . but the coherence of the [Middle Saxon] settlement plan suggests that it was organised on this large scale from the beginning.'[38]

The settlement involved, for the first time, substantial timber buildings in addition to the more traditional building form of the Early Saxon period, the SFB or sunken feature building, which essentially consisted of a single-storey structure with a wooden floor over a cellar-like space beneath.[39] This space probably served to keep the floor dry and would have helped the floor joists resist wet-rot.

The large buildings were a series of post-built rectangular halls and their outbuildings, including an impressive circular poultry house. These buildings were set within enclosures that were defined by ditches, and perhaps by hedges too. Gill notes that from the eighth to the tenth centuries the use of space within the settlement became increasingly formalised. She suggests that this may have been a reflection of two things: greater social control and authority, coupled with a growing shortage of land.

The changes visible in the layout of the settlement are mirrored in the surrounding countryside, where analysis of botanical samples suggests that farming was changing quite rapidly. Hay meadows were being laid out, major boundaries between larger holdings were being constructed, and manuring (using manure from farms and settlement) was introduced as a regular part of the farming cycle. Farming, in other words, was becoming more organised and intensive, yet at the same time it was also more diverse, with a greater variety of crops being grown. Technological improvements included the probable introduction of the mouldboard or heavy plough, which allowed soil to be cast to one side to form a true furrow.

The new form of plough was invented sometime in the mid-first millennium AD, and was one of the great unsung technological developments of the early medieval world. Suddenly proper ploughing became possible: the soil was cut, lifted and folded back on itself. This had all sorts of beneficial effects. The top growth of weeds was denied light beneath the surface, and died. Any manure spread on the surface was taken down into the ground, where the earthworms could give it their undivided attention. Earlier, non-mouldboard ploughs were known as 'ards' or scratch-ploughs. They were invented in the Near

East in the fifth millennium BC, and were most effective if used in two directions, a pattern known as 'cross-ploughing'. The best British example of the marks left by cross-ploughing with an ard was found below the mound of the South Street long barrow, just outside Avebury in Wiltshire, and dating to the fourth millennium BC.[40] I once had the doubtful pleasure of actually using an ard. It was pulled by two oxen, took all my strength and weight to keep it in the ground, and I only managed to make it penetrate about four inches deep. It really was a struggle, despite the fact that the two oxen were remarkably tame and behaved themselves excellently. I concede that ancient farmers would have had generations of skill and practice to guide them, but even so, I found it extraordinarily difficult. These earlier ploughs acted more like a huge hoe or a modern tractor-towed sub-soiler, which simply breaks up and lifts the soil as it passes through. All the effort goes into encountering the soil's initial friction and resistance; less attention is paid to what happens as the ploughshare passes through. It's a subtly different way of looking at the problem and the process of ploughing.

This pattern of intensification coupled with new technology is also seen at other Middle Saxon sites in the Thames Valley. It echoes, too, what we saw in the Fens of the Norfolk Marshland – and there are many other examples that show how the Middle Saxon period was one of stability, increasing social control and rapid economic development, at home and abroad. These changes in the countryside were combined with the growth of the first towns and the spread of international trade. It must have been a remarkably dynamic time in which to have lived.

Michael McCormick's view of early medieval Europe accords well with what we now know about the Middle and Late Saxon period in southern Britain. Increasingly archaeological evidence is revealing this as a time of vigorous change, trade and development, with regular communication over long distances. It seems no exaggeration to say that in the four centuries before the Norman Conquest, Later Saxon southern Britain was very much a part of Europe, and not just as a matter of economic convenience. The ties were also cultural, scholarly and ecclesiastical. Perhaps rather surprisingly, given the fact that William the Conqueror was a Norman with Viking family ties, the close relationship between Saxon England and its Continental neighbours failed to develop much further under him or his offspring. If anything, the Plantagenets and other high medieval monarchs took England in a more insular direction – whatever they might have claimed by way of territory across the Channel.

There is now no doubt that close links existed between Later Saxon southern Britain and its neighbours around the southern North Sea basin. Further north and west the situation was rather different. As we have seen, development here was slower and less affected by outside influences, a situation which was soon to be exploited by those remarkable entrepreneurs the Vikings. Our understanding of the period has changed in two important respects. First, we now see the Middle Saxon period in southern Britain as altogether more dynamic and cosmopolitan than hitherto. Second, we no longer see the Vikings as just being a force for evil – a view, as we will see, that was fostered by King Alfred, who is increasingly being acknowledged as a master of political propaganda. So what were the Vikings really like?

CHAPTER TWO

Enter the Vikings

THE LATE SAXON PERIOD (850–1066) has been poorly taught at schools, and I cannot blame the teachers altogether for this. There are too many kings with strange names beginning with Æ. Viking armies seem to whizz about the place generally wreaking havoc, and worst of all, it seems somehow rather uncivilised. In actual fact, and largely thanks to archaeology, we now realise that many of the advances made in Middle Saxon times were consolidated and built upon in the Late Saxon period. Indeed, it must now be seen as one of the most creative periods in English history. Certainly there was strife and conflict, but at the same time the administrative framework of the country was being established. The Church was gaining a firm foothold, patterns of land ownership and tenure were being established, and urban life was to be transformed by the setting up of the first *burhs*.

Maybe the neglect of archaeology is a reason why so many popular history books relegate the entire Saxon period to a single introductory chapter which usually reads as a prologue to the main business, which happened after 1066. Having considered the Middle Saxon period in the barest outline in Chapter 1, I plan to devote this and the next two chapters to the Late Saxon period. Although it will be impossible to avoid some degree of overlap, the present chapter will mainly be about the Vikings and the historical events surrounding their conflict with the Saxons. Chapters 3 and 4 will consider more general themes, such as the changes that took place in the administration of town and country.

The Late Saxon period is very much better documented than the Middle Saxon period, largely thanks to *The Anglo-Saxon Chronicles*, which as we will see shortly were set up in the late ninth century. But in both the Middle and Late Saxon periods evidence from field archaeology is having a most dramatic effect on the way we now view the first four centuries of medieval Britain. If one takes the historical record at face value, it would appear that people thought about Dane and Viking raids almost obsessively. Little else, it would seem, occupied their thoughts. But it now appears that the reality was rather different. Yes, raiding did affect people, especially in eastern and northern Britain, but as we have seen, farming, trade and communication were very much more important. But now we must come to grips with the bare bones of the political history – which is another way of saying that it is time to introduce the Vikings.

At first glance there is something wonderfully romantic, even 'prehistoric', about those wild Scandinavian warriors. They are strangely attractive, in a horribly bloodthirsty way. I remember on my first visit to Denmark meeting a university colleague who specialised in the archaeology of the Earlier Neolithic. Like me he was fair-haired, with an orange beard. As he shook my hand he said with a broad smile, 'So you are Viking, I think?' Suddenly – and quite irrationally – I felt I was part of a Band of Brothers. Had he offered me a horned helmet I would have grabbed it with both hands.

In fact horned helmets are part of the romanticising of the Vikings which began in the nineteenth century. Sadly, despite their evocative profile and terrifying appearance, they were never worn by Nordic warriors. I do, however, know of a very fine Late Iron Age example (probably first century BC), complete with rather fat, straight horns, which was dredged from the River Thames at Waterloo Bridge in 1868.[1] Its Celtic-style decoration firmly marks it as being some eight centuries earlier than the first Viking raids.

The word 'Viking' does not appear in any contemporary accounts of the period. Instead we read of raids by Danes or Norsemen. Sometimes they simply referred to their attackers as 'heathen'. The word (which is Old Norse in origin) gained public acceptance in the nineteenth century with the publication of the Icelandic Sagas, and the heroic deeds of the semi-mythical Viking sailors and warriors that appear in them. The Sagas were enormously popular and influential in Victorian Britain, and indeed across much of northern Europe. Today archaeologists tend to use 'Viking' as shorthand for 'Anglo-Scandinavian', which is the correct way of describing the Norse-influenced way of life to be found at places such as Jorvík (York). In general terms, what one might term the 'Viking Age' ends in England in the mid-eleventh century with the Norman Conquest, but we should not forget that places like the Western Isles of Scotland and the Isle of Man remained under Viking rule until 1266. Orkney and Shetland were Norwegian until as late as 1469.

The warlike reputation of the Vikings was justified, because we do know that they raided extensively in northern Europe, and even crossed the Atlantic to Greenland and Newfoundland in Canada. But there was a great deal more to them than that. Raiding was part of what they did, but it was probably a relatively minor part. In fact they were very much more constructive and, dare I say it, useful. Today many archaeologists question whether there was ever a group of people who saw themselves as distinctively Viking, as opposed to something less immediately identifiable, such as Nordic or Norse. It is also questionable to what extent the term Viking can actually be attached to a defined ethnic group. This is perhaps understandable: viewed from the perspective of a Saxon peasant in eastern England, it wouldn't matter a jot whether the raiders were members of the same tribe, nation or kingdom, because they were all equally unwelcome.

The Vikings are as popular in print as they have ever been, and some of the more recent accounts are also very well illustrated.[2] *The Anglo-Saxon Chronicles* contain the earliest account of a Viking raid on a British monastery, which took place on 8 January 793 on the island of Lindisfarne, just off the Northumberland coast. The 'heathen' raiders sacked the buildings, killed several monks and took others captive. They also desecrated altars and helped themselves to valuables which may have included the richly decorated original covers of the world-famous Lindisfarne Gospels, now in the British Museum.

The picture of heathens from abroad mercilessly raiding Christian shrines is a vivid one, but raiding was characteristic of the times. We know of many raids, especially around the Irish Sea, by British on Irish and *vice versa*. The Vikings were not the only people doing it. We also tend to think of northern and eastern England – what was soon to be called the Danelaw – as the main object of Viking depredations. But in fact other parts of the British Isles also received many and repeated visits from Viking raiders and settlers. It was a complex

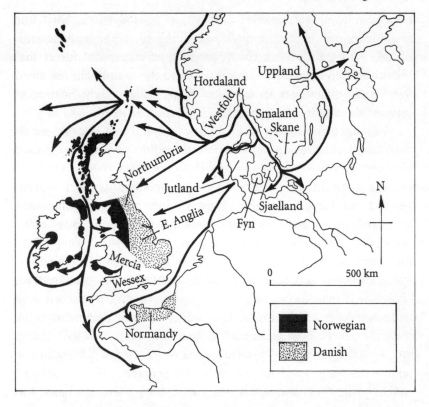

FIG 7   *The general pattern of Viking raids and migrations in north-western Europe from just before* AD *800 until the eleventh century.*

picture, not least because the Vikings were coming from many parts of Scandinavia. As a rule of thumb, people from Norway colonised the north and west of Britain, and Ireland. Danes came to eastern England and north-west France (Normandy).

Their non-existent horned helmets aside, the Vikings are justly celebrated for their superbly graceful, clinker-built sea-going vessels, known as longships. The tradition of clinker building in northern Europe predates the Vikings, and was to persist until the fifteenth century for large sea-going vessels, when it was replaced by carvel or frame construction.* The Viking longship was a superb vessel. I

---

* Clinker building is a strong and flexible technique which uses planks that overlap downwards. In carvel or frame construction the planks are placed edge to edge.

remember coming across one in a rather run-down state, very dusty and liberally spattered with pigeon droppings, in a shelter on the shore of Lake Michigan in Chicago. A faded plaque declared that she was a full-scale replica that had been sailed across the Atlantic for the World Columbian Exposition of 1893. The *Viking*, as she was named, was a copy of the Gokstad ship which was discovered in Norway in 1880.[3] Nobody was around, so I had a Viking longship that had crossed the Atlantic all to myself for an hour or so, until it started to get dark. It was an experience I will never forget.

The first thing that struck me about the *Viking* was her size. She seemed tiny for a vessel that could take the worst that the North Atlantic had to offer. I was reminded of this ten years later when I visited the Viking Ship Museum in Roskilde, Denmark, in 1987. I was on a circuit of Continental tourist attractions as part of the feasibility study I undertook before we opened Flag Fen to the public. I had spent the morning sampling the delights of Legoland, and was eager to escape clever things made from plastic bricks, so I headed out to Roskilde. I was looking across the harbour when I noticed that in amongst the yachts and pleasure craft was a replica Viking ship (a large one, but not one of the ocean-going warships), with another, much smaller boat moored at the shore. By modern standards they were tiny.

Maritime archaeologists have realised that many of the handling characteristics of full-sized vessels can be replicated in half-scale models, with the help of some simple mathematics.[4] These smaller vessels also present the shipwrights involved in their construction with most of the technical challenges faced by their ancient counterparts, but at considerably reduced expense. So far half-scale models have been constructed of a smaller Viking-age vessel, the fourteen-metre clinker-built Graveney boat, which it is estimated could have carried a cargo of six to seven tonnes. This vessel, which was abandoned in the mid-tenth century, was carrying a cargo that included (presumably Kentish) hops – comprehensively destroying the myth that all medieval ale was unhopped. The half-scale model of the Sutton Hoo ship, a twenty-eight-metre vessel, has been named the *Sae Wylfing*. I have seen her in action, and I was particularly impressed by her lightness – she could easily be dragged up onto a sloping beach by her crew, and would not require a quay unless heavily laden. The constructors of the *Sae Wylfing* were so impressed with her handling in rough water that they were inclined to attribute much of the political success of the builders of her original to such vessels.[5] It is thought that the Sutton Hoo vessel was buried within a barrow mound to commemorate or conceal the last remains of King Raedwald of Essex, one of the *Wuffingas*, the early kings of Saxon East Anglia.

Boat or maritime archaeology has become a sub-discipline in its own right, and landlubbers are advised to walk its companionways with extreme caution. Its practitioners can be as ferocious as Captain Bligh. So the point I want to make has to be simple: yes, ocean-going Viking longships were quite probably the finest open clinker-built vessels ever built, but they were not the only ships afloat at the time – we know of many humbler boats from Viking Britain – and they were not 'the reason', as I was taught at school, that the Vikings voyaged abroad. The Vikings came first, the ships second. In other words, the longships were built because the men who sailed them wanted to travel and had the necessary skills to build them.[6] It was not the other way around.

It should also be stressed that Viking longships did not appear, as it were, out of the blue. They can be seen to form part of an evolutionary tree whose roots probably extended back to the Early Bronze Age, around 1900 BC, when the first plank-built boats (found at Ferriby on the Humber) made their appearance. These boats could have crossed the Channel, and were probably used for trade along the coast. By the Late Bronze Age (say 1000 BC) trade and exchange around the North Sea was taking place on a regular basis. During Roman times Britain exported huge amounts of grain across the Channel to feed the later Roman field armies. We know that the Anglo-Saxons were excellent sailors, and we have evidence for this in the clinker-built ship from Sutton Hoo, dating to around AD 625. This vessel superficially resembles a Viking longship, and would have been perfectly capable of crossing the North Sea. And of course in the previous chapter we saw the extent of trade throughout northern Europe in the Middle Saxon period and afterwards. So Viking ships, like the Viking phenomenon in general, were part of a process that had roots many centuries old.

Viking warships, and some Viking art, were intended to strike terror into their enemies, and in this they undoubtedly succeeded, because images of Viking ships, such as that in wrought iron on the door of Stillingfleet Church, North Yorkshire, continued to appear even after the immediate threat had passed.

If we are to appreciate the impact of the Vikings on southern Britain, we must briefly go back to the Middle Saxon period and say a few words about the relationship of the Vikings, in what would later be known as the Danelaw, to the two major Saxon territories west of them, the Mercians in the Midlands and the West Saxons in Wessex. Many will know of Wessex and King Alfred the Great in the ninth century, but Mercia, under great rulers such as Offa, was of comparable power in the previous century.

Those of us who have the good fortune to live in the middle of England have always believed that we live in the belly of the place. What the Midlands digests, England consumes; this is the part of the country where we are proud to make and grow things, and where you find the best beer and the warmest people. In the Saxon period the Midlands was synonymous with the kingdom of Mercia. It was the most powerful kingdom of Anglo-Saxon England in the first part of the Middle Saxon period (late seventh and eighth centuries). The heart of Mercia was the middle Trent Valley. This is where its episcopal centre, Lichfield (founded 669), and two royal sites, at Tamworth and Repton, were located. As we will see, Repton is currently being excavated, and is producing very exciting results. Mercia's early kings Penda and his son Wulfhere were aggressive soldiers, and managed to exact tribute payments from all around: from southern Anglo-Saxon kingdoms, from British kingdoms to the west, and from Northumbria.

Mercian power peaked in the eighth century with two kings, Æthalbald* and Offa (757–96); the latter is mainly remembered today for the construction of Offa's Dyke, a massive earthwork which runs north–south for 192 kilometres between England and Wales. It consists of a bank to the east and a ditch to the west, so defenders could stand atop the bank and shower attackers with rocks, spears, arrows and

---

* I have used 'Æ' to indicate the Anglo-Saxon or Old English vowel 'ash', which was pronounced like the *a* in 'hat'; but I have been deliberately inconsistent in not applying it to King Alfred the Great, who ought more correctly be referred to as Ælfred. See Bruce Mitchell and Fred C. Robinson, *A Guide to Old English*, fourth edition (Blackwell, Oxford, 1986), p.13.

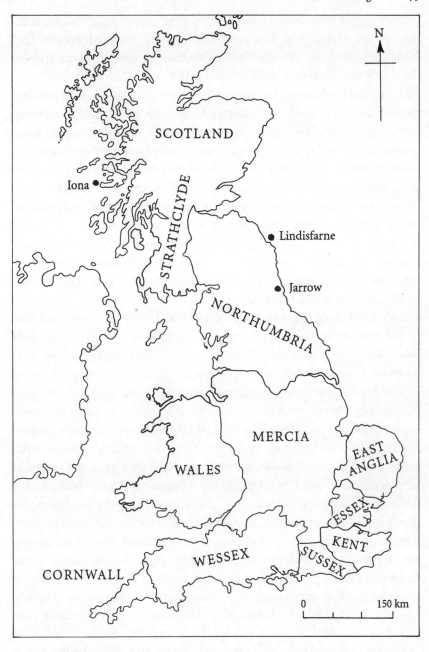

FIG 8 *The principal kingdoms of Britain in the late eighth century (Middle Saxon period).*

anything else that came to hand while they struggled across the ditch and up the steep slope. The positioning of the bank behind the ditch clearly suggests that the earthwork was built to defend the territory of Mercia from attacks from Wales and the west. At first glance Offa's Dyke seems like a single massive construction, but research by Sir Cyril Fox in the 1950s showed it to have been built in a series of sections, some of which don't marry up too well.[7] Fox suggested that it was essentially a symbolic 'line in the sand' created by the might of Mercia against the altogether more puny Welsh. More recently, detailed survey and excavation by Dr David Hill of Manchester University has shown that it was constructed in earnest as a defensive work against concerted attacks from the powerful Welsh kingdom of Powys.[8] It was a serious piece of military engineering, probably regularly patrolled by Mercian troops and linked to a system of warning beacons. Anglo-Saxon beacons were an important military tool and consisted of large thatched bonfires which were always at the ready.

Contrary to popular belief, Offa's Dyke does not extend from sea to sea across the entire eastern approaches to Wales. In fact the original Mercian earthwork is only found across the central part of Wales – a stretch of just over a hundred kilometres. The rest is unprotected, and David Hill believes that this stretch represents the boundary between Mercia and Powys, the source of the principal recurrent threat. Mercia was not at war with the kingdoms of Gwynedd to the north, or with Ercing or Gwent to the south. So that was the boundary Offa defended – there was no point in doing any more. This tells us that boundaries and political treaties were generally honoured. It also tells us that Offa was a pragmatist, and was not about to do anything that was not strictly necessary. It is known that Offa lost Mercian land to the kingdom of Powys in the mid-eighth century, and David Hill regards the Dyke as a fallback position to ensure that there were no further incursions into his territory.

The massive expansion of Mercia in the eighth century gave it control of land to the south and east, including, as we have seen, London, Kent and Sussex. If not actual control, Mercia also managed to impose significant influence on Essex, Surrey and East Anglia. Wessex somehow retained its independence. After Offa's death these new territories were kept within Mercian control by Cenwulf (796–821), but his successor, Beornwulf, could not stem the tide of increasing resentment against Mercia. In the year 825 he was defeated by King Egbert of Wessex at the Battle of Ellendun, and with the battle went Kent, Sussex, Surrey and Essex.

We have seen how the Norse raids began a few years before 800, and for the next three centuries Scandinavian raiders, soldiers and settlers were to play an active part in the development of early medieval Britain. It would be a mistake to think of this time as some sort of 'Viking Period', because many parts of Britain remained largely unaffected by these events. It would also be an exaggeration, because although Scandinavian people did influence certain areas a great deal – Viking York or Jorvík, which was captured by the Danish 'great army' in 866, is the obvious example – the language and basic culture of most of Britain remained fundamentally the same. In England, families born to the new arrivals often adopted Christianity and soon spoke the native language (Old English). The changes brought about by the Scandinavian 'presence', as J.D. Richards* has termed it, were much less far-reaching than the earlier adoption of an Anglo-Saxon way of life, which happened in the three or so post-Roman centuries.

The earliest Viking raids were essentially hit-and-run affairs aimed at rich coastal targets such as monasteries. Monkwearmouth, made famous some sixty years previously by that extraordinary genius the Venerable Bede, was just such a site. After persistent raiding it, and its twin monastery at Jarrow, were abandoned by the monks around 800. Scandinavian raiding turned to settlement quite rapidly in certain outlying areas of Britain, such as the north-western isles of Scotland and the Isle of Man. Strangely, perhaps, Wales seems to have been missed. The story of Norse raiding and settlement in England is recorded in some detail in *The Anglo-Saxon Chronicles*. This, or rather *these*, accounts are a fascinating mixture of history and propaganda.

The Anglo-Saxon Chronicles is one of the most important pre-Norman histories of Britain.[9] It was established by King Alfred sometime in the 890s. In form it was an annal written in Old English, which was maintained and updated at major ecclesiastical centres, where the

---

* To avoid confusing the two Julian Richards of Viking studies, I will refer to Julian D. Richards (of York University) as 'J.D.' and Julian Richards (of the BBC) as 'Julian'.

monks' choice of the events worthy of record often reflected local concerns, such as the appointment of a new bishop. Happenings in more distant parts of Britain often failed to get a mention. Julian Richards describes his excitement on being allowed actually to read a copy of the *Chronicles* in the library at Corpus Christi College, Oxford.[10] Like most archaeologists he was extremely keen to read at first hand the account of the Lindisfarne raid of 793. But he was to be sadly disappointed. The copy before him had been made in Winchester, where such far-off events were not thought worthy of inclusion.

The *Chronicles* begin with the Roman invasion, the account of which was mainly based on Bede, and they were still being updated in the mid-twelfth century, when the project was dropped. Surviving manuscripts are associated with Canterbury, Worcester, York and Abingdon. As Julian Richards discovered, the *Chronicles* can be patchy as a reliable source on early events, but are much better in their later coverage of the reigns of Alfred (871–99), Æthelred (865–71), Edward the Confessor (1042–66) and the Norman kings. Initially King Alfred set the project in motion for political ends. It was written to glorify his deeds, his reign and the emerging English nation. It does not give the other side of the story. For that, we will shortly turn to archaeology.

We learn from *The Anglo-Saxon Chronicles* that there was a 'great army' from Denmark in eastern England from 865. This force was highly mobile, and it took York the following year. It then went on to capture additional territory in the north of England (Northumbria), the Midlands (Mercia) and East Anglia. This was the land which became known in the eleventh century as the Danelaw – the area in which customary or day-to-day law (for example the rules of land ownership and local government) was influenced by Danish practice.

Alfred, King of Wessex, who ruled from his capital at Winchester from 871 to 899, is generally acknowledged as the first king of England. According to *The Anglo-Saxon Chronicles* his reign was largely given over to wresting eastern England back from Viking domination. Historians have painted him as an appropriately heroic figure. He is seen as the Great Man who founded England. As the *Chronicles* which he so astutely set up portray him, he is very much the English hero to the Viking villain. His principal contemporary biographer, Bishop Asser, was a churchman who was recruited to the royal court by Alfred.

He wrote his *Life of Alfred* by 893, and this is the source that most historians draw upon. Laying aside the question of its authenticity, it can hardly be seen as unbiased, written as it was by someone who enjoyed the fruits of royal patronage. Moreover it draws heavily upon *The Anglo-Saxon Chronicles*, which were themselves a source of pro-Alfred propaganda. Subsequent historians and politicians have added much to this already impossibly noble image. We probably lack the independent sources to form a truly balanced picture of Alfred, but recent work suggests that he may at least have been human rather than superhuman.[11] It cannot be denied that while he was a sufficient master of 'spin' to make many modern politicians green with envy, his real and lasting achievements were many. He was a ruthless ruler who understood the importance of public opinion. He was the right man for the times in which he lived.

The bare facts of Alfred's life are clear. He was the youngest brother of King Æthelred I of Wessex. Æthelred fought the first Danish waves of attack on Wessex, which were launched in the autumn of 870 from bases in East Anglia. Eventually he was killed on campaign in April 871. Alfred inherited the throne of Wessex aged just twenty-two. He had already assisted his elder brother in his campaigns against the Danes, and he continued the war vigorously. The Danish Great Army was to be no pushover, however.

In 873–74 the Great Army overwintered at Repton on the Trent. It was not an accident that the Danes chose the Mercian capital. Their presence made an important political statement. According to *The Anglo-Saxon Chronicles* the Great Army at Repton consisted of two elements. The first was the remainder of the original Viking Great Army that had arrived in East Anglia in 865; these men were under the leadership of Halfdan. The second force was the Summer Army of Guthrum, which had arrived two years earlier, in 871. Between 875 and 877 the army campaigned in Wessex. Meanwhile members of the Great Army were settling down, and in 877 a sizeable contingent settled in Mercia when the Great Army divided the province between itself and the Mercian ruler Ceowulf. So the opposition to Alfred may not have been as numerous as was once thought, because significant numbers had taken to farming. But it was battle-hardened and very well led by Guthrum.

In January 878 Alfred was defeated after a surprise attack by Guthrum at Chippenham. From there he fled to Somerset, where he waged guerrilla war in the marshes of the Levels. By May he had regrouped his forces and attacked Guthrum's troops at the Battle of Edington, near Westbury. This was to prove one of the turning points in the early history of England. Guthrum was forced to sue for peace, and provided the victorious Alfred with hostages. The Battle of Edington was followed in the same eventful year by the Treaty of Wedmore. This required the Danes to abandon their stronghold in Wessex (at Chippenham), which they did, eventually withdrawing to East Anglia. In a way that seems strange to us today, the victors of Edington also insisted that Guthrum should be baptised a Christian. He then retired to be King of East Anglia.

So the West Saxons of Wessex were the only southern British royal house to survive the threat posed by the Viking invaders. Alfred went on to form an alliance with the large kingdom of Mercia, that had fallen to the Vikings a few years earlier. The royal house of Mercia ceded London to Alfred after its recapture from the Danes in 886. Alfred was plainly an able administrator, and he instituted some important reforms. From an archaeological perspective his greatest innovation was probably the development of a network of *burhs*, or defended settlements, which served as permanent defences against the Danes and as secure places for coin mints and administration. I shall have much more to say about *burhs* later.

Although the vast majority of the population was still English or Saxon, many Scandinavian families settled peaceably within the Danelaw and seem to have gone out of their way to 'fit in' and adopt the Saxon way of life. A wealth of evidence now indicates that these settlers were more concerned with avoiding conflict than causing it.[12] Raiding resumed, however, in the last two decades of the tenth century, culminating in the final Norse invasion of England by the Danish King Svein (or Sweyn) Forkbeard in 1013.

Svein ruled in Denmark from about 985 until his death at his recently established English headquarters in western Lincolnshire in 1014. He became King of England in 1013, but had been involved in heavy and persistent raiding for some twenty years prior to that. His conquest of England was rapid, and it is interesting that instead of entering the country by the 'traditional' route across the Channel, he landed in the Humber estuary – a plan, incidentally, that the Nazis had in mind in World War II. He possessed a fleet of excellent sea- and river-going vessels that penetrated up the Humber to the Trent, which took him straight into the heart of England. His invasion base and headquarters on the Trent at Gainsborough was well inland – just a short distance north-west of Lincoln. It was here that he was acknowledged King by most of Anglo-Danish England. His mobile forces then moved south and west, where they took Oxford and Winchester rapidly. London followed by the end of the year, and the Saxon King Æthelred II fled to Normandy. This left Svein in control of England for about six weeks, before his death on 3 February.

Svein Forkbeard would only have been an interesting, if rather bellicose, footnote to English history had he not been accompanied on his English adventure by his younger son Cnut (Canute). To most English people King Canute is famous for the most misinterpreted anecdote in British history, his non-attempt to stem the tide, which, being an intelligent person, he knew would fail. His reign started badly when he mutilated his English hostages before taking his army back to Denmark. He returned to England in September 1015, and after defeating the stiff opposition provided by Æthelred's son Edmund Ironside, he took the throne. From 1016 until 1035 he provided England with a much-needed period of stable rule.

In the language of the comic version of history *1066 and All That*, Cnut was by and large a Good Thing: he retained many Saxon advisers, and made a Christian second marriage to Æthelred's widow, Emma of Normandy. Apart from his initial excesses, he seems to have been a pious man and a good judge of character. He died quite young in 1035, and both his sons (Harold I 'Harefoot' and Harthacnut) had short reigns and died in their twenties. The throne returned to the Saxon line in the person of Edward the Confessor, who ruled from 1042 to 1066. Cnut was an effective ruler not just in England and Denmark, but in Norway too (which he took in 1028). He fostered the English economy and realised the importance of regular taxation, or *geld*, in maintaining stability and an efficient administration. Had he not been a Dane he would almost certainly have been treated by historians as a ruler of comparable stature to Alfred.

The final throes of the long struggle between Vikings and Anglo-Saxons in England undoubtedly contributed to Harold's defeat at the Battle of Hastings. I have always rather admired Harold II, and not just because he was the archetypical Englishman defeated by William. He must have been a great leader who naturally inspired loyalty in his followers. He was made Earl of East Anglia in 1044, before following his father as Earl of Wessex in 1053. Edward the Confessor announced that he was to be his successor on his deathbed, doubtless because he knew there was no other person who could command so much respect across the country. Harold II was crowned the day after Edward died in the first week of January 1066. The events of that momentous year are well known. Harald Hardrada, King of Norway and a most able soldier, arrived in Britain and joined forces with Earl Tostig, Harold II's exiled brother. Their motives were simple: Harald Hardrada wanted the throne, and Earl Tostig wanted the return of the earldom of Northumbria.

At first Tostig and Harald Hardrada were successful. They sailed up the River Ouse, and on 20 September heavily defeated Harold's brothers-in-law, the Earls Edwin and Morcar, at the Battle of Fulford, south of York. Harold then rapidly marched his troops north and engaged Hardrada and Tostig, both of whom were killed at the Battle of Stamford Bridge, just east of York. The death of Harald Hardrada marks the political end of the Viking presence in England. It also contributed to the political demise of the Saxons. Not only were Harold's forces exhausted by the three-week march to and from York, but his presence there gave William's forces a chance to rest and regroup after crossing the Channel before they had to fight the Battle of Hastings on 14 October. The two sides were evenly matched, but the Normans possessed cavalry, their troops were fresh, and they were commanded by a superb and cunning tactician. Harold commanded the loyalty of his men right up until his death late in the battle. Then all was lost.

Those then are the main historical events of the period. Inevitably I have so far discussed the Vikings in generally abstract terms. We have seen how they established themselves in Britain, but what can one see of them out and about in the real world? As one passes through the countryside of eastern England with a road atlas or map to hand, it's almost impossible not to notice that a high proportion of place-names in Lincolnshire, Yorkshire and Norfolk end in the letters '-by' – places like Grimsby, Selby or Wragby. This comes from the early Norse word for a farmstead or village, *bý*, although sometimes the place-name can be a hybrid of Old English and Norse, for example Welby in Lincoln-shire, which means a farmstead or village by a spring or stream (from the Old English *wella*).[13] No less than 48 per cent of the place-names in the East Riding of Yorkshire have Norse origins. Fengate in Peter-borough, my first major excavation, derives from two old Norse words meaning 'fen' and 'road'.

Place-names are one thing, but what about actual, tangible physical evidence? Given the extent and duration of the Viking presence in England, there are remarkably few buildings or major structures that are of undeniably Scandinavian inspiration. This certainly does not apply in those northern parts of the British Isles where trees have trouble growing and where fine building stone is readily available. The stone here survives far better than wood. The best-known of these sites is the Viking settlement at Jarslhof, on the southern tip of the mainland island of Shetland. These are possibly the best-preserved Viking remains in Britain. Originally this farmstead was a small native Pictish settlement, which was replaced by a series of Viking longhouses in the ninth century. The houses are substantial structures, about twenty metres long by five metres wide, and they employ a cavity-wall technique of construction, with stone facings on the inside and the outside, and soil on the inside. Broadly similar techniques can be found on houses of the Neolithic some 5,000 years ago, on Orkney.[14]

Perhaps the relative rarity of stone monuments to the Viking age reflects the fact that the Vikings were master craftsmen in wood rather than stone. Maybe it also reflects the fact that they often adopted British ways of doing things when they arrived. When it comes to artefacts, perhaps the best-known are the hoards of Viking silver which are found across the British Isles, including Scotland and the Isle of Man. By far the biggest was assembled in the early tenth century (probably 905). It was found in 1840 in a lead-lined chest on the banks of the River Ribble at Cuerdale in Lancashire, and consists of a large number of smaller objects (many of them chopped up) such as brooches, bracelets, clasps, buckles and coins, which together weigh an extraordinary forty kilos.[15] I sometimes struggle when I carry a twenty-five-kilo feed sack for my sheep, so I know what forty kilos feels like.

The coins included Arab, Byzantine and Anglo-Saxon issues. It is likely that the most recent Arab coin reached England from Baghdad, by way of Scandinavia, in about nine years.[16] The eclectic mix of coins gives an impression of the variety of coinage that was in current circulation in the Viking world, because Arab and Byzantine coins are frequently found in Viking hoards from Scandinavia. The best explanation for this hoard is that it represents the pay chest of a Viking army, recently arrived from Ireland. Other explanations would apply to smaller hoards. Some may represent personal wealth buried for safekeeping in times of trouble. Others may follow the old Scandinavian tradition of making offerings to the gods that were never intended to be recovered. As a prehistorian used to dealing with the very much more numerous hoards of the Bronze Age, I suspect that a one-size-fits-all explanation probably won't work.

It would be a great mistake to view the Vikings as a bunch of illiterate warriors. The great passage grave at Maes Howe on Orkney was constructed around 3000 BC as a magnificent tomb-cum-temple aligned on the midwinter solstice. Four thousand years after its first use its main chamber was occupied or visited from time to time by Viking men and women who left behind a rich and fascinating series of inscriptions on all four walls of the tomb.[17] They are written in runes, a type of script that was based on vertical lines with a combination of attached strokes and loops. It's a style which is well suited to be carved into wood or stone. One of the writers, named Erlingr, wrote in two types of runes, which suggests that he was a well-educated man.

The thoughts behind these carvings seem strangely modern when translated. The Norse equivalent of 'Joe Bloggs was here' would be 'Arnfithr Matre carved these runes'. Perhaps this is something from behind the Viking equivalent of the school bicycle shed: 'Thorni bedded Helgi carved' (Thorni being a woman's name). Sometimes the humour could be subtle: 'Ingigerth is the most beautiful of women' – next to the rune is a carving of a slavering dog. The modern obsession with finding treasure was expressed several times, for example: 'It is surely true what I say that treasure was taken away treasure was carried off in three nights *before those . . .'.* The longest inscription makes repeated reference to treasure: '*This mound was raised before Ragnarr Lothbrok's her sons were brave smooth-hide men though they were. Crusaders broke into Maes Howe Lif the Earl's cook carved these runes. To the north-west is a great treasure hidden. It was long ago that a great treasure was hidden here. Happy is he that might find that great treasure. Hakon alone bore treasure from this mound.'* It is signed '*Simon Sirith*'. If the reference to Crusaders seems odd, it should be remembered that the Orkneys remained a Norwegian possession until 1469.

FIG 9   *An example of Viking runic humour on the wall of the south-east side chamber of the much older Neolithic tomb of Maes Howe, Orkney. The rune, carved to the right of a slavering dog, reads 'Ingigerth is the most beautiful of women'.*

The best examples of Viking art are the carved stones in church-yards which are widely distributed across northern Britain, Ireland and the Isle of Man. Viking carved stone art occurs quite frequently in those areas where it is present: there are approximately 115 examples in Cumbria, and around four hundred in Yorkshire. The Isle of Man has yielded forty-eight stone crosses which were produced in a rela-tively short time (between about 930 and 1020). These sculptures are undoubtedly Viking, but they are also affected to a greater or lesser extent by Anglo-Saxon and British ('Celtic') influences. This vigorous new hybrid seems to have been a creation of the insular British Vikings, because carved stone sculpture is not known in Scandinavia until the end of the tenth century, by which time the British tradition was flourishing. Stone sculpture was being made in Britain before the Viking raids, and it seems that the newcomers were quick to adopt it, but in their own fashion.

Because most Viking crosses are today found in churchyards, we tend to assume that they always stood there marking graves. In fact none have been found at graves, and it seems entirely possible that they were in fact memorial stones, some of which may originally have been erected in public places. A good example is the figure carved on the Middleton Cross in North Yorkshire, which probably represents a Viking warlord sitting on his throne – which is not the sort of sculpture one would put on a grave-marker. This would be more appropriate on a memorial in, say, a marketplace.

Further south in Yorkshire there is a group of distinctive Viking grave-markers known as hogback tombstones. The name comes from their curved profile, and they are mainly confined to the Viking kingdom of York. They are believed to have been tombstones, but none has actually been found over graves, and their decoration, which can be very elaborate on the best examples, is in a distinctively Viking style, with bear-like beasts at head and foot and elaborate interlacing patterns. Their shape and design – some have carvings of roof tiles on their upper surfaces, and their bowed sides resemble those of boat-shaped houses – recall, for example, the pre-existing English tradition of small, house-shaped stone shrines. They are usually found in parts of the country which were settled by Norwegian Vikings. Although they are undoubtedly Viking creations, no examples of hogbacks are known from Norway, and along with much of the stone art of this period they are best seen as a colonial creation of Anglo-Scandinavian culture. Hogbacks seem to have been a short-lived phenomenon, being confined to the middle decades of the ninth century.

Another uniquely Anglo-Scandinavian development are the early sundials that appear on country churches in Yorkshire. These sometimes record the names of Viking lords who were benefactors of the church. A good example can be seen at Old Byland (high in the east side of the tower above the southern doorway), but the best is undoubtedly that at St Gregory's Minster, Kirkdale. Here the inscription in Old English reads: 'Orm, son of Gamal, acquired the church of St Gregory when it was tumbled and ruined, and had it rebuilt from the ground in honour of Christ and St Gregory, in the days of Edward the King and Tosti the Earl.' This is a remarkable historical cameo: Orm is a Norse name, King Edward was Edward the Confessor (1005–66), and Tosti(g) was the ruler of Northumbria and younger brother of Harold who was briefly King of England (in 1066). Tostig was killed at the Battle of Stamford Bridge in the same year that his brother died at Hastings. The inscription on the sundial probably dates to 1055–65.

Archaeology is often as much about archaeologists as it is about the past. As the subject becomes avowedly more professional, many within it would also like it to become more anonymous, feeling that less attention to individuals will lead to better teamwork. They may be right, but my belief is that a good team is composed of strong individuals with their own identities. They may well have a higher-profile leader, but that is normally a short-term arrangement, because when the team breaks up they can then follow their own interests, having gained confidence and experience from being part of a well-led team. In my experience anonymity is often a way of avoiding decisions, whereas good archaeology is all about having to make uncomfortable choices. All of which is my way of introducing the highly charismatic Professor Philip Rahtz.

The first time I met Philip was at a conference in York. The paper he delivered was a model of how to hold your audience. Afterwards we introduced ourselves, and he interrogated me closely about my then current Bronze Age dig at Fengate, near Peterborough. On that first encounter he got far more from me than I did from him – which is the sign of a true pro. In 1986 Philip retired from being Professor of Archaeology at York University and returned to his home near Helmsley in Yorkshire, a short distance from Kirkdale minster, which he decided would make an excellent retirement project for himself and his wife Lorna.[18] Of course he knew about the famous sundial, but the church now stands in the beautiful open country of Ryedale with no village around it. The obvious question was, how and why did it get there? Another friend of mine, Richard Morris, who was Director of the Council for British Archaeology, is a leading authority on the early Church in Britain; he is also a trained musician and in his spare time writes enormous biographies.[19] Richard had suggested that a large field immediately north of the churchyard might contain earlier remains, perhaps relating to a pre-Viking Saxon monastery.

Philip and Lorna were able to demonstrate that Richard's hypothesis was almost certainly correct. Early graves near the church were orientated on a 'natural' alignment which reflected the local topography and was the same as features in the north field. Later graves were arranged east–west, reflecting a stricter 'canonical' structuring of the graveyard. In addition to a fine Saxon stone sarcophagus, they also found a fragment of so-called 'filigree' coloured glass rod which may have formed part of an elaborately decorated vessel, which was probably made overseas. They point out that this provides evidence that the early monastery at Kirkdale was part of the great seventh–ninth-century pan-European trading networks that I discussed in Chapter 1.

There was evidence too that the early monastery fell out of use and became derelict before it was rebuilt, probably in the eleventh century – just as it said on the famous sundial. So the Viking noble Orm Gamalson (as he would probably have called himself), who rebuilt the minster 'from the ground [up]', was indeed reconstructing an earlier ruined church. By choosing such a place he was deliberately allying himself with what had gone before. In anthropological terms he

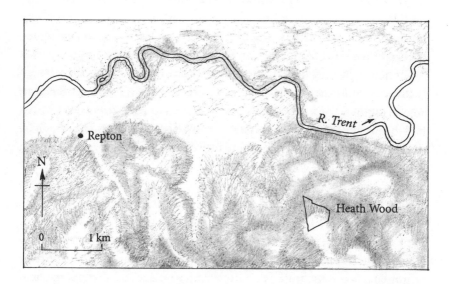

FIG 10   *Map showing the location of Repton, where the Viking Great Army spent the winter of 873–74, and the Heath Wood pagan Viking barrow cemetery. Both sites lie on the southern slopes of the Trent Valley, and are separated by a low knoll. Repton is shown on the general location map to Part I.*

was 'legitimising' his claim to the area around the minster. This was a way of seeking local goodwill, and is not the action of a person who did not wish to become part of the community. Gamalson's rebuilding of the minster was part of a widespread process in both Viking and Late Saxon England, whereby an emerging nobility was making its mark by rebuilding – effectively 'privatising' – rural churches, using their own money. In the next chapter we will see something similar happening at the church at Earls Barton, Northamptonshire.

Viking burials were once notoriously hard to track down in Britain, but recently things have changed with two important excavations. The first of these at Heath Wood, near Ingleby in the Trent Valley of Derbyshire, is the only known Viking cremation cemetery in the British Isles.[20] It can also be closely linked to the Viking Great Army between the years 873 and 878. As in many modern research projects, the team (which was directed by J.D. Richards and Marcus Jecock) reassessed the results of much older excavations which had given rise to a number of theories which didn't make a great deal of sense, given what we now know about Viking archaeology. There was an urgent need both to 'pull the site together' and to determine how much damage was being done by rabbits and the roots of the trees in Heath Wood, which covered the cemetery.

It became clear, when finds from the twenty barrows that had been excavated in the old excavations were examined, that the cemetery was solely Viking. The finds were not particularly spectacular, and most had been damaged by fire. The impression they gave was that the cemetery had been used for a short time and by a relatively restricted group of people. It was also substantial, comprising fifty-nine barrows arranged in four quite distinct clusters.

The barrows of the cemetery sit on a bluff or headland on the south side of the Trent Valley. Four kilometres to the north-west is Repton. Repton has been a major research project directed by Martin Biddle and Birthe Kjølbye-Biddle, who have excavated extensively around the church of St Wystan and the priory beside it.[21] Possibly their most exciting discovery was a massive D-shaped ditch and bank which incorporated the church and which is thought to have been the headquarters of the Viking Great Army when it overwintered at Repton in 873–74. Today the medieval church of St Wystan is plainly visible from the barrow cemetery, despite an intervening ridge. Admittedly, the Saxon church would have been smaller and lower, but even so, computer-aided visibility calculations carried out as part of the Heath Wood project have suggested that anything higher than 2.5 metres would have been seen from the barrows. The project has also shown that the barrows were erected in open country. Any funeral pyres there would have been clearly seen from Repton, especially at night, when they would have dominated the skyline. The two sites *have* to have been closely related.

The earlier excavations were of twenty barrows. The first five were 'opened' (excavated would be too grand a term) in one day on 22 May 1855 by the local antiquarian Thomas Bateman. He correctly identified the remains of funeral pyres and guessed that the barrows had been 'the scene of a sanguinary conflict between the Saxons and their Danish enemies'. A remarkable judgement.

The finds from earlier excavations included fragmentary swords and pieces of scabbard and the loops that attached them to the sword belt. There were also numerous iron nails, part of a spur and some finer items, such as two fragments of silver wire embroidery. The recent project mostly confined its attention to the excavation of just two mounds (50 and 56) and the area between them. Although neighbours, the two barrows turned out to be rather different. I will take Mound 50 first. Once the topsoil and upper mound material had been removed the excavators came down on evidence for a cremation hearth: there was an area of burnt sand, indicating intense heat, and within this were large quantities of ash, charcoal and burnt bone. The fire had been positioned near the centre of a carefully fashioned flat-topped platform.

Unlike Mound 50, there were no indications of extreme heat on the platform of Mound 56, and the only evidence for cremation was a shovelful of charcoal and cremated bone at the very edge of the plat-form. The composition of this cremation deposit, and the fact the ground around it had not been reddened by fire, suggests that it had been brought to the barrow from somewhere else. At all events, unlike the cremation within Mound 50, this was not an *in situ* funeral pyre. Finally, just like Mound 50, the cremation deposit had then been buried under more material from the shallow, scoop-like ditch around the barrow. This was the final act that marked the end of the funeral ceremonies.

On the basis of his own team's work and the earlier excavation,

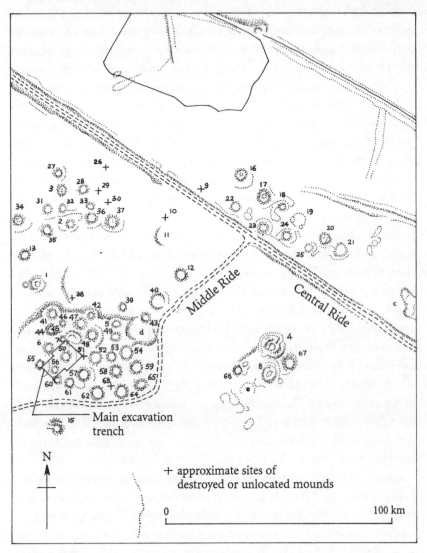

FIG 11 *Plan of the Viking barrow (burial mound) cemetery at Heath Wood, near Ingleby, Derbyshire. This pagan cremation cemetery of fifty-nine barrows was in use between 873 and 878 and was probably a war cemetery of the combined Viking Great Army which overwintered nearby at Repton in 873–74.*

Richards concluded that there were some twenty barrows like Mound 50, with clear evidence for *in situ* funeral pyres. The rest, like Mound 56, resembled token barrows that perhaps commemorated people whose funerals had taken place elsewhere. The relationship of Mounds 50 and 56 could possibly suggest that the smaller, token barrow represented the remains of a person or people who were either related to or were somehow subservient to the group represented by Mound 50.

The team that dug the site decided to see how long it would take to back-fill half an excavated mound. It took a dozen people, armed with wheelbarrows and modern spades and shovels, a full day to finish the job. This suggests that the construction of the barrows would have been a very labour-intensive process.

Some of the human bones recovered were of women and children. This would fit with the discovery of dress fittings and ornaments that are known to have accompanied female burials in Scandinavia. Several mounds showed evidence for more than one burial, and it is quite possible that some of the bodies represent human sacrifice – where a slave would be killed to accompany his or her master to Valhalla. The majority of the bones found were from domesticated animals, such as sheep, cow, horse, dog and pig. In Mound 50 these bones had been cremated along with the human bones, which suggests that the animals had been sacrificed, the horse and dog to accompany their owners on the journey to Valhalla, while the sheep, cow and pig provided food along the way. Sometimes uncremated pig and cattle bones were found in the mounds, which suggests that pork had been eaten either during the funeral ceremonies or by the people who had the job of erecting the mounds afterwards.

The finds were interesting, but not spectacular, and there was evidence to suggest that the pyres had been raked through when the flames had died down. Many of the objects suggested warriors. There were shield fragments and numerous scabbard fittings. With one exception the swords were fragmentary and showed clear evidence for ritual destruction or 'killing' before being thrown into the fire. Such practices were probably intended to remove the swords from the world of the living, and have roots that extend back 3,000 years, to the Bronze Age. Most of the barrows produced large quantities of nails, many of which had been plated, which would suggest they had been used ornamentally – perhaps to decorate wooden chests. It is quite probable that some of the bodies had been placed in such chests before cremation.

How are we to interpret this fascinating site? Is the link to Repton real or imaginary? It certainly isn't the latter, but neither is it simple. There are some obvious problems. If the barrow cemetery represents a war cemetery of the Viking Great Army, as Thomas Bateman half-suggested in 1855, then how, for example, does one explain the presence of women and children there?

It would be a mistake to view an early medieval army as being composed of soldiers alone. This applies with added emphasis to an army some of whose members had been in England for almost ten years; even the Winter Army component of the Great Army had been there for three. Inevitably they would have been joined by family members from overseas; either that, or they acquired families in Britain. The eagerness with which many settled down in Mercia from 877 surely shows that a significant proportion of the men had eyes for farming rather than fighting.

I said earlier that Viking burials are remarkably rare in England. J.D. Richards records fewer than twenty-five burial sites, of which most are single graves.[22] It is also well attested that Viking settlers and their descendants converted to Christianity soon after arriving in England. Yet Heath Wood is almost aggressively pagan. Sometimes, for example at the earlier royal burial at Prittlewell, people 'hedged their bets' and included both Christian and pagan elements in their burials – just to be sure. Many of the Viking burials at Repton are within the church-yard, and some of these may well have been members of the Great Army. As we have seen, many of the Great Army veteran soldiers had been in Britain for almost ten years, and it is highly likely that they had converted to Christianity. So why have a deliberately pagan barrow cemetery at a distance from the church, but within sight of both the church and the headquarters?

I find Richards's explanation entirely convincing, partly because it borrows ideas from prehistory and partly because its subtlety rings true. He suggests that the key to understanding the relationship of Repton and Heath Wood lies in the dual composition of the Great Army when it overwintered in 873–74. The men of the original force, under Halfdan, took over the mortuary chapel which was the Saxon precursor to the present church. They buried their dead around it and established their winter camp there. They were Christian. The Winter Army under Guthrum, which had arrived more recently to reinforce them, was still pagan. Richards goes further; he argues that they were pagan because they wanted to make a forceful statement about themselves: 'Is it possible . . . that the Heath Wood Vikings maintained, or even reinvented, pagan sacrifice and cremation to assert their difference from the native population, or even those comrades who they saw as losing their identity?'[23]

The finds and other evidence suggest that the Heath Wood cemetery was in use from the winter of 873 until 878, when warriors, as Richards puts it, became farmers. Men killed in the Wessex campaigns would have been buried here – and this would help to account for the many 'token' cremations where the location of the actual funeral pyre is unknown. The siting of Heath Wood now makes sense: it would have dominated Repton, and the funeral pyres of the original 'founder' cremations would have lit the night sky. I wonder how many newly-converted Christians down there in Repton changed their minds when confronted by the symbolic fires of the final throes of paganism in Britain?

In the previous chapter we saw how the cumulative results of metal detectorists' finds are having a dramatic effect on our understanding of an entire period. Sometimes 'one-off' finds can also have important archaeological implications, provided they are reported promptly and action is taken. Although I still find it hard to be enthusiastic about the hobby, some of its archaeological shortcomings can be repaired if the detectorists follow the rules laid down in the voluntary Portable Antiquities Scheme (*www.finds.org.uk*). One example is relevant here. Peter Adams and George Robinson were very prompt in reporting their discovery of two Viking brooches to Faye Simpson, the Scheme's Finds Liaison Officer for Lancashire and Cumbria, in March 2004. Their action led directly to the excavation of the first complete cemetery of individual Viking graves in England, in open arable farmland just outside the Cumbrian village of Cumwhitton.[24]

The two brooches came from the grave of a woman of high status.

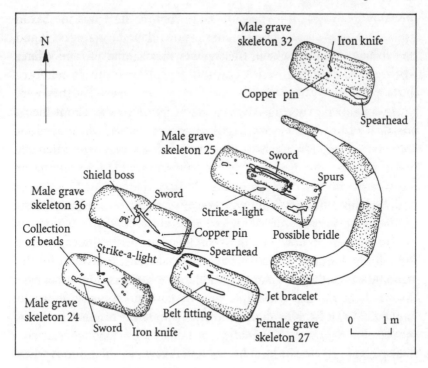

FIG 12 *Plan of the early-tenth-century pagan Viking cemetery at Cumwhitton, Cumbria.*

In the grave with her were the remains of a wooden chest, an iron knife and what is probably a sword-like implement used by weavers. The detectorists continued to search the field, and discovered more finds in the topsoil a few yards away. These objects, like the two original brooches, had been removed from the graves below by modern ploughing, which had also (presumably) removed any traces of barrows. The new area was excavated and five shallow graves were found, aligned east–west. This might suggest that they were Christian, were it not for the fact that the graves contained all types of grave goods – a practice frowned upon by Christians.

The finds dated to the mid-tenth century and indicate that the cemetery contained the bodies of four men and two women. James Graham-Campbell, one of the leading authorities on the Viking age, has suggested that the settlement where these six people lived was probably in or near the village of Cumwhitton. He was also able to explain the east–west orientation of the graves. Pagan Vikings believed that if they stood upright in their graves they should face the village where the community lived. It was this that dictated the arrangement of the graves.

Despite being damaged by modern farming, the Cumwhitton burials were of wealthy people, and people, moreover, who had probably arrived recently. Graham-Campbell reckons they were probably first-generation immigrants. This recent discovery tends to play down the role of the first Vikings as bloodthirsty raiders. Another recent find, this time during a commercial excavation, throws even more light on the first generation of Viking settlers.

We have seen how the mass of metal detector finds, revealed through the Portable Antiquities Scheme, has transformed our understanding of southern Britain in Middle Saxon times, but it has also thrown light on the vexed question of *how* the Vikings settled in England. Was it by 'elite domination', as some have suggested? In this model, elite figures such as soldiers or nobles move into an area, take their pick of high-status local brides, and everyone in that society then aspires to mimic the new upper class. The result is that everything rapidly changes on the surface, but ethnically the people remain largely unaltered. An alternative, perhaps simpler, explanation is the military one: large numbers of soldiers swamp an area, take all the marriageable women at the expense of local men – and society changes. We have known for some time that the Vikings were efficient, highly mobile warriors, but armies at the time were generally quite small, and the idea of them 'swamping' a region seems improbable. So the 'elite domination' model has generally found the most favour among academics.

A recent paper by Kevin Leahy, who advises the Portable Antiquities Scheme for north Lincolnshire, has however suggested a rather unexpected third option for a part of the country which we know was attacked by the Viking army in 877.[25] Anyone driving through the Lincolnshire Wolds will immediately be struck by the number of place-names ending in '-by', which was derived, as we have seen, from the Norse word for a farmstead or village. In fact some 38 per cent of place-names in Lincolnshire have Viking roots, and in the Domesday

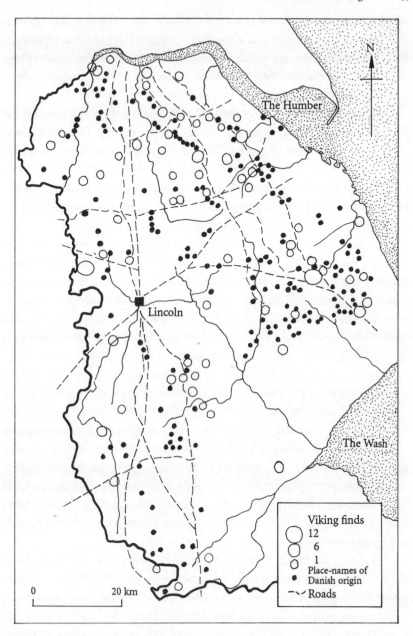

FIG 13 *The distribution of Scandinavian place-names and finds of Viking metalwork in Lincolnshire. Most of the finds were made by metal detectorists and are generally rather inexpensively produced small objects such as brooches.*

Book (1086) no fewer than 140 out of 220 Lincolnshire landowners had Danish names. There is a wealth of other evidence, too, to suggest that the Viking presence in the county was widespread, and potentially involved large numbers of people. But how did this take-over happen – if, that is, it did happen?

Kevin Leahy has so far examined over 260 Viking metal finds from the area. One might expect most to have come from certain key strongpoints, the sort of places that may have been favoured by warrior noblemen. One might also expect the objects to be things that such men would have treasured: fragments of daggers, swords or scabbards, belt fittings, harness trappings and so forth; but no, instead the vast majority of the finds are the sort of items one would normally associate with peasant farmers – and not just any peasants, but specifically women. Most of the objects are, as Leahy puts it, of strikingly poor quality: cheap, mass-produced trinkets that include large numbers of brooches, which we know formed part of the dress of ordinary Danish women. Male objects are found, including swords, but some show clear links to Scotland and Ireland, which might suggest that members of the Viking army were Viking in name only.

The distribution of Viking finds in Lincolnshire coincides with the occurrence of place-names with Danish roots, which would suggest that Danish families settled widely in the countryside around the principal towns, such as the famous Five Boroughs, which I will discuss shortly. So in Lincolnshire, if not elsewhere, it would appear that settlement did in fact mean settlement from abroad, and not 'elite domination' or simple military conquest alone. At first glance it is hard to avoid the conclusion that large numbers of civilian settlers must have travelled to Lincolnshire from Denmark, and presumably in many, many ships.

Or is it? This raises an argument that is as old as archaeology itself. Kevin Leahy's position is that the brooches and other trinkets, which nobody would deny can be linked to women, came over, as it were, attached to women. The modern version of this argument would be that the many Mercedes-Benz and BMW cars on the roads of Britain, and elsewhere, came with Germans at the wheel. The cars and the Germans within them stayed put when they arrived – and presumably formed relationships with the Japanese population who came with the

Sony television sets and the Italians who brought the Gucci handbags. I don't want to reduce a complex issue to the ridiculous, but none the less there is a great danger in leaping to the conclusion that objects = people.

In *Britain AD* I discussed the so-called 'fibula event horizon' of the century or so prior to the Roman Conquest.[26] This was a time when people over southern Britain were looking across the Channel to the spread of Classical influences brought about by Caesar's conquest of Gaul (France). There can be no doubt that people in Britain liked what they saw, and mimicked many Continental ways. Wine was imported by those who could afford it, and clothing and female fashions changed too. The archaeologist J.D. Hill described it as 'the end of one kind of body and the beginning of another kind of body'.[27]

As in Viking Lincolnshire, 'trinkets' were an important part of the new look, and a particular type of rather elaborate safety-pin-like brooch, known as a fibula, became very popular – hence the rather unlovely term 'fibula event horizon'. I would guess that the quantities of trinkets involved were very much greater than even those of Viking Lincolnshire. Just flipping through the pages of the report on my own excavations of a medium-sized Later Iron Age farm at Fengate, I spotted no fewer than fourteen (which would merit a big circle on the Lincolnshire distribution map).[28] But nobody, not even in their wildest imagination, would suggest that there was a massive invasion of eastern England in the Late Iron Age.

There are dangers, however, in slipping from one period to another too readily. While I remain slightly sceptical about some of Kevin Leahy's claims, it cannot be denied that the Vikings were great sailors, and that travel was part of their way of life; which is possibly more than can be said for the inhabitants of Iron Age Britain. A recent item in the Society of Antiquaries' email newsletter, *Salon*, suggests that DNA evidence taken from five hundred men and women living on Shetland demonstrates that the original Viking settlers brought their womenfolk with them, although the male–female balance tended to favour men more the further one moved from Scandinavia.[29] All in all, I think the old vision of warlike Viking warriors pointlessly raping and pillaging their way through Britain is well and truly dead.

More *bona fide* evidence for women travelling long distances comes from just across the county boundary of Lincolnshire, to the west, where contract archaeologists working ahead of the construction of a sewer at Adwick-le-Street in Yorkshire, just north of Doncaster, came across the grave of a woman aged thirty-three to forty-five.[30] She was wearing the clothes of a free-born Scandinavian, consisting of a full-length chemise under a strap dress which was held in place by two tortoise-shaped brooches, similar in style and date to the pair found at Cumwhitton. Bone survived poorly at Cumwhitton, but preservation at Adwick-le-Street was very much better, and Dr Paul Budd of Durham University was able to carry out stable isotope analysis of her tooth enamel. This technique allows scientists to pinpoint where a person grew up, because tooth enamel ceases to be formed after the age of twelve, and while it is being laid down it incorporates certain characteristics of the local water – which can in turn be mapped using modern sources of information. Paul showed that the woman with the two brooches spent her childhood in Norway, possibly in the Trond-heim area. She had been given a pagan burial with grave goods that included a bronze bowl, an iron knife and a latchkey – a symbol that she was a married woman. Again, this first-generation immigrant hardly seems very fierce or warlike.

One final thought before we leave the realms of Viking death. The Holy Grail of Viking funerary archaeology in England has to be the discovery of a ship burial. In 1945 a superb and *bona fide* ninth-century Viking ship burial was excavated at Balladoole on the Isle of Man by the great German archaeologist Gerhard Bersu, who was interned on the island as an alien despite the fact that he had fled from Germany before the war.[31] His internment was very free and easy, and he was allowed to excavate a number of Manx sites, which he did meticulously and with enormous flare.

In 1985 a rich Viking ship burial was discovered on the foreshore on the north side of the Orkney island of Sanday, at a spot known as Scar.[32] The archaeologists had to work in the most appalling conditions, being constantly lashed by driving winds and salt spray. But it was well worth the effort. The shape of the boat could be made out by the rust marks of some three hundred iron rivets which held the timbers together. Part of the boat had been lost to the sea by the time the archaeologists were alerted to it. The eastern part of the boat had been weighed down with packing stones, but the western part was a burial

FIG 14   *The clothes worn by a first-generation Viking woman whose grave was found at Adwick-le-Street, near Doncaster. She wears the clothes of a free-born Scandinavian, a full-length chemise beneath a strap dress which was fastened high on the chest by a pair of large, oval 'tortoise' brooches. Late ninth century* AD.

chamber which contained the bones of a man, a woman and a child. Although somewhat disturbed by an otter's nest, the finds were very rich indeed, and included a sword and scabbard, a quiverful of arrows, a bone comb, an iron sickle and an elaborate ninth-century brooch of Norwegian type – far superior to the cheap and cheerful trinkets from Lincolnshire. This was high-status stuff. The finest find was a large carved whalebone plaque, thought to have been an ironing board. According to legend these plaques were carved by young men and given to their brides as betrothal presents. There is something rather sad about this little family group.

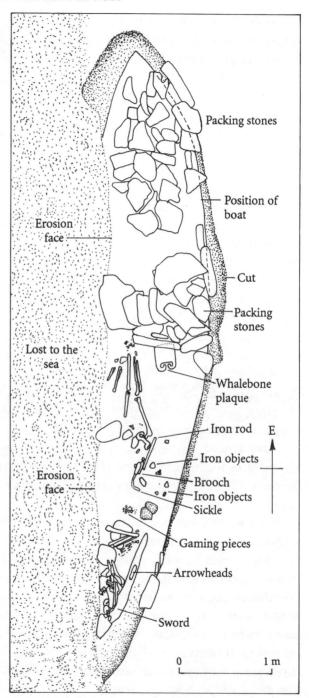

FIG 15 *A plan of the ninth-century Viking boat burial at Scar on the north coast of the Orkney island of Sanday. Approximately a third of the boat had been lost to the sea when the archaeologists arrived on the scene. The east portion of the boat has been weighed down with rocks. The west part was a burial chamber which held the bodies of a man, a woman and a child.*

Packing stones

Position of boat

Erosion face

Cut

Packing stones

Lost to the sea

Whalebone plaque

Iron rod

E

Iron objects

Erosion face

Brooch

Iron objects

Sickle

Gaming pieces

Arrowheads

Sword

0   1 m

So far no Viking ship or boat burials have been found on the British mainland. The nearest we have come is the magnificent seventh-century Anglo-Saxon ship beneath the barrow at Sutton Hoo in Suffolk. Recently about 130 pieces of metalwork were found by two unidentified detectorists in Yorkshire.[33] They reported their finds to Simon Holmes of the Portable Antiquities Scheme. There was speculation in the press about a possible Viking ship burial, but some of the finds, according to Arne Emil Christensen, the retired curator of the Viking Ship Museum in Oslo, were not what one might expect to find from such a burial. They did find nails – which are everywhere when the timbers of a ship eventually decay – but not very many of them. Peter Addyman, until recently Director of the York Archaeological Trust, thinks there might possibly be something to the story. Time will tell.

J.D. Richards points out that despite Britain being a war zone, or perhaps because of it, the three centuries of the Viking 'presence' were also a period of major social and economic change for the Anglo-Saxons.[34] As we have seen, the administrative organisation of the landscape altered quite rapidly to accommodate changes in both how and where people were living. Another important product of the continuing conflict was the new *burhs*, or fortified towns. We will see in Chapter 4 how the establishment of Saxon *burhs* has had an enduring influence on the urban geography of England.

I well remember the time I first became aware of this. I had just learned how to drive, and had gone for a trip in my father's car up the Great North Road to see the stone-built town of Stamford, which has to be one of the most beautiful places in Britain. In those days the A1 did not bypass it; instead traffic ground its way across the River Welland and up the hill towards the centre of town. Towards the top of St Mary's Hill the road makes a very sharp turn to the left and then follows a gently curving, almost circular path. That sharp bend and the subsequent route was where the road met the early Danish defences of the *burh*. What I didn't know then was that there was another, Saxon, *burh* on the south side of the river.[35] Even more remarkable, my two favourite pubs in Stamford, St Mary's Vaults and the George Hotel, are in the Danish and Saxon *burhs* respectively. I often wondered why they have contrasting clienteles. Even today the clothes they wear are different: smart tweeds at the George and grubby blue denim at the Vaults. Now I know why.

The Danish *burh* at Stamford was constructed on a prominent valley terrace and overlooked the probable site of the original Saxon settlement on the north side of the Lammas Bridge, a couple of hundred metres upstream of the main Town Bridge. The original Town Bridge, which consisted of five arches, was built in the twelfth century and lasted until the mid-nineteenth, when it was replaced by the current Norman-style bridge. The earlier crossing-place was at a spot where the river flowed in two smaller channels which could have been forded or bridged with more ease. Today these streams are crossed by two modern footbridges, the Lammas and the George Bridges; earlier versions of both appear in the Domesday Book (1086) – about which much more later. The line of the two footbridges suggests the route of the original Saxon road to the settlement, which was probably quite substantial given that it controlled the river crossing. The fact that the Danes saw fit to construct a major *burh* directly overlooking it must also be significant.

The Danish *burh* may have been established about 877, when the 'Great Army' conquered Mercia and retained half of it for its own use. It used to be held that Stamford was one of the Five Boroughs set up by the Danes to consolidate their hold on Mercia – the others (listed in the *Anglo-Saxon Chronicles* entry for 942) were Derby, Leicester, Lincoln and Nottingham. Richard Hall has pointed out that there is no direct evidence for such an early foundation for the Five Boroughs, and it is just as probable that they did not come into Danish hands until sometime after 910, in which case they would have been modelled upon Alfred's earlier Wessex *burhs*.[36] They all share certain points in common, being located on navigable rivers and/or major roads. Derby, Leicester and Lincoln made use of Roman fortifications, and all five have provided evidence for Middle Saxon occupation. The *Anglo-Saxon Chronicles* for 918 record that the northern, Danish, *burh* at Stamford fell to forces under Edward the Elder, son of King Alfred of Wessex, who then constructed the southern, Saxon, *burh* to control both sides of this important crossing.

There has been some dispute as to the extent to which the Danes founded truly urban fortifications when they established the Five Boroughs. While it can be shown that they were positioned on or close to earlier settlements, with the possible exception of Lincoln, none of these could be said to be true towns with wharves, extensive industry and commerce, and it is quite possible that they acquired their urban status, encouraged by Edward the Elder, after he had freed them from Viking control.

Although the origin of the *burhs* lay in the warlike times of the late ninth and tenth centuries, they grew, developed and flourished in Late Saxon and Saxo-Norman times. So I will consider them in the next chapter, when I cover the growth of towns in more detail. I have mentioned the Five Boroughs here because they were products of the Danelaw, albeit under Saxon influence. But what was the actual Viking contribution to the growth and development of towns in Britain? Everyone knows about 'Viking York', but to what extent was it Viking in the sense of 'people' and 'culture', rather than Viking the period?

J.D. Richards sees the role of the Vikings in the origins and growth of towns in Britain as being essentially indirect.[37] He does not view them as instigators, but rather as facilitators, to use an ugly term he would never employ himself. So in places, such as the Isle of Man, which the Vikings had more or less to themselves, they did not establish towns. In Ireland it is well known that Dublin and Cork are Viking foundations, but Richards makes it clear that these were English-style towns 'exported' to Ireland by the Vikings. In York the Vikings encouraged the growth of the town, but are unlikely to have instigated it. One way in which they facilitated the growth of towns was entirely accidental: simply by being a hostile presence in the land they encouraged others to create the fortified *burhs*.

Unlike the rulers of the Danelaw, the kings of Mercia and Wessex actively encouraged urban growth in the *burhs*. These new centres provided protection for royalty, administration and local government. As a result of this security and administrative convenience, trade, industry and commerce flourished. The *burhs* provided an ideal climate for the rapid economic growth that characterised the eighth and ninth centuries. They were fundamentally different from the *wics* that preceded them because of this new element of planned location, administration, security and control.

Richards also suggests another indirect way the Viking presence might have aided urban growth. Within the countryside of the Dane-law, security problems led many of the Saxon people, and especially those with 'mobile' skills such as artisans and tradesmen, to seek the protection of the towns. Their arrival in places like York would have added to the towns' economic prosperity. As Richards points out, 'It may not be coincidence that the fastest-growing ninth-century towns were in those areas most affected by Scandinavian land-taking.'[38]

We saw in the previous chapter that our ideas about the *wics*, trade and the Middle Saxon period have changed a great deal, largely as a result of the mass of new information provided by metal detectorists and commercial excavation. I want next to examine the extent to which this has this altered our perception of the Vikings, because trade and commerce did not simply stop when the first raids started in the late eighth century. Put simply, were they quite as disruptive as they have traditionally been painted?

A leading authority on the Viking period, Richard Hodges, pub-lished two papers in September 2004 which view the Vikings through positively rose-tinted spectacles; one indeed was entitled 'Goodbye to the Vikings?'.[39] The title was plainly intended to provoke, but the thoughts behind it are interesting. Hodges' second paper was a review in a more academic journal of recent work on early medieval Europe, in which he included his ideas on the interpretation of 'productive' sites. These views are a substantial development from those he expressed in his classic and highly influential study of the period, *The Anglo-Saxon Achievement*.[40] Most authorities now regard the earliest centuries of medieval Britain and Europe as a time of rapid change, trade and expansion. Inevitably, too, there was conflict – there almost has to be in such situations – but this ultimately mattered far less than the underlying processes of state-formation and communication.

Being an archaeologist, Hodges takes a long view of the period. He stresses the links between the earliest medieval states and the late Roman Empire. He has little time for the presumed total chaos, anarchy and disruption during the 'Dark Ages' of the fifth and sixth centuries. There has to have been continuity of government and social order, much of it supported, as we saw in *Britain AD*, by the early Church.[41] Hodges lays great stress on communication, and cites the work of Michael McCormick, who has provided historical and archaeological evidence for regular communication between Europe, Arabia and Byzantium (the remains of the eastern Roman Empire, with its centre at Constantinople – now Istanbul – in modern Turkey).[42] The coin evidence alone shows that this must have been a cosmopolitan world – an interpretation that flies in the face of what students were taught in the decades after the war, when early medieval Europe was seen to consist of a series of disparate, isolated regions.

Turning to 'productive' sites, Hodges describes the volume of archaeological material as 'quite astonishing' – strong language indeed for an academic.[43] He sees the picture in Middle Saxon southern Britain as essentially the same as that in contemporary southern Scandinavia, where trade and distribution were controlled by an elite operating from centres such as Hamwic, London and even (he suggests) York. He concludes that the Vikings were major players in the rapidly developing social, economic and political networks of early medieval Europe. As we saw in the previous chapter, Northumbria lagged behind southern Britain in terms of economic development in the Middle Saxon period. We now realise that the Vikings – or perhaps we should say peoples from the southern Baltic region – played an active part in developing the trading networks around the southern North Sea basin, the English Channel and further afield.

So, were those raids in Northumbria, Ireland and elsewhere simply destructive, or can we see them in a different light? Could we not be looking at something more akin to opportunistic entrepreneurship (albeit with a spot of rape and looting on the side)? The northern raids of the Vikings could be seen as the expansion of already-existing trading networks. This expansion was not wholly warlike, because in the process they established colonies of settlers and rapidly adapted to local customs and religion – especially Christianity. We know for a fact (as we will see in Chapter 4) that York prospered under Viking rule. As Hodges puts it, the Vikings were already stakeholders in an early medieval Europe that was realigning itself following the death of Charlemagne in 814. Viewed strategically, we must now see their place in European history as being constructive rather than disruptive. It has taken us a very long time to realise just *how* one-sided was King Alfred's version of English history, as he gave it to us in *The Anglo-Saxon Chronicles*.

CHAPTER THREE

Rural Life in Late Saxon Times

ONE DAY I PLAN to write a book about the archaeology of the twentieth century. As a part of this project I want to consider the many concrete pillboxes and other wartime defences that still litter – as some would say – the countryside. When archaeologists started to study the archaeology of the Second World War in the 1980s and nineties they assumed, because it was the received wisdom of the time, that the orders, permissions and other paperwork required to build these things had all been lost. But when they started to look they found many of them, and they have profoundly affected our understanding of the period, not least by revealing where sites (such as pillboxes) had once stood, because many had been demolished and cleared away in the post-war years. This is a sort of reconstructive documentary archaeology that doesn't necessarily require excavation, other than to confirm or deny its results.

Another type of reconstructive history has been named 'administrative archaeology' by Andrew Reynolds in his excellent recent survey of Later Saxon England.[1] Most of us are used to navigating our way around the counties of England. We take them for granted: 'Is old so-and-so still living in Shropshire?' 'No, she found the house too much trouble, so she moved to Sussex.' It never occurs to an English person to question where Shropshire or Sussex might be, because they are within their own personal geographies of England. They have become part of their identity at a profound level. I can see no reason why most reasonably well-educated people in Saxon England should not have possessed their own personal geographies too. Many would have resembled those of our own time surprisingly closely. This is why I now want to look at Andrew Reynolds' work on the earliest 'administrative archaeology' of England.[2]

The term 'administrative archaeology' sounds dreary in the extreme, but if one thinks about it for a few moments, it ceases to be. After all, what can be more personally relevant than the place where one was born and raised? As I have just noted, one's personal geography is essentially about a sense of place. Sometimes we express this in artistic terms, such as A.E. Housman's 'blue remembered hills'. But we describe people as coming from certain places that are named and defined, albeit quite freely. Although it is starting to break down as society becomes both more urban and more mobile, the person you are is synonymous with the place where you grew up. I remember once discussing someone I had just met at a conference with a colleague, and we were trying to decide where he came from. To our embarrassment we failed to realise he was standing directly behind us, which we soon discovered when he announced with a huge grin and a strong cod-Birmingham accent: 'Me? Oi'm a Brummie, me.' He was joking, but he was also both fond and proud of that great Midland city and what it had taught him about life.

So administrative boundaries are about personal identities. They are also about the way we govern our locality and administer justice. As a prehistorian I would dearly like to attempt an administrative archaeology of the Bronze and Iron Ages, but we lack the basic raw materials for reconstructing one. There are, for example, very few surviving roads or boundary markers. We cannot even be sure that we know the existence of all the major centres of settlement. In the end our best window on the administrative geography of prehistoric Britain is provided by coin distribution maps and the accounts of Roman authors such as Tacitus. The administrative organisation of Roman Britain changed in the latter part of the Roman period, but the major administrative centres, the so-called *civitas* (cantonal or county) capitals, remained broadly similar.

It was once thought that Roman roads were avoided in Early Saxon times because they would have been the haunts of bands of marauding bandits. We now realise that the Dark Ages were far less chaotic than they were once painted, and it does not seem reasonable to suggest that when faced with a long journey, a drover or carter should choose to cope with wet, muddy winter fields when he could use a proper, well constructed road, albeit in some need of repair. We have already

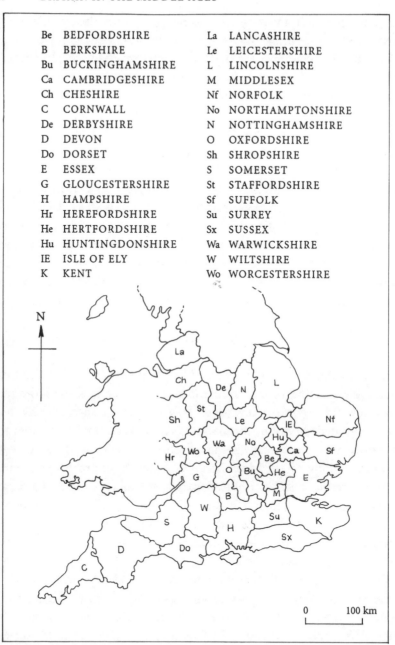

Be	BEDFORDSHIRE	La	LANCASHIRE
B	BERKSHIRE	Le	LEICESTERSHIRE
Bu	BUCKINGHAMSHIRE	L	LINCOLNSHIRE
Ca	CAMBRIDGESHIRE	M	MIDDLESEX
Ch	CHESHIRE	Nf	NORFOLK
C	CORNWALL	No	NORTHAMPTONSHIRE
De	DERBYSHIRE	N	NOTTINGHAMSHIRE
D	DEVON	O	OXFORDSHIRE
Do	DORSET	Sh	SHROPSHIRE
E	ESSEX	S	SOMERSET
G	GLOUCESTERSHIRE	St	STAFFORDSHIRE
H	HAMPSHIRE	Sf	SUFFOLK
Hr	HEREFORDSHIRE	Su	SURREY
He	HERTFORDSHIRE	Sx	SUSSEX
Hu	HUNTINGDONSHIRE	Wa	WARWICKSHIRE
IE	ISLE OF ELY	W	WILTSHIRE
K	KENT	Wo	WORCESTERSHIRE

FIG 16 *The shires of Late Anglo-Saxon England. These are essentially the same counties that existed prior to the local government reorganisation of 1974.*

A view of Offa's Dyke in Shropshire. The Dyke was built by the Mercian King Offa (757–96) as a military defence against the Welsh kingdom of Powys. The deep ditch and high bank were clearly intended to repel attackers coming from the west. This view, which is looking south-west, shows the Dyke as it approaches its highest point at Llanfair Hill, near Clun in Shropshire.

Part of the Yarnton (Oxfordshire) Anglo-Saxon settlement as it might have appeared in the eighth century AD. This painting by Peter Lorimer shows a timber hall with a lower annexe in front of a circular henhouse or dovecote.

The magnificent pre-Norman, Saxon tower of All Saints' Church, Earl's Barton, Northamptonshire. This massive tower was constructed in the later tenth or earlier eleventh century, and the distinctive strip-like stonework probably echoes timber construction (the topmost, castellated level is later). It was constructed during the period when the first manors were being formed, and it seems probable that a main purpose of the tower was to proclaim the importance of the Saxon nobleman (*thegn*) who built it. That lordly significance survives in the name of the modern village, Earl's Barton, although the 'Earl' in this instance would have been the later Earl of Northampton.

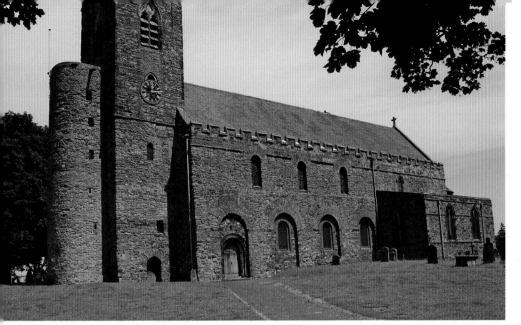

All Saints' Church, Brixworth, Northamptonshire. When you visit this imposing church it is hard to believe that most of it was constructed in the eighth century. It makes use of Roman bricks taken from buildings that were still standing in the area. Its ground plan is an aisled hall, which recalls basilicas, the principal public buildings of Roman times.

Above Three Viking period hogback tombs at St Thomas's Church, Brompton, North Yorkshire. These finely carved grave-markers were made in the tenth century and are mostly found in northern England and central Scotland. They get their name from the curved central ridge which resembles a hog's back. They are thought to represent houses, as some (like the two lower ones here) have carved shingles or roof tiles. Mythical beasts, often muzzled and usually resembling bears, support the ends.

Right St Andrew's Church, Middleton, North Yorkshire. This carving of an Anglo-Scandinavian lord sitting on his throne of office was carved on a stone cross in the tenth century. The circular bosses just above each shoulder are decorations on the back of the throne. He wears a long knife at his belt and is surrounded by symbols of rank and power: a spear, sword, axe and shield.

Clifford's Tower, York. This two-storey stone tower was constructed in the mid-thirteenth century on top of the original Norman (twelfth-century) earth mound of York Castle. It probably replaced an original timber keep, known as the King's Tower. William the Conqueror built York Castle, and another on the other side of the River Ouse, as a military response to a rebellion by the townspeople of York in 1069.

Two late-medieval buildings at 28–32 Coppergate, York. These partially-surviving fifteenth-century houses were probably built on the site of two slightly earlier buildings constructed before 1420 by William Alne, a prosperous merchant and former mayor of the city. They share the same parallel arrangement to the road, an alignment that was unusual for York, where most medieval buildings were set with their gable ends towards the road. This arrangement caused drainage difficulties for the neighbouring properties, which proved expensive for Alne to sort out.

Opposite Maisie Taylor standing beside the original south-west door of the Church of St Helen, Stillingfleet, a few miles south of York. This superb door is probably contemporary with the building of the Norman church in the twelfth century, although there are indications that it might even be slightly earlier. The iron-work is most remarkable and includes two fine 'C' hinges, various figures and a Viking ship. Traces of lost iron strapwork can just be seen in low relief on the door's weathered surface.

Donington-le-Heath Manor House, near Coalville, Leicestershire. We know from tree-ring and other evidence that this building was constructed some time between 1288 and 1295 by one Robert de Herle. We also know that Robert's widow, Isabella, was still living in the house in 1332. Robert and Isabella would have used the door with a pointed arch on the first floor, which would have been approached by a wooden staircase (the long slot left of the door may have been part of this). The very narrow lancet windows are original, but the downstairs door and the two rectangular windows were added in the seventeenth century.

A view of Stokesay Castle, Shropshire, from the adjacent churchyard. Stokesay is a fine example of a fortified manor house. Here the fortifications amounted more to a military 'style' that was primarily intended to impress the medieval visitor. The elaborate post-medieval (probably early seventeenth century) timber gatehouse replaces a medieval one (left); the superficially similar upper storey of the north tower (right) is in fact original, and thirteenth-century. The fine south tower (with flagpole) and hall (between the two towers) were constructed by Lawrence de Ludlow shortly after 1291.

Grace Dieu Priory, Leicestershire. These ruins are a good example of a small monastic house, in this instance a nunnery. In the early fifteenth century there were fourteen nuns, with several local girls boarding there. The population at Grace Dieu remained stable throughout the fifteenth and into the sixteenth century. Income (£92 in 1535) was derived from landholdings in the region, amounting to some 100 acres. This land also produced food and other materials needed for subsistence. Life was frugal, but far from impoverished. Grace Dieu was abolished in October 1538.

Fountains Abbey, North Yorkshire, seen from the south-west. This magnificent Cistercian abbey is now a World Heritage Site, and would have been a world away from humbler foundations such as Grace Dieu. Its construction made use of sandstone quarried from the north side of the narrow valley of the River Skell. An outcrop of that stone can be seen here immediately left of the Abbey Church's west front (built about 1160). The exterior of the west range of the cloister (built after 1140) runs up to the Abbey Church from the right.

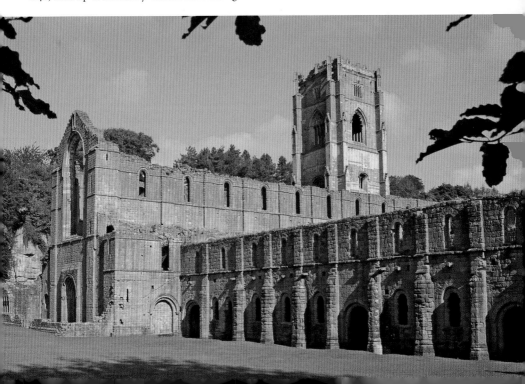

Fountains Abbey: a view south along the ground floor of the west range, from the Outer Parlour immediately outside the Abbey Church. The far end of the range was constructed over the River Skell when the range was extended in the later twelfth century. This magnificent long view would not have been seen in medieval times, as the range was originally divided by a number of partitions.

Fountains Abbey: Mill (ground floor) and Abbey Granary (above it). This building, which was constructed about 1140, is the oldest still visible at Fountains. It would have been operated by the lay brothers. These monks were an important part of the Cistercian system. Their job was to tend to the running of the Abbey and its estates. They were distinct from 'choir monks', who led a more reclusive life, with additional church services and less sleep.

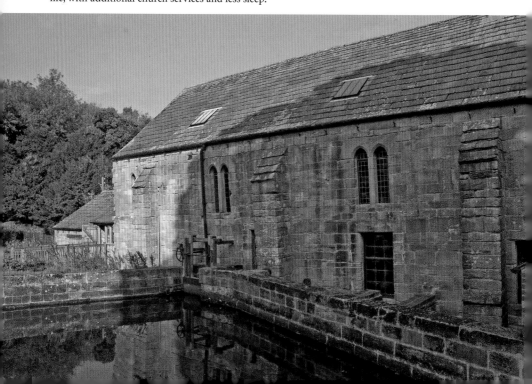

seen that Roman roads continued in use throughout the Middle Saxon period and into medieval times – and beyond, as many are still in use today. Many major Romano-British towns and cities were reoccupied in Saxon times. Some of these towns, such as London, York and Lincoln, then became county towns and major administrative centres.

The system of shires (the word derives from the Old English '*scir*', meaning share) that is familiar to most English people today is the same system that the Normans would have encountered in the mid-eleventh century. That is why people became so angry when the government 'rationalised' the ancient counties in 1974. Some very ancient and deeply held identities were affected: at the time I was working near Rutland, and I can well remember the strength of local feeling. Happily that county is now back where it belongs.

Many counties have roots that extend back to the sixth and seventh centuries. The best way of seeing this is by examining the administrative subdivisions within a county, the equivalents today of the districts and parishes; but to do that we need to go back well before the eleventh century to that early tax assessment list with the strange name, the Tribal Hidage, which I briefly alluded to in Chapter 1. This extraordinary document gives us a fascinating glimpse of England in its very earliest stages. The main political/administrative groups are already apparent: the Myrcenes (Mercians – Mercia), the East Engles (East Angles – East Anglia), East Sexena (East Saxons – Essex), Suth Sexena (South Saxons – Sussex), etc.

The Tribal Hidage survives to us in the form of an eleventh-century manuscript (now in the British Library) which, to judge from the places mentioned, is based on much earlier information. The term 'hidage' refers to a hide, which was a holding of land considered sufficient to support a family. It would seem that this document is a copy of a much earlier list which itemises the holdings of thirty-five named tribes, whose whereabouts and geography coincide with what we know about England in the late seventh century (say 680). Andrew Reynolds suggests that the Tribal Hidage is best seen as a one-off snapshot of Middle Saxon England, rather than some sort of developing historical document.[3]

The earlier history of county development suggests that some administrative subdivisions could go back as far as the late fifth century

FIG 17 *The approximate position of the groups listed in the Tribal Hidage. The Tribal Hidage was probably compiled about 680 and is a list of tax assessments based on 'hides' (the amount of land needed to support a single family).*

– the century that began with the official collapse of Roman rule in Britain (AD 410). The Venerable Bede, writing in Latin about 731, records the existence of administrative units called *regiones* (regions), and describes the Isle of Ely as a *regio*. Andrew Reynolds considers that these *regiones* represent the boundaries of smaller late-sixth- and seventh-century sub-territories; other examples may include the counties of Norfolk and Suffolk, within the larger kingdom of East Anglia.

FIG 18 *Diocesan boundaries in 850. These boundaries have origins that extend back to the later seventh century, and probably represent the territories of early kingdoms at the time they were converted to Christianity.*

These relatively large sub-territories were themselves composed of smaller 'micro-kingdoms' that grew up and were in turn absorbed by expanding neighbours from the late fifth to the eighth centuries.

I find administrative archaeology particularly satisfying, because it lays stress on continuity and evolution, rather than disjunction. It is also closely linked to the development of the landscape and the way that the people who lived there related to each other. We see this in other aspects of spatial administration, for example the arrangement of the ecclesiastical landscape.

The very early history of the development of the ecclesiastical landscape is not particularly clear. It essentially consisted of minster ('mother') churches, which sat within large parishes known by the Latin name *parochiae*. Both minsters and *parochiae* had origins in the later seventh century and the Middle Saxon period. *Parochiae* and minsters were grouped together within a diocese. After the tenth century we see the development of smaller parishes (as opposed to *parochiae*), but this was part of a much larger set of landscape rearrangements that must await the next chapter. It has been suggested that the earliest diocesan boundaries probably coincided with (i.e. were the same as) the boundaries of later-seventh-century and Middle Saxon kingdoms. This would make much sense if, as seems probable, the conversion of the English to Christianity happened 'from the top down': convert a king or tribal leader and his territorial boundaries became those of the church he has sponsored.

If we apply the principles of administrative archaeology to the territories occupied by the Vikings and Saxons, we find that by and large territorial subdivisions within Wessex and Mercia are very much more archaic than in the Danelaw. The sizes of subdivisions such as 'hundreds' (in theory a unit comprising one hundred hides) within the counties of Wessex varied enormously, whereas those within the Danelaw are more uniform. Hundreds, incidentally, existed until very recently. At first glance this contrast would suggest that land within the Danelaw was apportioned afresh when the Viking settlers arrived, but this is probably misleading. The general consensus is that the uniformity reflects the fact that an 'ideal' Wessex-style administrative geography was imposed on the Danelaw when it returned to English control. In the Danelaw the equivalent of a hundred was the *wapentake* (a term derived from the Old Norse *vapnatak*, which refers, as Andrew Reynolds puts it, to the brandishing of weapons in consent at an assembly). I am writing this book in a farmhouse near the Wash in the *wapentake* of East Elloe, in South Holland, Lincolnshire. Both *wapentakes* and hundreds were used to convene men and courts for the purposes of administering and enforcing justice.

If administrative archaeology can make a big contribution to the way we think about the organisation of the English landscape and local scene, what about more traditional styles of archaeology – can excavation and survey address some of these issues? In other words, to what extent can essentially small-scale techniques be used to throw light on the bigger picture? Here I must introduce an old friend who has probably done more to popularise our subject than anyone in Britain since the great Sir Mortimer Wheeler, Glyn Daniel and *Animal Vegetable, Mineral*, in the 1950s. I refer, of course, to Professor Mick Aston. Mick – he answers to no other form of address – is a pioneer of landscape archaeology. In fact he co-edited, with his friend Trevor Rowley, one of the first books devoted to the subject, appropriately if unoriginally entitled *Landscape Archaeology*.[4]

Mick is known to millions as the lead archaeologist in Channel 4's long-running *Time Team*, the first series of which was screened in 1993. I am writing this in March 2005, and the twelfth series has just finished. That's a remarkable record by any standard. A few archaeologists are still inclined to sneer at *Time Team* because it gives the impression that worthwhile archaeology can be done in just three days. According to these critics, some new students arriving at university apparently believe that archaeology *must* be done in that time. Laying aside the fact that this seems improbable, I don't believe it is a difficult task to correct such a false impression, if it has indeed taken hold. For what it's worth, short investigations of a few days' duration are commonly undertaken by commercial archaeological companies as part of the early 'assessment' phase of a commercial project. So sometimes 'real' archaeology has itself to be done rapidly. Short assessment excavations size up the scale of the problem and allow a reasonably well-informed brief to be drawn up, which other contractors can then tender for.

Time Team has hugely widened the appeal of archaeology to the public at large. When I was a student in the 1960s all my co-students were white and middle-class, and many had one parent or more who worked in academia, libraries or museums. It was a very closed world. *Time Team* prised this world open and revealed it (warts and all) to other people – millions of other people.

Time Team's three-day formula is a format which builds a sense of urgency into the programmes. It also puts a limit on the costs of making each programme. There are three camera crews, a fully staffed 'Incident Room', a skylift 'crane' for overhead views, and a helicopter. All of these things cost money. What some critics fail to grasp is that *Time Team* brings with it a huge battery of experts and special techniques, ranging from instant tree-ring dates to computer analysis, state-of-the-art surveying, graphic reconstruction, aerial photography, geophysics and every excavation procedure known, from trowels and toothpicks to earth-moving machinery, and from time to time the Team goes underwater. Geophysicists use various techniques that measure soil electrical conductivity, magnetism and so forth, to in effect 'see' beneath the surface.[5] Mick Aston has always insisted that each site is placed within the context of its landscape, which is why one of the key members of the Team is the landscape archaeologist Stewart Ainsworth. Like all other *Time Team* archaeologists Stewart has a 'day job', in his case surveying landscapes for English Heritage.

I have mentioned the techniques and approaches employed by *Time Team* partly to dispel some of the strange myths I've heard over the years, but also to show how the programme's multi-stranded approach can be used to tackle some of the complex issues surrounding the early development of landscapes. Mick's principal recent landscape research has been through the Shapwick Project, which was established in 1988 to examine a 1,284-hectare (3,171-acre) parish in central Somerset.[6] The parish was selected because it covers a variety of landforms, ranging from the marshy ground of the Somerset Levels to the Polden Hills, three or four kilometres distant.

The actual fieldwork of the project has largely been carried out by volunteers under the watchful eyes of Mick and his collaborator and fellow-academic (Mick recently retired from Bristol University) Chris Gerrard of King Alfred's College, Winchester. Sometimes the 'public involvement' of research projects can be, at best, token; often it's something added to lottery grant applications to allow bureaucrats to tick the box labelled 'social inclusion'. But not at Shapwick, where more than five hundred people have so far taken part in the project.

To my mind this type of professional/volunteer project is ideal. The energy of enthusiasts can be harnessed to answer specific research questions. They are not, as it were, 'out for themselves', trudging alone across open fields with a metal detector and hoping for a valuable find. Projects like Shapwick offer so much. They have an active social life, and everyone can become part of the team. Nothing is better than collapsing in the pub after a wet, windy winter's day spent criss-crossing a ploughed field with other field-walkers. While the beer in the glass sinks, one's spirits rise as the results begin to come in. Today somebody usually has a laptop with them, and you can see the distribution patterns of the finds you all picked up earlier in the day. 'Hot spots' appear, while other areas remain stubbornly blank. Why was this? All sorts of explanatory ideas fly around. Then you relate what you found that afternoon to the general picture revealed in previous years. Slowly all the pieces begin to fall into place and start to form the outlines of a coherent pattern. It's a man-made pattern that reflects the way people lived their lives and farmed the land many centuries ago. It can be amazingly gratifying.

Why is this process so very rewarding? I think the answer is quite straightforward: in essence what we are witnessing in the pub is genuine happiness not brought about by beer (although that helps), but through taking part in *the creation of knowledge*. That's why the team are so close. There is another lesson to be learned here, which is that fieldwork means nothing unless it is analysed, studied and then published (anywhere – on the internet, in a newsletter or academic journal). Archaeology is about a great deal more than mere digging. That is what separates it from metal detecting, which is just about searching and finding. I suppose in the final analysis it's the thrill of the chase, versus creative research.

The team at Shapwick did very creative research. One of the techniques they pioneered was first used in America, and is known as 'shovel-pit testing'. In eastern England, thanks to the vast expanses of arable agri-desert bequeathed us by the EU's Common Agricultural Policy, there are remarkably few fields of permanent pasture. So when

I do field-walking I wait for the field to be ploughed, then wait a further three or four weeks for the soil to be washed by a few showers. Rain is vitally important, because without it very few finds will show up on the surface. Then the actual process of field-walking is relatively straightforward: one walks slowly up and down the field, with head down and nose and eyes running freely (if a north-easter is blowing). When you find something interesting you pop it in a bag and a surveyor records its findspot and allocates it a number, which is recorded electronically on his instrument. With modern laser technology, such recording is much quicker than it was in the past. However, in much of Somerset conventional field-walking is impossible, because there are many more fields of pasture than in the Fens, where I work. This is why the Shapwick team adopted the idea of shovel-pit testing.

Good ideas are often simple. Shovel-pit testing merely involves digging a small, shovel-sized pit, and then sieving the soil from it for finds. The samples must be large enough to be significant, but not too large, or the work won't be worth the effort. Above all they must produce the same volume of soil, or one will not be comparing like with like. At Shapwick they sieved two bucketfuls at each sample location, and there were five of these in each fifty square metres. It sounds a slow business, but the team reckoned it was about as fast as straight field-walking. They also used various geophysical means of sensing beneath the surface. Most of the field-walkers were untrained in archaeology, so it was decided that everything on the field surface should be kept, from Neolithic flint tools to modern plastic. Up to 1999 the project recorded a staggering total of over 70,000 objects.

So, with geophysics, shovel-pit testing and conventional field-walking, carried out on a huge scale, they were able to discern some general trends in the changing pattern of settlement within the parish. Perhaps surprisingly, these changes did not seem to coincide with the obvious big political events, such as the Norman Conquest or the Viking wars. But that is not to say either that they were caused by purely local phenomena. It would seem that the changes observed there were not confined to Shapwick alone, but were happening at many other places in Later Saxon southern England. The steady rise in population and prosperity was probably the main driving force behind the changes.

Good research projects must have some idea or hypothesis that they want to examine. It's no good just to say 'Let's go and look at Shapwick,' because where do you start, what methods and techniques do you use? If the question is simple enough – for example: was there settlement at Shapwick in medieval times? – you could probably answer it in half a day, using the simplest techniques: a few field-walkers rapidly surveying one or two ploughed fields. But Mick and the team were intrigued by a more complex and intriguing idea that had been put forward in 1982 in an unpublished thesis by Nicholas Corcos, an MA student at Leicester University.[7] Corcos suggested that the roots of the medieval Open Field system of farming at Shapwick lay in the Late Saxon period. This was the time when earlier settlements, which were small, dispersed and surrounded by their own fields, were replaced by a larger, centralised village with its Open Field system. It was a major change in the way people organised their landholdings, their farming practices and probably their daily lives too. I will discuss the medieval Open Field system more thoroughly later, but all we need to know at this stage is that it was a parish-based system of arable farming, involving two or three large open fields which were subdivided into small strips of about half an acre each. Groups of strips were known as furlongs.

The arable land of the open fields was managed by common agreement among the tenants, each of whom would have possession of several strips and furlongs scattered through the open fields. Disputes were settled at the manorial court, where the tenants also met to decide which furlongs were to remain fallow and where animals could be grazed. It was realised that grazing, manuring and leaving land fallow were important if the arable land was to be rested to regain its fertility and minimise plant diseases. Animals were also grazed in the woods and on open pasture, often on heavier clay land around the fringes of the parish. The arable land was closest to the village, and was usually the best-drained, lightest and most fertile ground. The big drawback to the system was the fact that individual holdings were so widely dispersed, but as time passed there was a tendency to rationalise them into groups of furlongs. After the Black Death this process gathered pace as land became more freely available and the rules governing the Open Field system grew less rigid.

That at least was how the system operated in theory. In practice it differed from village to village and from region to region. The origin of the Open Field system is particularly intriguing, because it involves so much major reorganisation of the rural landscape. The Shapwick Project was multi-period, and we will return to it when we come to discuss the later medieval landscape, so the team spent due time and effort examining the Roman and prehistoric landscapes. They were surprised to find that many of the settlements and farms of the earlier medieval landscape actually had Roman and even earlier antecedents.

It would be difficult to prove that all these individual spots were occupied continuously without resorting to extensive excavation, which would be very destructive and probably not worth the effort or expense, but the fact that earlier finds came from the places that we know were occupied in the early medieval period (i.e. in the eighth–tenth centuries) does suggest that these places had already been favoured for a very long time, for various reasons – probably to do with drainage, water supply, access to good arable land and so forth. The sheer longevity of the pre-Open Field landscape at Shapwick shows how far-reaching and dramatic were the changes that led to its reorganisation. This was not something that would have been undertaken lightly.

Research into the origins of the Open Field system of the Middle Ages advanced by leaps and bounds in the last three decades of the twentieth century. But this work was not always either straightforward or simple. At Shapwick the testing of Corcos's original idea was made difficult by the fact that Later Saxon pottery was extremely rare, and did not survive well in the soil. In a couple of instances where it did survive as surface scatters these coincided precisely with concentrations of post-medieval rubbish, which would suggest that somehow the earlier pottery had become mixed up with the later material – and presumably was spread on the fields with it. Such things can be very perplexing.

As early medieval and Saxon pottery was so rare when it did occur, it was potentially important. So the team concentrated on other forms of evidence to track down the likely areas of Later Saxon settlement. They used a careful study of field names, together with analysis of maps and aerial photos, to suggest that the village and its two open (or common) medieval fields came about through the amalgamation of at least four (and probably more) earlier farms and settlements. This process of concentration – or 'nucleation', to use the jargon word – left the earlier church isolated from the new village, which now lay to the west. All of this happened quite suddenly sometime in the tenth century.

At present the team are trying to tie down the 'moment' of nucleation more precisely. It was completed by the end of the tenth century, and if other parishes in southern Britain are any guide, it probably began in the earlier tenth. So far this date would fit the available evidence best, but it remains to be proved absolutely. The way that the change happened is also beginning to become apparent. As one might expect, the shape and layout of the new village and its open fields was largely determined by what had gone before. The new village is aligned at right angles to the wetland, with its East and West open fields on good dry land. The survey showed that lines of communication to east and west, along the land sloping down to the wetter ground, had been established since at least the Iron Age, or possibly even earlier. At some time, probably in the earlier tenth century, intermittent settlements were established along a stream which ran south–north towards the wetland from another watercourse a few metres away. The land here sloped sufficiently to allow good drainage. Plots in the new village were laid out in multiples of twenty and one hundred feet – clear evidence for planning and careful layout.

The new system of Open Field farming would only work if communal labour was employed, which again suggests planning and oversight. It could also be argued that it would only work if the people concerned were willing and wanted it to be successful. The Church would seem to be the institution most likely to have encouraged and coordinated the required reorganisation. The project established that there had been a minster church on the block of land known as 'Olde Churche' since at least the eighth century. This church appears in Domesday, with an estate large enough to sustain a small group of priests. Clearly this was a place of some importance, which was part of the much larger estate of the extraordinarily wealthy Abbey of Glastonbury, nearby.

Recent work has provided evidence for further village nucleation in Somerset which, like Shapwick, can be linked with scatters of tenth-

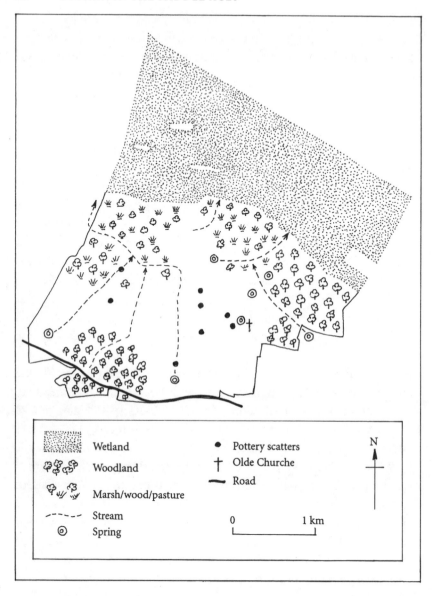

Wetland

Woodland

Marsh/wood/pasture

- - - - **Stream**

◎ **Spring**

● **Pottery scatters**

✝ **Olde Churche**

⌐ **Road**

N

0　　　　　1 km

FIG 19　*The landscape of the parish of Shapwick, Somerset, in the early
medieval period (before 1100). A series of settlements, some of them occupied
more or less continuously from Roman or even earlier times, are distributed
along the higher ground to the south of the wetlands, known as the Somerset
Levels.*

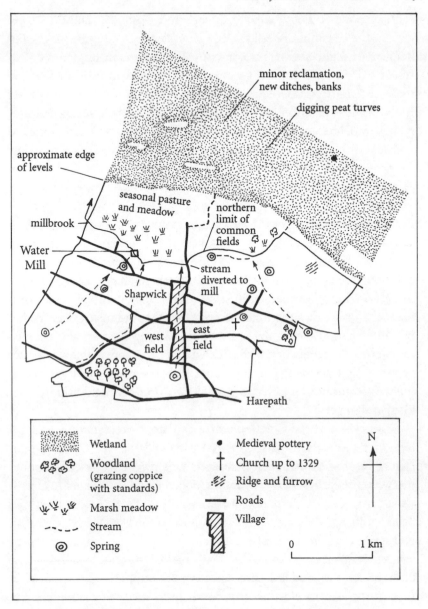

minor reclamation, new ditches, banks

digging peat turves

approximate edge of levels

seasonal pasture and meadow

millbrook

Water Mill

northern limit of common fields

Shapwick

stream diverted to mill

west field

east field

Harepath

	Wetland		•	Medieval pottery	N
	Woodland (grazing coppice with standards)		†	Church up to 1329	
	Marsh meadow			Ridge and furrow	
	Stream		—	Roads	
	Spring			Village	

0   1 km

FIG 20   *The landscape of the parish of Shapwick, Somerset, in the later medieval period (1100–1550). The earlier landscape was reorganised in the tenth century, when the separated settlements were drawn together into a single village with two large open arable fields, the East and the West Fields. Many of the boundaries and alignments of this new landscape were inherited from earlier periods.*

century pottery. These villages, Meare and Compton Dundon, were also on the Glastonbury estate. As a general rule, medieval villages and hamlets in Somerset were accompanied by irregular, unplanned field systems. This was in contrast to, for example, Midland counties, where the vast majority of parishes were laid out on the Open Field system. But this new evidence would now suggest that 'on selected arable estates, a deliberate decision was made by some large monasteries to reorder both landscape and settlement on an impressive scale, probably to increase revenue. The context for this might be the reinvigoration of monastic life under Dunstan in the 940s and subsequent monastic reforms.'[8]

The establishment of the new settlement was a major project which also involved the digging of some substantial boundary ditches, which were first revealed in 1996 by commercial excavation ahead of the construction of a pipeline. I should add here that although I have sometimes been less than enthusiastic about the quality of some commercial archaeology, there can be no doubt that the steady drip-feed of new information such as this is slowly building up a remarkably detailed catalogue of local history. The trick will be to establish Shapwick-style projects right across the country that will make sense of these seemingly unconnected discoveries. Somehow I doubt whether that is ever likely to happen.

If Mick Aston and Christopher Gerrard are correct in their assumption that the early monastic church provided the main stimulus for changes to the landscape at Shapwick, one might reasonably wonder just what the earliest Saxon churches looked like, as buildings. We know what Later Saxon churches looked like, and they could sometimes be magnificent. The best-known examples, such as Earls Barton in Northamptonshire, which I will touch on shortly, are mostly late (usually tenth or eleventh centuries), but one early example stands alone both in its size and its completeness: the church of All Saints at Brixworth, also in Northamptonshire. Even now it's a large church, but its age is truly astounding, and is very hard to accept as one stands in the churchyard. Excavation has now proved what is apparent on the outside: that this is a building of the late eighth–early ninth century, and it is now generally considered to be the largest and finest building of that period in Europe north of the Alps. Its layout is essentially that of an aisled hall, a design whose roots lie in the commonly occurring public building of the Roman world, known as a *basilica* – a word that was adopted by the early Church for its own use.

Recent research has shown that the builders of All Saints, Brixworth visited presumably ruined Roman buildings over a large area of the countryside roundabout and robbed them of tiles and stonework, which they incorporated into their new building.[9] It's a remarkable thought that the people who built this large church were inhabiting a world in which numerous Romano-British structures were still standing, albeit in a tumbledown state – rather like the abandoned farms and villages one can still see in the Scottish Highlands, after the enforced 'Clearances' of the later eighteenth century. This part of eastern England was quite well advanced in such things, because one of the greatest abbeys in the entire country had been established in the late seventh century at Peterborough in Cambridgeshire, just across the county line to the north-east. Other very early monastic foundations are known at Oundle and Weedon, and although the churches have gone, Middle Saxon Ipswich Ware has been found in excavated ditches at Weedon – which would link it in to the trading networks of that period which we discussed in Chapter 1. Communication would have been via the River Nene, which runs like a blood vessel through the middle of the county.

It was institutions such as the Church and the developing power of a rising aristocratic elite that lay behind a major transformation in the arrangement of the Later Saxon landscape of the English Midlands and the surrounding regions. We have seen hints of it already at Shapwick, but we now come to the second major change to the story of medieval Britain that has been brought about by archaeology. I am tempted to use the word 'seismic' to describe its impact, but colleagues in geology can become indignant at the misuse of their term. Nevertheless, in some respects I believe we can count it as *the* major change. We considered the first change – the recognition of 'productive' sites and the reassessment of *wics* and *emporia* – in Chapter 1. Now we come to what Dr Paul Stamper in the standard textbook of British archaeology has described as one of 'the great discoveries of British archaeology of the later twentieth century'.[10] Over large areas of central and southern Britain the early tenth century witnessed a major replanning of the countryside which was, to continue Stamper's words, 'at least equal in importance to the Enclosure movement of a millennium later'. Both altered the appearance of the rural landscape and the way it operated. As we began to see at Shapwick, both of these major changes were about significant shifts in the power structure of those who controlled the most productive land.

In this chapter I will be concerned with the origin of the medieval Open Field system, which was the principal result of the great resurveying that took place over large areas of central Britain in the earlier half of the tenth century. The establishment of manors in the various parishes was also an important part of this process, which has acquired the rather unlovely label 'manorialisation'.

Most modern archaeology is the result of teamwork, and solitary scholars – loners, I suppose you could call them – are few and far between. But there are always exceptions, and the greatest pioneer in the archaeology of medieval field systems is just such a person. I've had the great good fortune to know David Hall since the mid-1970s, when he worked for English Heritage's Fenland Survey. He's an extremely sociable person, and like most good archaeologists he can do many things. After reading science at Oxford and then working for several years as a food scientist, he decided to concentrate on the main love of his academic life, archaeology. Soon he landed the Fenland Survey job – and he never looked back. But the main love of his academic life continued to be the archaeology of medieval Northamptonshire.[11] Anyone who has driven through this beautiful county of 'spires and squires' will know that the gently undulating countryside still preserves huge areas of ridge-and-furrow fields. These strange-looking rounded ridges are the physical remains of those strips and furlongs I mentioned earlier. Until quite recently this important evidence for the agriculture of the Middle Ages was unprotected by any legislation, and during the 1960s to 1980s a vast acreage was flattened by modern power-farming. It was a terrible loss, because unlike a hedge, we can never 'replant' ridge-and-furrow, as to do so would probably cause even worse damage.

Northamptonshire is the place where medieval field systems survive better than almost anywhere else in Britain, largely in the form of those ridge-and-furrow fields. One of David's skills is reading medieval

Latin. He is one of those rare archaeologists who is equally at home in County Records Offices or out on a grassy field. He does most of his fieldwork in the winter, when the soil is bare and sheep have nibbled away the long grass to reveal the contours of even the faintest ridge-and-furrow. Then in the summer he chases up his documentary sources. Over the past thirty years David has spent most weekends, when not doing his archaeological 'day job', trudging across the North-amptonshire landscape. Usually you will find him dressed in a heavy tweed overcoat with a long, multicoloured scarf wrapped several times around his neck; sometimes he will be on his own, but often he takes his long-term friend and colleague Paul Martin along with him.[12] David's extended research into medieval fields and settlements, which now includes many more than just those of Northamptonshire, means that nobody knows as much about the subject as him. I should note here that much of David's research has been actively encouraged by Glen Foard, formerly the County Archaeologist, who shares David's interest in the Saxon and medieval landscape. It was Glen who helped put together the huge Raunds Project (see page 133), which has done so much to substantiate and flesh out David's theories.

There have been many theories about the origin of ridge-and-furrow and the medieval Open Field system. Some have been out-and-out guesses, others have been better informed.[13] It has even been suggested that ridge-and-furrow was the result of nineteenth-century steam ploughing, but this is manifestly absurd, because the steam plough draws a straight furrow, and one of the most characteristic features of ridge-and-furrow is the gentle S-shaped curve of the indi-vidual ridges. In 1957 the historian Maurice Beresford suggested that they were the remains of medieval agriculture, and this has been proved many times simply by comparisons between the pattern of ridge-and-furrow on the ground and maps made before the widespread changes of the Enclosure movement. The two are almost always identi-cal. The Later Saxon nucleated systems of the Midland counties rapidly developed into a style of intensive arable farming, usually based around two or three large Open Fields, that was later to be described as 'champion'. I will have a great deal more to say about champion landscapes in Chapter 6. Here we are concerned with the origins of the system.

Now that we have proved the general date of the first Midland Open Fields, the next question has to be about their origin. Did the ideas behind the Open Field system come over from the Continent with the earliest Anglo-Saxon culture, or was it invented independently in Britain? At first glance, the early or original Anglo-Saxon theory has a great deal of appeal. After all, this was the time when English culture was created, and agriculture is almost as fundamental to a society as the language it speaks – and we know that Old English came into being in the seventh–ninth centuries.* The early origins theory was first put forward in 1883 by the great landscape and economic historian Frederic Seebohm in his book *The English Village Community*.[14] Other historians have wrestled with the problem; some have followed Seebohm, others have opted for start dates as late as the twelfth century. Over the years, however, there has been a growing appreciation that the Open Field system did not just happen and stay put, but like many farming systems it grew and evolved to meet the constraints and opportunities of landscape, history and technology. It was also increasingly realised that the problem could not be sorted out simply by poring over maps.

After the war it was realised that the development of the landscape cannot be studied without paying close attention to the actual physical landscape itself. This is where archaeology and people like David Hall enter the stage. By closely studying the relationship between ridge-and-furrow and other features on the ground – churchyards and roads, for example – David has dispelled earlier theories both that the Open Field system arrived intact, as it were, with the first Anglo-Saxon culture, or that it survived from Roman times. He points out that Early Saxon settlements, like their Roman and prehistoric antecedents, were mainly confined to lighter soils. People then simply did not possess the technology to cope with the heavier clay soils of, say, the Midland counties, which are the heartland of the Open Field system.

Common sense might suggest that the Open Field system developed piecemeal from the Earlier Saxon landscape, as population grew and farming technology improved. But in this instance common

---

* Linguists prefer the term 'Old English' to 'Anglo-Saxon' because it emphasises the essential continuity between the three principal stages of the language's development: Old, Middle (the language of Chaucer) and Modern English.

sense would appear to be wrong. As we saw at Shapwick, the shift from earlier settlement patterns to the new Open Field system happened quite suddenly. It is very difficult to be precise about dates, but taking central Britain as a whole, the process would seem to have started in Middle Saxon times, and was actively under way in the early tenth century.

The new system often involved large areas of new arable land, which was sometimes arranged in huge, long strips. Long fields are particularly well suited to the mouldboard plough, which is not particularly simple to turn around and would not have been easy to use in the smaller paddock-like fields of Earlier Saxon England. Similar developments were happening on the Continent, in the Carolingian Empire, where in Austria and Germany, for example, long, strip-like fields were being laid out in the later eighth and ninth centuries. The German examples can be dated to between 775 and 850. Again, these strips were set out for the efficient use of the mouldboard plough, but they involved major landscape reorganisation – it wasn't just a matter of accommodating new technology: both ploughs and people had to change. As we saw at Shapwick, other social and agricultural changes would also have taken place.

Huge strip-like open fields are also found in Britain. David Hall points to examples of furlongs in the Yorkshire Wolds that are an astonishing 2,000 metres long. Other very long strip furlongs are found around the periphery of the Midlands, in South Yorkshire, around the Humber and in the silt fens around the Wash. Some of these large-scale strips may have been laid out during the main life of the Open Field system, but the evidence on the ground suggests that most were arranged in this fashion from the very outset.

I mentioned a few paragraphs ago that these major changes in the management of the landscape were helped by the influence of the Church, as we saw so clearly at Shapwick. They were also aided by the emergence of a new aristocratic elite. These are the people I want to discuss next. Like *nouveaux riches* almost everywhere, they needed to ally themselves to the establishment, while at the same time proclaiming their power to lesser mortals. One good way of achieving both these goals was through the construction of large and fancy church buildings.

As a student I remember reading about the famous tower of the parish church at Earls Barton in Northamptonshire. It was, and still is, perhaps the best-known example of Saxon architecture in England. The rest of the church is somewhat later and rather less distinguished, but the tower is quite out of the ordinary. It is decorated with strip-like stonework which is believed by most people to echo the style of timber construction that would have been used by most parishes. It was built in the tenth or eleventh century, and was clearly intended to impress. The church stands on high ground, and dominates the landscape round about. It looks particularly impressive from the new Peterborough to Northampton road which runs along the Nene Valley beside it.

The magnificent tower of Earls Barton Church is one of the glories of surviving Late Saxon architecture, and was constructed during the manorialisation process. The tower itself could have held bells, and might also have served some defensive purpose, but its main reason for existing was undoubtedly to proclaim the importance of the *thegns* who built it. Indeed, some of that early lordly significance survives in the name of the modern village, *Earls* Barton (Barton is from the Old English *bere-tun*, meaning a barley farm or place where grain is stored[15]). The 'Earl' in this instance would have been the Earl of Northampton, but the clear signal of aristocratic possession emphasises the continuing importance of the place within the social landscape of the region.

The Middle and Late Saxon periods saw the establishment of the power structure that would ensure that there was governance, whether good or bad, in the regions of Britain. Both country and urban areas were settling down. There were, of course, exceptions, such as the English–Scottish borders and the regions where Viking strife was happening, but the general tendency was in the right direction. Meanwhile the population and the economy, especially in the south of Britain, continued to grow. These pressures, allied to improving communications, were making Later Saxon society successful. As we have seen, the Church played an important part in that success by providing good rural governance, a stimulus for trade and a focus for learning and scholarship. But there was an emerging power in the land that would eventually prove to be at least as significant as the Church.

A couple of paragraphs ago I slipped in the word '*thegn*' when discussing Earls Barton. Now I owe an explanation. The word is pronounced 'thane' but is spelled in its original form to distinguish it from the Scottish thanes, who were senior aristocrats – usually the leaders of whole clans. The *thegns* of Saxon England were an emerging nobility, many of whom obtained their estates through grants of royal land. They first begin to appear in the Middle Saxon period, and were becoming a real force in the land in Late Saxon times. In theory a *thegn* was a person who owned at least five hides of land and was obliged, in return, to serve the King in times of war. The middle rank of society were the *cnichts*, or knights, a rank that grew in importance in the Middle Ages. As time passed society became ever more hierarchical.

Thegns and knights were significantly more important than the lowest form of freeman, the *ceorl* (pronounced 'carl'), who was in effect the head of a free peasant household. These social divisions varied between the different kingdoms of Later Saxon England, but *ceorls* too were liable for military service. Although in the country at large things may have been beginning to settle down, these were still turbulent and often violent times. The payment of blood money, or *wergeld*,* was a means of containing the worst of the violence, and amounts were set according to rank. So the size of *wergeld* payments gives us some idea of social status. In Wessex and Mercia, for example, *thegns* were obliged to pay on average six times as much *wergeld* as a *ceorl*.

If *thegns* ruled the roost, the people towards the bottom, whose labour ultimately supported the entire system, were the villeins. These were tenants who were said to be in a state of serfdom – in other words they were tied to a particular landlord, and owed him a lifetime's obligation of labour. In return they had rights to work land in the Open Fields for themselves. Today I suppose we would think of these people more as 'bound-over' slaves than as workers. Having said that, they were not slaves, and they were the most numerous group in society. True slaves did exist: their rights were non-existent, and depended

---

* *Wergeld* was a payment by a killer and his family to a victim and their family. Relatives were obliged to avenge a death, and *wergeld* was a means of avoiding a prolonged blood feud.

entirely on the whim of their owners. Unlike *ceorls*, villeins were not freemen, and the name had not yet acquired any pejorative overtones – it simply referred to the fact that they were the inhabitants of '*vills*', or villages. There were at least two other groups of serfs: 'bordars' and 'cottars', who had rights to even less land than villeins. It was the villeins whose labour kept the landlords' wholly-owned, or '*demesne*' (pronounced 'demean'), farms prosperous and in business – and it was the *demesne* farms that gave the landowners their main income.

Slaves were more common in Earlier Saxon times than in the Middle Ages proper, but they did exist, having been either captured during raids or warfare, or the offspring of slaves. Slaves were for life, but villeins could escape their ties and obligations by various means. If they were particularly successful and astute they could buy their way out by paying the lord an agreed sum. They could also join the Church (with their lord's permission), or escape to a town and live there undetected for a year and a day, after which they would legally be at liberty. These were the means that were employed at the end of the fourteenth century, when serfdom broke down and villeins gradually became transmuted into 'copyholders': tenants who owed rights to their land through a lease and rent – a binding agreement that was copied into the manorial court rolls. That, in a nutshell, was the social system that was established in Later Saxon England and which remained substantially unaltered until the later fourteenth century, when the knock-on effects of the Black Death began to have a profound effect on the way people organised their lives and labour. We will see later that one could argue that medieval Britain began to come to an end when the social system established in Later Saxon times started to change itself so radically in the later fourteenth century.

The rise of *thegns* and the new regional elites went hand in hand with the process known as manorialisation. This began in earnest in Late Saxon times, and becomes evident from the early tenth century, which is when England becomes what we would recognise today as medieval, a full century and a half prior to the Norman Conquest. Once established, the manorial system was to last throughout the Middle Ages and into Tudor and Stuart times. In effect it was the basis of local government in rural areas. Manors were established by local landowners as a means of managing their estates, and manorial courts met to decide everything from who was to farm what furlong to the rotation of crops to be adopted that season in the great Open Fields. They also sorted out boundary disputes and other business. So in another important respect the medieval period continued to exert an influence long after it was supposed to have ended.

Manorial courts were presided over by the lord of the manor, who was usually the landowner himself, but some very powerful nobles would appoint a deputy to sit in their stead. Everyone, whether tied tenant or freeman, was expected to attend. Most of the business transacted at manorial courts related to the village's Open Fields, where most people had their holdings of land, but certain farms were run directly, and sometimes from outside the parish. These included the in-house or grange farms belonging to monasteries and the *demesne* farms belonging to great landowners. The word '*demesne*' is a legal term to describe land that was farmed for the direct benefit of the landowner – although this was not a rigid arrangement, and when economic conditions merited it such farms could be wholly or partly let to tenants. *Demesne* farms were usually run by a deputy, known as a reeve, who was appointed by the landowner through the manorial court.

So far we have looked at two Northamptonshire churches, and of course at David Hall's pioneering research in the same county into the origin of the Open Field system. One of David's many discoveries was in and around the central Northamptonshire parish of Raunds, and it led to one of the most important archaeological research projects of the late twentieth century. The Raunds Area Survey took place between 1985 and 1993, and covered an astonishing area of forty square kilometres in Raunds and the parishes around it. In those days developer-funded archaeology was in its infancy, and although coercion by the planning authorities was not to begin officially until 1989, certain counties such as Berkshire and Northamptonshire realised that it was inevitable, and took steps to ease it in gently. Raunds was part of that easing, and here the pill was sugared by the addition of several heaped teaspoonfuls of English Heritage cash.

The project was a model of its sort. It involved huge amounts of field-walking and documentary research. We saw at Shapwick how a small amount of excavation helped to sort out some of the problems that were raised by the field-walking surveys. But there Mick Aston and his team were limited in what they could excavate – in some respects this sharpened their wits and gave their digs extra 'edge'. Their approach was more lean and hungry than all-singing and all-dancing – and was none the worse for it. At Raunds it was the other way around. Here the scale of the field-walking survey was more than matched by a series of major excavations on the gravel terraces of the Nene Valley. These sites were threatened by the digging of gravel quarries that were to provide the enormous quantities of aggregates required by the growth of Northampton and the road system around it, which was then being improved and enlarged. If you drive through the area today most of the archaeological sites are either fishing lakes, watery nature reserves or places where water-skiers whizz around like mosquitoes.

The downside of an elaborate, expensive, approach is that it creates big organisational challenges which cannot be sorted out by a cosy chat between members of the team in the pub, which is the way Mick Aston and I prefer to work. When large sums of public money are involved, with them come accountants and administrators. Big projects may also have staff problems, and Raunds has had its share of them. There have also been publication production difficulties. The upshot has been that we still lack full reports of the excavations, although they are promised shortly. So was it worth all the time, expense and effort? I think the answer has to be a firm 'yes', simply because to have done nothing would have been unacceptable. The people behind the project had the guts to think big, and to place the various digs within a well-worked-out landscape setting. But it's a great shame that the reports have been so delayed, because archaeology has come a long way in the thirteen or so years since the diggers laid their trowels aside.

As I hinted earlier, I think the ideal way forward would be to have a series of Shapwick-like projects in which the public could, and indeed should, be involved. These could be supervised by professionals and commercial work could take place as a part of the larger survey – just as it did at Shapwick. I believe that public involvement is the key. With public and commercial involvement the professionals could set research questions that could actually be answered. Situations such as the non-appearance of the Raunds reports would, I suspect, be avoided if members of the public felt that their own efforts were in danger of being wasted. I know from experience that a hostile crowd in a village hall can make even the most lethargic and disorganised professional jump around in a very frisky fashion. Public pressure would keep the professionals on their toes and ensure that the dead hand of bureaucracy was kept at bay. At present archaeology is becoming more and more divided between client-funded commercial excavations, where the public is wholly excluded, and the so-called 'amateur' projects, where people are looking for academic guidance because, quite rightly, they want their work to address real research issues. Somehow the two must be brought together.

The Raunds Area Project revealed a great deal about the Bronze and Iron Ages, which is why I used to visit the excavations quite regularly. I can well remember being impressed by the scale on which things happened. Some of the digs put one in mind of those epic Middle Eastern projects in the pages of an Agatha Christie mystery, with huge teams of people busily scurrying around. Nobody was carrying dry soil in baskets, but the areas opened were huge, and in the hot summer months the dry gravel surfaces did indeed resemble the deserts of Sumeria. All the while huge dumper trucks thundered around in the distance, leaving behind them tall plumes of orangey dust. Gravel quarry digs have a sort of romance and brutality all their own.

As I have already hinted, Raunds was very important to me as a prehistorian, but it also revealed at least two high-status Roman villas, both with mosaic floors. One of these, at Redlands Farm, was most remarkable because 'an entire rear gable wall of one of the wings had collapsed outwards and was almost completely intact'.[16] I cannot think of another example, certainly from Roman Britain, where the entire profile of a building has survived in this way. Even these extraordinary discoveries were eclipsed for most archaeologists by the demonstration at West Cotton and North Raunds, two major sites within the project, of the sheer scale of Late Saxon changes to the landscape. Here we were seeing changes that recalled Shapwick, but this time they were across whole landscapes and involved a great deal of extra work and reconstruction. Shapwick was unusual for Somerset, where the process of nucleation was generally piecemeal. At Raunds the trend was more universal, and reflected what was happening across the English Midlands in the Late Saxon period. Paul Stamper's claim that this was one of 'the great discoveries of British archaeology of the later twentieth century' does not seem over the top.

I want to leave the operation of Open Fields to Chapter 5, where it belongs, but the question of their origins is important and I cannot leave it hanging. The main point to note is that great changes to the southern British landscape took place well before the Norman Conquest. What do the Raunds projects reveal about the beginnings of the 'classic' British medieval farming system? We will see that the origins of the 'champion' landscapes lay fairly and squarely in Later Saxon times. But first, some brief thoughts on surveying.

The point has already been made that the major changes to the landscape of Later Saxon times were carefully thought out and precisely surveyed. The basic measure of land was still the hide, which had now become a defined unit of taxation rather than a rough-and-ready estimate. The new system was introduced with a clear aim in view, which Tony Brown and Glen Foard have described as self-sufficiency and the regulated sharing of resources. In the Midlands version of the Open Field system, arable land was apportioned by means of the ridge-and-furrow strips, and it is this important but rapidly vanishing feature of the Northamptonshire landscape which has allowed the timing of the great resurveying to be pinned down chronologically.

When fields of ridge-and-furrow are examined closely they are found to overlie, and therefore to post-date, spreads of Early and Middle Saxon pottery. The Late Saxon period also witnessed the introduction of a mass-produced style of pottery known as St Neots Ware, which first appears in Northamptonshire in the late ninth century, and is found there in quantity from the mid-tenth. Broken-up small sherds of St Neots Ware are found in the soil of ridge-and-furrow, where they were almost certainly introduced with farmyard manure that was spread over the fields. Such sherds are not found in features that predate the ridge-and-furrow. The evidence taken together suggests that ridge-and-furrow generally came into being in the early tenth century – i.e. in Late Saxon times.

To return to surveying: we now know when it happened, but can we prove that it was necessarily planned and deliberate? There are many examples that show how the very long strip fields of the first systems were subsequently shortened or subdivided, which would suggest that the original layouts could be modified during use – which in turn is significant, because it demonstrates that the system worked and was flexible. The changes would of course have happened through the manorial courts, by common agreement, and with the approval of the landowner. Brown and Foard point to the Open Fields in the parish of Daventry in the southern part of Northamptonshire as a clear example of careful surveying to meet prearranged criteria.[17]

The research at Daventry was carried out by Tony Brown, whom I first encountered in the early 1980s when he was editing the new county journal *Northamptonshire Archaeology*. He examined the documentary evidence, along with the shape of the actual fields as they survived in the form of ridge-and-furrow, and noticed some remarkable coincidences. The parish was divided into two townships (the smallest unit of communal land ownership), each of which consisted of twenty taxable hides. Each hide had four *virgates* (the Latin term for the standard individual farm unit or yardland), and each *virgate* had thirty taxation acres. Thus the two field systems of the individual townships together contained 2,400 acres. Tony discovered that the documents, which were prepared for taxation purposes, and the evidence from the ground agreed precisely. It was an extraordinary discovery. As he and Glen Foard put it, the Anglo-Saxon surveyors had laid out a system of exactly the size they wanted.

At Raunds, as elsewhere in the Midlands, the process of resurveying and manorialisation was well under way in the Late Saxon period. This process was an important indication of the increasing power of the landowners who owned the estates. At Shapwick occupation appears to have been continuous, but at Raunds there was a break in settlement between the Middle Saxon farm and the first Late Saxon settlement, which consisted of four rectangular timber buildings, one of which was larger and better-built than the others, and was probably a hall. These were the sort of ordinary buildings that one would usually associate with a peasant farm which was occupied at a time when this part of the county was under Danish control. The big change happened sometime around 950–75, when the area had returned to English rule, and it didn't just involve buildings, but dramatic changes to the way the landscape was organised.

The first clear evidence for the changes was found when the excavators revealed a ditch at least 230 metres long which ran through the open-area excavations and out at each end.[18] This formed one side of an enclosure of exactly an acre in area. Within the enclosure was a large rectangular timber building, part of which was a large hall. Next to this enclosure was another ditched yard, probably for livestock. Further to the south there was a series of smaller enclosures, which were also linked to the big ditch; these contained timber buildings and other domestic structures. This development did not take place in isolation. On the other side of the valley there were further rectangular enclosures, similar to those south of the main enclosure. These were probably the remains of tenant farms belonging to the main system, because they were laid out on the same alignment, and at the same time. It was all part of the same well-coordinated and well-surveyed process of manorialisation. But can we prove it?

Normally the evidence as presented here would be sufficient on its own to make a pretty convincing case, but there are also later documents to back it up. There can be little doubt that the large hall in the imposing enclosure was a manor, and we know from Domesday that the manor here was held by the king's *thegn*, Burgred. Later the place was known as Furnells, after the de Furneus family which held it in the twelfth century. The buildings in the smaller enclosures, both south of the manor and across the valley, were probably the lord's tenant farms. So Raunds demonstrates conclusively that the manorial and Open Field system which operated so well right up to the Black Death, when so much was forced to change, had its roots within the Saxon period.

This is not to say, of course, that all manors were founded at this early period. Some appeared later, along with their villages, but in the English Midlands the process which had begun around 850 had been completed by the end of the twelfth century. Manorialisation is a horrible word, and the only substitute I have come across is hardly any better. The process of founding manors and coming together to live in villages with Open Fields is sometimes also referred to as 'nucleation', a word which reflects the fact that dispersed farms and settlements were drawn together into a central nucleus formed by the new village. Perhaps this is a better term to describe the process as a whole, because not all villages with Open Fields did in fact possess a manor. In some instances the manorial courts were located in neighbouring settlements, or in the case of *demesne* farms the lord or his deputy, the reeve, ran them directly. Incidentally, it seems likely that people such as me with the name Prior or Pryor were ultimately descended from a reeve or agent of the Prior – the Prior's man – whose job it was to manage and run the estates belonging to a monastery.

What were the underlying causes of these sweeping changes? We will never know for certain, and it is probably safest to judge each case on its own merits, but I have already hinted at some of them. We saw at Shapwick, for example, that Glastonbury Abbey had a big interest in rationalising its estates. The same would have applied in areas controlled by other well-off early monastic foundations, such as Peterborough Abbey. Powerful lords also exerted a huge influence on the process, as we saw at Raunds. But can we not go any deeper? Surely the monasteries and lords were merely the agents, rather than the fundamental causes, of change? In a most important book, Carenza Lewis, Patrick Mitchell-Fox and Christopher Dyer have suggested that nucleation was part of a new economic system, in which villages were created as institutional communities: landholdings, tithes (Church taxes), taxes and tenancies were all connected.[19] This new system was made necessary by various factors, including population increase and the resultant market forces. If you add to the mix the fact that the changes were also in the interests of two increasingly important forces in the land, namely the Church and the new regional elites, then one can begin to appreciate not just how it happened, but why it was so well planned and competently executed. It was in everyone's interest to get it right.

In certain parts of the country the old dispersed system continued much as before. The economic requirement to change was not there, and although settlement patterns did alter at this time, the changes were nothing like as profound as those associated with nucleation. I shall discuss life in these areas with a more dispersed settlement pattern later, when we come to consider the impact of the Black Death on the rural population.

I sometimes have the impression that people think of the Saxon period as essentially backward. In popular imagination it is seen as lying deep within the 'mists of antiquity' – a time when people had strange names like Burgred and lived a life that had changed little since the Iron Age, despite the best efforts of those civilised Romans to set them on the right track. As we have seen, archaeology is rapidly debunking these half-truths: there is abundant evidence for long-distance trade and communication in the Middle Saxon period; even in the turbulent times of the Viking wars normal life continued and the first towns prospered; the Late Saxon period saw the process of manorialisation and the wholesale reorganisation of the countryside. But what about technology – to what extent did this advance?

If I had been asked that question even two years ago I would probably have answered 'Not much,' but my eyes were opened when I attended the Annual General Meeting of the Council for British Archaeology in Belfast in 2004. I was very struck by an exhibition in the Ulster Museum which used archaeology to show how people through the ages had managed to resolve their bitterest disputes, and on a site visit to the stone foundations of an early medieval tide-mill I was astounded by its sophistication. Tide-mills use the rise and fall of the tides to generate their power, and I resolved to learn more about watermills when I returned home.

It just so happens that there has been something of a renaissance in the study of watermills. Early ones, like the example I saw in Ulster, are of the horizontal sort, rather than the vertical, overshot or undershot types we are more used to today. They were generally smaller than vertical mills, and continued to be used in the Scottish islands and western Ireland into the nineteenth and twentieth centuries.* The mechanism of a horizontal mill is simpler and in some respects more elegant, without the need to transfer power through a right angle, which with wooden gearing is not always very efficient. Their main disadvantage is that the weight of the millstones has to be carried in a substantial structure above the water. Plainly this limits their size. Examples of twelve Irish horizontal watermills have been dated by tree-rings to the three centuries AD 630–930.[20]

I have already mentioned the importance of imported lava quernstones from central Europe to Middle Saxon England. They were

---

* Click Mill, near Dounby in the Northern Isles, was still working in the twentieth century.

part of the trade networks that thrived at the time. Quernstones are revolved by hand, but Continental lava was also used to make the smaller stones needed in horizontal watermills, such as one excavated by Philip Rahtz at Tamworth in Staffordshire.[21] Local stone was also used there, and Philip was amazed at the extraordinary persuasive powers that must have been possessed by the salesmen who sold the Tamworth miller their expensive imported products.

One of the earliest mills from England was found during the course of a commercial excavation at Ebbsfleet in Kent.[22] The timbers were found during the construction of the north length of the Channel Tunnel Rail Link from north Kent to its eventual destination at London's St Pancras station. The line crosses the Ebbsfleet River, and here archaeologists working for Rail Link Engineering found two parallel oak chutes – in effect boxed-in square pipes – which took water to drive a horizontal wheel, which sadly has not survived. A much better preserved, though slightly later, horizontal mill has been found at Earls' Bu on Orkney.[23]

The mill at Earls' Bu formed part of a larger Viking settlement, dating to the late eleventh and early twelfth centuries, but the engineering and construction would appear to be broadly similar to, and as sophisticated as, the Ebbsfleet example – and the tide-mill that first aroused my interest when I was in Northern Ireland. Preservation at Earls' Bu was outstanding, and it was possible to work out how the mill operated. Unlike at Ebbsfleet, the water that powered the horizontal wheel at Earls' Bu was conducted along a single wooden chute. A pond at the top of the head race, or lade, that fed the chute would have given the water added pressure. The tail race out of the mill was also carefully constructed from stone and capped over with slabs. The design of these so-called 'Norse' mills was clearly well-thought-out, and remained remarkably constant through time. I've put the word 'Norse' in quotes because some of the examples from Ireland, and those from Tamworth and Ebbsfleet, are plainly pre-Viking in date. The smaller horizontal mill was a design that is found quite widely across northern Europe in early medieval times, and one must beware of attaching misleading quasi-ethnic labels too readily.

Over the years I have spent some time visiting a working watermill at Sacrewell near Peterborough, and I have been struck by the degree

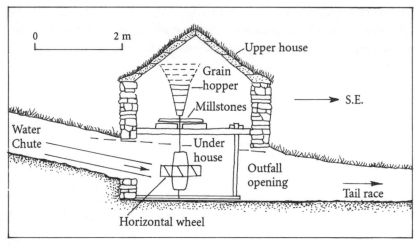

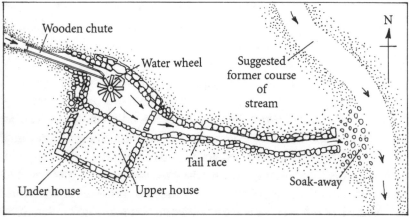

FIG 21   *Plan and cross-section through the Viking period horizontal water mill at Earls' Bu on Orkney. This mill, which probably dated to the early twelfth century, formed part of a larger Viking settlement. The principal advantage of a horizontal mill is that no gearing is required to drive the millstones, which are located in an upper mill house above the stream.*

of control that the miller is able to achieve. The spacing of the stones, their speed, and the supply of grain all need to be carefully supervised, which would explain why elaborate arrangements like boxed-in chutes and the carefully constructed tail and head races were needed. The speed/pressure of water passing through the mill could be controlled by means of sluices leading up to and out of the chute. Milling is a very skilled business, and both the construction and the design of the mills had to reflect this.

CHAPTER FOUR

Urban Life in Late Saxon Times

BEFORE I WROTE THIS CHAPTER, all my archaeological instincts told me that it would be a great mistake to separate lives in Later Saxon towns from those of the Middle Ages. They were, after all, part of the same phenomenon. Apart from minor changes in pottery styles there was very little to distinguish what went on in, say, York or London before or after the Norman Conquest. For Wales and Scotland the decision was easier, because true towns are less easy to pin down prior to the eleventh century. In Scotland there were indeed centres of population before that – one thinks in particular of the large settlement at Whithorn in the south-west – but it is still generally held that the main impetus towards urban life there happened with the widespread introduction of burghs by King David I (1124–53) and his successors. We know a great deal about the development of Scottish burghs thanks to a series of important urban excavations, especially at Perth and Aberdeen, since the 1970s. This work has been summarised in an excellent review of medieval archaeology in Scotland by Peter Yeoman.[1]

Despite this wealth of good material, I plan to confine my attention largely to England. My justification is that I want to dispel some long-held and erroneous popular beliefs. First I want to look at the nature of towns and cities that had Roman roots. Most people know that York, London and Lincoln, for example, were important Roman towns. But how did they develop after AD 410, when the Roman troops had withdrawn? Did life simply continue much as before, or were the former ways abandoned? If they were abandoned, why did they restart? There are also many misleading myths about the Normans, whose handiwork has all but obliterated the achievements of their Saxon predecessors. Did their arrival suddenly swamp the Saxons, who were unable to compete with them at any level? That may be the impression given by the buildings that survive, but it is far from the truth.

It is well known that most English parish churches, castles and cathedrals have those wonderful heavy, round Norman arches somewhere in their structure – even if they have only been bricked in by later builders and improvers. They are so easy to recognise. Often Norman stone structures have replaced earlier Saxon buildings, which were sometimes, but by no means always, made out of timber – as we saw at Brixworth and Earls Barton. To what extent did Norman builders build, or rebuild, English towns? That's a question I will return to in Chapter 5; here I want to establish the size and importance of those pre-Norman Saxon towns, whose buildings were indeed mostly constructed from timber. I don't want them to be lost beneath tons and tons of later stonework and history. Over the past fifty years my colleagues in urban archaeology have sweated blood revealing the remains of Saxon towns, and in the process they have transformed our understanding of English social history. So whether it's academically correct or not, I shall devote a separate chapter to their discoveries.

Both archaeologists and historians of urban life have worked together to produce a series of fascinating plans that show the development of Britain's major towns and cities. They will also help me sidestep some of the problems of arbitrarily separating the Saxon from the Norman and later periods. I will include a series of maps of Colchester in this chapter, and of York and the City of London in the next. These maps will begin with the Roman period and end with the late Middle Ages. My aim is to paint a picture of overall development, and I will not dwell on individual buildings or institutions. I could write another book, for example, on London's remarkable and diverse medieval monasteries, but sadly I lack the space – and it is the general impression which concerns me here.

To understand the earliest towns of Late Saxon England we must briefly return to the continuing conflict between Saxons and Vikings. The three main provinces of Later Saxon England were the Danelaw, a somewhat reduced Mercia and the territory of the West Saxons, known as Wessex. We have already discussed the rise and sudden sharp decline of an over-enlarged Mercia, but now I must return to that rather sorry tale.

FIG 22 *The three principal kingdoms or provinces of central and southern Britain at the time of the establishment of the Danelaw in the later ninth century.*

The loss of the southern territories did not seriously affect the Mercian heartland, which Wessex could not impinge upon. But all of that was to change when the Viking Great Army overran the entire kingdom in 874, after their winter at Repton. This left the rulers of Mercia with no alternative but to look south-west for help from their old enemy Wessex. Anything would be better than the heathen Vikings. As often happens in history, closer political relations became cemented by royal ties of blood. King Alfred's daughter Æthelfleda (herself the result of Alfred's union with his Mercian wife Ealhswith) married the ruler of Mercia, Æthelred, sometime in the late 880s. She was a remarkable woman, who ruled Mercia herself after her husband's death in 911. She died in 918, and during her reign she fought successful military campaigns against, among others, the Danes of York and the Welsh. She also established a defensive ring of *burhs* around the western parts of the province. After her death, her daughter Ælfwynn was almost immediately deposed by her uncle Edward the Elder of Wessex, who then took control of the province.

In Chapter 1 I discussed the *wics* and *emporia* of Middle Saxon southern Britain, and we saw how they fitted into a much larger, pan-European trading network. We also poured cold water on the idea that there was a significant hiatus, when trade, communication and commerce ceased, between the time when the *wics* had lost their central role, which happened by, and just after, the end of the eighth century, and the construction of the first *burhs* in the late eighth and early ninth centuries. Indeed, there is evidence to suggest that some of the new *burhs* were located at places which we know were already occupied when the settlement was given the status of a *burh*. London and York are both examples of this.

King Alfred's idea of constructing fortified towns as part of a network was a good one, because the defensive sum of the component parts of a linked system is far greater than a series of individual strongpoints. The first *burhs* were constructed in the late eighth century by that remarkable ruler Offa, King of Mercia. He probably based his idea on Continental examples in the Carolingian Empire. However, I will concentrate on the better-known and more thoroughly studied *burhs* founded by King Alfred of Wessex and his successors in the ninth century.

Like the earlier Mercian *burhs*, Alfred's were built in response to the threat posed by the Vikings. They were carefully positioned so that no part of Wessex was more than thirty klilometres or so from one of these new fortified towns. These places were in effect privileged settlements that the King wanted to succeed. At first their main aim was to defend the territory around them and the townspeople within them. But soon both trade and the new towns prospered, partly because of the security they enjoyed, but also because administrative, commercial and financial services were all concentrated within the walls of one town – and that town possessed excellent lines of communication, by road and river.

Many of the later *burhs* that are mentioned in Domesday were positioned on roads or navigable rivers and possessed minster churches, probably founded in the seventh or eighth centuries. So, as I have already noted in passing, some of these new *burhs* were not created completely afresh, out of nothing, but may represent an enhancement or refounding of an existing settlement. But most *burhs* were new foundations or refoundations of Roman towns and cities. Their changed locations *vis-à-vis* the *wics* and *emporia* may in part reflect the years of Viking strife, but the ninth century was also a time of rapid development and change. Monasteries and the Church were of growing importance, as were the regional elites. These new political and economic conditions gave rise to new social and trading networks.

As we saw in the previous chapter, processes of nucleation were gathering pace in the countryside. Smaller regional centres, such as Colchester, were becoming more prominent. So we must see the establishment of the *burhs* in the context of an increasingly 'layered' landscape, of small tenant farms, larger *demesne* farms and monastic granges, villages, small towns and market towns – with *burhs* and cities close to the top. I say 'close to' because it is hard to judge whether the most powerful royal or ecclesiastical centres were actually at the very top. But whether they were at the highest pinnacle or not, *burhs* formed an important part of several social and trading networks, and they were not placed on the map simply by royal whim. The selection was both planned and thoughtful. The *burhs* were certainly given royal blessing, which helped them to thrive, but their subsequent prosperity depended to a great extent on their position within the landscape and the quality of the communications they could draw upon. A great deal of this successful planning can be attributed to Alfred and his advisers.

Alfred may have known how to blow his own trumpet by way of *The Anglo-Saxon Chronicles* and a sycophantic biographer (whose text may not be 100 per cent genuine), but it cannot be denied that he was an effective and imaginative ruler, even if his government was rather expensive to the taxpayer. It probably took upwards of 27,000 men to garrison the *burhs*, and the peace he made with the Vikings was also paid for in gold. These payments were not part of the infamous

Danegeld taxes which happened later, under Æthelred and Cnut; the *Danegeld* consisted of annual contributions towards a mercenary and resident Danish force, and had nothing whatever to do with Alfred.

We saw in the previous chapter that Alfred's historical reputation has recently slipped from the godlike to the merely human, but even so his achievements were considerable. He is believed to have laid the foundations of the English Common Law system that appeared formally under Henry II (1154–89). He supported the Church, even if he did help himself to the wealth of smaller monasteries from time to time, and above all he supervised the West Saxon take-over of England. This political stability was the context which encouraged the economic growth that is such a prominent feature of tenth-century England.

We have seen how the Tribal Hidage can provide us with a pretty good idea of the geography of England in the late seventh century. Somewhat later, probably between 911 and 914, we have another important tax assessment document, the Burghal Hidage. Like the Tribal Hidage, the content of which also survived in a later document, the Burghal Hidage survives as a sixteenth-century copy of an eleventh-century text from Winchester.[2] As in the earlier document a 'hide' was a unit of land sufficient to support a household, so the Burghal Hidage was an assessment to allocate financial responsibility for the upkeep and manning of the *burhs*. It provides the best evidence we possess for the location of *burhs* in the early tenth century.

The archaeology of towns is a subject that has come into its own since the mid-twentieth century. There is now so much information that it is impossible to know where to begin, so I have decided to start with the town that bills itself as 'Britain's first town', namely Colchester in Essex. It can make that claim because it was the capital of the most powerful tribe in southern Britain at the end of the Iron Age. Whether it was in fact a town as we would understand the term today is a matter of debate, but it was certainly a very large settlement, if not a very dense or concentrated one. The Roman invaders realised the importance of Camulodunum (its British name) to the Britons, and made it a major administrative centre.

Happily for us, Colchester's archaeological fame has meant that it has been blessed with a persistent and very active group of archaeologists, based around the Colchester Archaeological Trust, at whose head and heart are Philip and Nina Crummy. Philip looks after excavation and the running of the Trust, while Nina deals with the finds. Philip came to the Trust in 1971, the year I began my own work in the Fens, and we share a passionate conviction that archaeology matters too much to be kept to archaeologists alone. He is a pioneer of what is now referred to as 'public archaeology', which has included many excavations to which public access has been encouraged, and numerous

N

- York

■ Lincoln

- Chester
Derby ■   ● Nottingham

Stafford ●   Leicester   Stamford   Norwich
Tamworth ●   ■   ■   ●

Warwick ○   Northampton
Worcester ○   ● Bedford   Ipswich ●
Hereford ●   Winchcombe ○ Buckingham

Gloucester ●   Oxford ○   Wallingford
Malmesbury   Sashes   London
Bristol   ○ Cricklade   ○   ● Canterbury
Axbridge   ○ Bath   ○ Chisbury   Southwark ○   Rochester
Pilton   ○ Watchet   Langford   ○ Wilton   Eashing
   ○ ○   ○   ○ Winchester   Lewes
Lyng   Shaftesbury   ○   ○
Exeter Bridport   Eorpeburnam
Lydford   Burpham   Hastings
Wareham   Porchester   Chichester
Christchurch
Hallwell   Southampton

■ 5 boroughs
○ Burghal hidage
● Towns

0   100 km

FIG 23   *Map of towns in the Viking Age. Towns mentioned in the Burghal Hidage and the '5 Boroughs' of the east Midlands are distinguished by separate symbols. The '5 Boroughs' were either Viking foundations or were set up by the West Saxons after the end of Viking control.*

exhibitions in the town museum in Colchester Castle, which is itself of course an archaeological exhibit. As I write, friends from Channel 4's *Time Team* are filming a one-off 'special' about the recent discovery in Colchester of a very early Roman racetrack or circus. Recently Philip and the Trust have published a beautifully illustrated book, *City of Victory*, which takes the reader through the town's complex early history in an altogether painless fashion.[3]

One of the other reasons why I want to begin this section on Late Saxon towns with Colchester is that it is most definitely *not* one of the places that academics look to when discussing the rise of towns in England. While it was famous in the Iron Age and Roman times, Colchester rather faded from the map thereafter, which makes me curious. In Middle Saxon times it was notable that nearby Ipswich, not Colchester, became the *wic*. Similarly, Colchester does not appear on maps of early defended *burhs*. Did occupation there simply cease at the end of the Roman period? And if so, what persuaded people to return? What was it about Colchester that prevented it from being abandoned for good, like so many other Roman towns in Britain, such as Wroxeter, Silchester or Durobrivae, near Peterborough, the largest and richest of the so-called 'small towns'? I think we must view the history of each Saxon town on its own merits, because it's hard to generalise without taking particular circumstances, populations, skills and locations into account. Colchester interests me partly because it has such a glittering early history, but also because of what Philip Crummy calls its 'new beginning' in the Late Saxon period.

The Romans clearly had high hopes for Colchester when they named it Colonia Victricensis (City of Victory) shortly after the conquest of AD 43. For a very brief period – a decade or so – it was the major city in Britain, and money was poured into it. The Roman conquerors intended it to become the administrative capital for the entire province of Britannia, but it never really took off in the way that a successful capital must. Maybe this reflected the fact that it possessed no deep-water harbour, or maybe its location was wrong – a bit off the beaten track. But it had superb city walls, which were later to prove an important asset.

The once-glorious Camulodunum undoubtedly became a very sorry place in the decades following the collapse of Roman rule. The

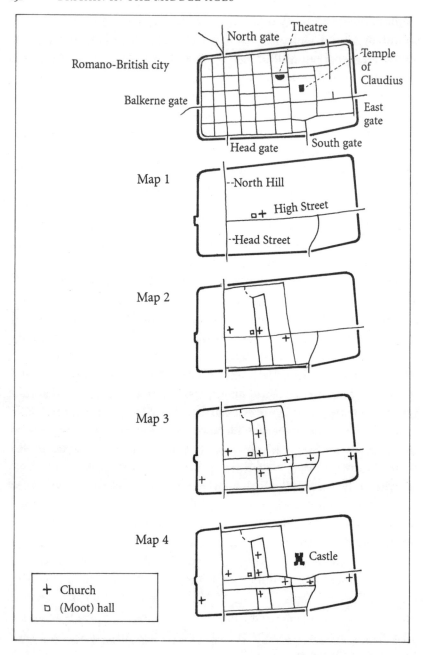

FIG 24 *Roman Colchester, showing the street layout, principal public buildings and gates through the walls. Map 1: eighth/ninth century. The main streets all*

foundations of three (Early Anglo-Saxon) houses of this period were found by Philip Crummy and his team. Two were on the famous Roman site of Lion Walk.[4] This is located within the Roman walled town, and Crummy dates its occupation, which seems to be more akin to a 'squatters' camp' than anything more urban, to about AD 440–50. We can't be certain about Early Saxon Colchester, other than to say the place was not entirely abandoned. Some sort of presence was maintained there, although the bulk of the population preferred to live in the rural landscape round about; this was a process that had begun in the final century or so of Roman rule, when significant areas within the city walls had reverted to farming or horticulture.

Crummy's 'new beginning' undoubtedly developed out of the Earlier Saxon settlement within the Roman city walls. But there was also a Danish element which included settlers and soldiers, although these fled or were killed when an English army from south of the Thames under Alfred's son, Edward the Elder, liberated the town in the year 917. Strangely, there is very little physical evidence for the Vikings' thirty-year presence in Colchester, so the vast bulk of the population is likely to have been English. In order to resist the possibility of Danish reconquest, Edward strengthened the town walls and quite probably laid out some new streets.

By now the town's 'new beginning' was well under way. It was considered sufficiently established for Edward's son Athelstan (924–39), one of the greatest of the Saxon kings of England, to hold his royal council or *witan* there in the year 931. This gathering was attended by at least seventy noblemen and fifteen bishops, including the Archbishop of Canterbury. Another *witan* was held there in 940. The town achieved assured urban status by the establishment there of a mint sometime around 991.

lead directly to gates in the walls and are still Roman. The settlement is village-sized and based around the church of St Runwald's. Map 2: the restorations of Edward the Elder in 917. The town walls were extensively repaired, and the network of new streets does not follow Roman alignments. Map 3: late tenth century. The High Street was widened to accommodate a market, and the area south of it was extensively redeveloped. Map 4: Norman (1075). The main development was the construction of the castle on the site of the Roman Temple of Claudius, and the diversion of the High Street around its outer bailey.

Although the Roman walls have survived to the present day, the layout of Roman streets was soon lost, because most were constructed from gravel rather than stone blocks, and would soon have become overgrown. In my experience too, wet gravel can be lifted and broken up by hard frosts, so the Early Saxon years of 'squatter settlement', when the roads were not looked after, would have seen their disappearance. The only exceptions were the two streets which ran north–south and east–west connecting four of the five gates through the walls. Presumably these survived because they served a practical purpose, so they were looked after. The well-known western or Balkerne Gate, which incorporated a magnificent stone double triumphal arch, was probably blocked either in late Roman times, as Philip Crummy prefers, or during the repairs to the walls by Edward the Elder, which was the conventional view, proposed by the great archaeologist Sir Mortimer Wheeler in 1917. This would explain why the early medieval east–west High Street stops short when it encounters the north–south road represented today by North Hill and Head Street.

Colchester in the eighth and ninth centuries would essentially have been a one-street village, with a church, a hall and a scattering of smaller houses. Around them would have been the largely grassed-over humps and bumps of the Romano-British town. The first major phase of construction of the modern town probably happened when Edward the Elder repaired the Roman walls in 917. This work involved the laying out of new roads and the allocation of new properties. Two new churches appear at about this time. The existence of the Saxon hall has yet to be proved, because it most probably lay beneath a magnificent medieval moot hall that was demolished in 1843 to make way for the present town hall. The two tenth-century *witans* would have taken place there.

The second series of major changes to Saxon Colchester probably happened in the later tenth century, when the High Street was widened to incorporate a new marketplace. This would have been a major operation which would have been coordinated by a civic authority. While this was happening it seems probable that the area south of the High Street was also extensively redeveloped; at least five new churches can be dated to about this period. Finally, after a period of two rather grim decades following the Norman Conquest of 1066, William I gave

Colchester to a man called Eudo Dapifer, a powerful baron who looked after the town well in the late eleventh century, until his death in 1120. He died in Normandy, but was buried according to his wishes in St John's Abbey, Colchester. Among other significant public works, he constructed the famous castle on the site of the early Roman Temple of Claudius. Like other medieval structures in the town, the castle makes much use of Roman bricks and masonry which were robbed from the many buildings that would still have been standing at this time. The High Street was diverted to go around the outer bailey (a defended enclosure around the outside of the castle's massive main building, or keep).

Although most attention is rightly paid to Colchester's glorious Iron Age and Roman origins, its later history is, for me at least, just as interesting. While it was not a deliberately founded Saxon *burh*, Colchester was listed as a Borough in the Domesday Book.* I won't attempt to define the word 'borough' at this stage, but its use in Domesday indicates quite clearly that Colchester was a fully-fledged town of some importance. At Colchester we see the Saxons or English essentially reinventing themselves, and setting about the creation of a town in a way that suited the pattern of life then. Towns were actually needed, for trade and to help the regional economy work. They were not imposed on the landscape, as it were willy-nilly. Maybe this is why so many earlier, Romano-British, towns – indeed like Camulodunum itself – never really took off. They were essentially a foreign idea that had its roots in the Mediterranean, a part of the world that had reached a stage of cultural and social development, in the mid-first millennium BC, where urbanism was the next logical step. Iron Age society in Britain was not ready for such changes. Nor was that of Early Saxon England. So when towns did appear in Later Saxon times they seem to have been created in two ways. Some, like Colchester, gradually grew up, while others, such as the defended *burhs* (and probably the earlier *wics* too), were deliberately founded by elite authority or royal command; but as we will see at Winchester, even these were sometimes placed on existing settlements.

I have heard it said by non-archaeologists that early English towns

---

* In fact Domesday uses the Latin form of the word, *burgus*, meaning a town.

owe their rather quaint character to their 'Englishness' – that they are an insular reinvention of an idea brought in from outside. This would be an attractive idea if it were true. Unfortunately, all the evidence points to the fact that both *wics* and *burhs* were built along lines that were already popular in Continental Europe. *Wics* formed a part of a closely integrated cross-Channel trading network, and the idea of defended urban *burhs* also had its roots across the Channel. We know that King Alfred, the first major *burh* founder, had Continental models in mind when he established his Wessex examples. Of course, each new foundation was a unique entity – none was a clone, like for example early Roman forts – and each had its own special circumstances and characteristics; but the underlying concept came from Europe.

I want now to head south-west, to one of the places where the discipline of modern urban archaeology can be said to have begun, in King Alfred's capital at Winchester. The archaeologist who directed and inspired this work was Martin Biddle, whom we have already encountered at Repton. But Winchester was where Martin's major work began, and it will be for Winchester that he will be remembered. It was excavations there (1962–71), and slightly earlier at Southampton (1953–69), that revolutionised our knowledge of the earliest English towns. I will return to Southampton when we come to discuss trade, but here I want to consider the capital of Wessex.

I had just finished being a student when Martin's last interim report on Winchester appeared in print.[5] Interim reports were very much in vogue in the 1970s and eighties. They were meant to show that the writing-up stage of the project was well in hand and was producing exciting results. Those results, you hoped, would ensure that funding continued. Sometimes, being human, one jumped to the wrong conclusions to make an otherwise dull interim report more memorable, but such mistakes could always be corrected in the definitive final reports. The Winchester interim reports were excellent, and probably contained few such errors of interpretation, but we still await some of the final reports.

All urban excavations take place opportunistically. Essentially, you dig where you can find either a gap between buildings, or a developer who wants to tear something down. You then have a brief opportunity to look at the place where a building once stood. Even today, when planning laws are far more favourable to archaeology, the interval between demolition and rebuilding is as brief as the developer can make it, for simple economic reasons. Allowing a building site in a place like Winchester or the City of London to stand empty and idle can cost millions of pounds.

So with large urban projects there may be several excavations at different sites within the town. Each will have specific aims and objectives. The smaller digs will usually try to clear up simple problems, like 'Did the High Street extend this far?', or 'Was there an earlier phase to the town hall?' The larger set-piece excavations will address the big issues. At Winchester sites were excavated at many places: at the castle, the cathedral, the walls and in residential and trading areas. One of the most important was located in an area known as The Brooks, in the heart of the town.[6] Here a number of trenches revealed an important series of medieval houses, but there was one discovery that was particularly intriguing and unexpected.

Winchester had been an important Roman town, known as Venta Belgarum, whose principal street plan was defined in the early stages of the excavations. One of the general aims of the project was to see how the medieval town plan related to this Roman ancestor. This was what the early work at The Brooks helped to clarify, and in a most unexpected fashion. The excavators discovered that the alignment of Middle Brook Street, the road that ran along the well-preserved foundations of the medieval houses, followed that of its Roman counterpart. This was a surprise, because in the previous season (1961) the foundations of a Dark Age post-Roman structure had been found on top of the Roman street below. That clearly meant that the street had been abandoned at some time after the Roman period. Further work showed that the alignment of nearby Upper Brook Street differed significantly from that of the Roman road beneath it. Lower Brook Street to the east did not appear to have had any Roman antecedent below it. What was going on?

Biddle came to the conclusion that the medieval street layout bore no relation to the Roman plan, apart from the High Street, which like that at Colchester happened to run between two gateways that had remained in regular use. Although it is not Roman, the arrangement

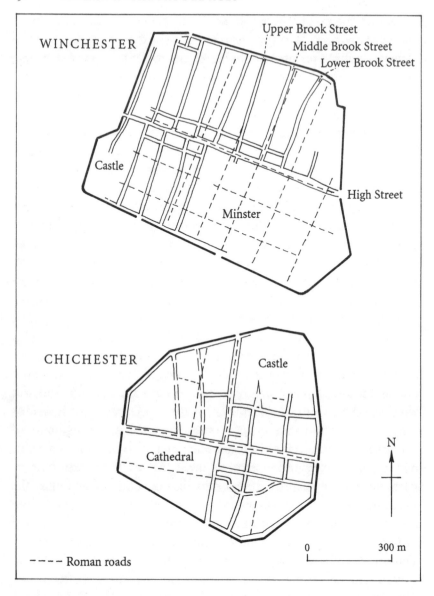

FIG 25 *Town plans of Winchester (Hampshire) and Chichester (Sussex), showing the arrangement of Roman and Late Saxon streets. In both instances the main east–west road follows the line of the Roman street. This probably reflects the fact that this was the most direct route between the two main gateways through the walls. Otherwise the Saxon town plan ignores the Roman layout.*

of streets in medieval Winchester was both regular and laid out on a grid pattern. It was far less haphazard, for example, than that of Colchester, which seems to have been laid out in at least two, and possibly more, episodes of pre-Norman development. At Winchester, Biddle was able to determine that the main grid of streets was in existence by the mid-tenth century, and was probably in use by about 904. He further suggested that the new layout happened when the Roman walls were rebuilt and refurbished when Alfred or his son Edward the Elder established the new *burh* in the late ninth or early tenth century. This would make sense, because the regularity of the new street layout strongly suggests that the entire venture was part of a single, well-planned operation – quite possibly with a strong military element. Biddle describes Late Saxon Winchester as a town of regular streets dominated by its great minster churches, full of wooden houses and enjoying contacts with western Europe and as far afield as the Byzantine empire.[7] English towns in the Late Saxon period could indeed be sophisticated, cosmopolitan places. But to what extent was Winchester a 'one-off'?

The best excavations produce discoveries that have implications that extend far beyond the site in question, and Winchester was one of these. In a well-known paper jointly written with J.D. Hill, Martin Biddle suggested the existence of a whole series of planned Saxon towns, with non-Roman grid-like streets.[8] In 1971 this was an astonishing revelation for everybody, except a few people like Biddle and Hill who were working in urban archaeology. For most of us, even in the profession, it came as a revelation, because it seemed to go against everything we had been taught about the Saxons, who we believed were an essentially rural people. It also showed how careful one must be in assuming continuity between one period and the next. Finally, it demonstrated how strong some of our archaeological prejudices are. As often happens when there is a major new discovery, we learn as much about ourselves and modern preconceptions as we do about the past. The Romans were seen as well organised and military in their outlook. Somehow we believed that they even thought in straight lines, just like some of their roads. But the fact that streets within a once-Roman town were laid out on a grid does not mean that they were originally Roman – any more than New York or dozens of other

American cities are Roman. As I was to discover myself in the 1970s, even Bronze Age Britons were capable of surveying straight lines and right angles.

One reason why it took so long for archaeologists to realise that many medieval towns with grid street plans were not following the Roman layout was due to what we saw at Colchester, where the High Street followed a straight line from the east to the west gate. For various reasons this road had remained in some sort of use throughout history. As a result, the streets laid out by Edward the Elder and others were more or less at right angles to it, and more or less followed the original Roman pattern. The key to solving the mystery lay in measuring the degree of 'more-or-lessness' of the two patterns, and that could only be properly done when people began to carry out modern excavations using up-to-date surveying techniques.

Biddle and Hill showed how Winchester and Colchester had been replanned in Later Saxon times, and they also showed how Chichester, Bath and Exeter, other walled Roman towns, had been given new street layouts in the medieval period. But for me the real proof of their theory was the demonstration that three Saxon defended towns at Wareham (Dorset), Wallingford and Cricklade (both in Oxfordshire) also had grid-based street plans. These three were 'new towns' that are mentioned in the Burghal Hidage, and this gives us an important clue to their origins – and indeed to their layout and construction. Biddle and Hill suggested that the eight towns they examined in Wessex owed their layout and construction to King Alfred's deliberate foundation or refoundation of a network of defended *burhs*. Alfred reigned between 871 and 899. Colchester was replanned and reinvigorated somewhat later, in 917, when Edward the Elder freed the area from Danish control. Other towns, such as Bedford, Chester, Gloucester, Hereford and London, provide evidence that they too were subject to replanning on their return to West Saxon control in the early tenth century.

The traditional view of Alfred's *burhs* was that they were intended to provide refuge for country people during periods of Viking attack. There may well be truth in this, but the fact remains that large parts of the interior space within the walled enclosure were partitioned into parallel streets which provided access to permanent houses. These were planned defended towns in every sense of the term.

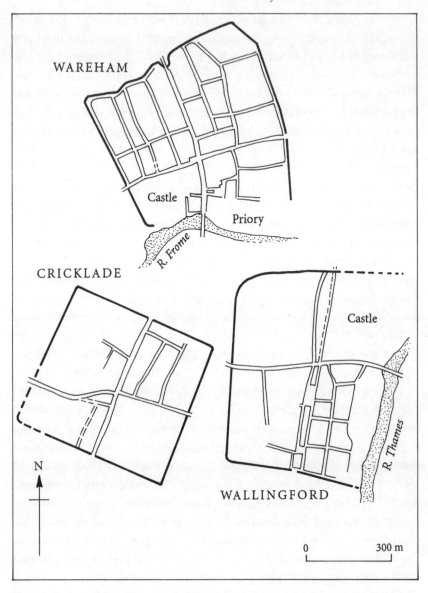

FIG 26   *Town plans of Wareham (Dorset), Cricklade and Wallingford (both Oxfordshire), showing the grid-like arrangement of the streets. Excavations have proved that these towns were constructed in Late Saxon times. Like Winchester and Chichester they were part of King Alfred's network of fortified towns known as* burhs, *which were established as a defence against the Vikings.*

I mentioned London in passing, but the capital city cannot be treated in so perfunctory a manner, especially since so much new information has appeared in the last four or five decades. In the 1950s and sixties the emphasis tended to be on Roman London, Londinium. More recently attention has been on medieval and post-medieval times, but perhaps the biggest, or most unexpected, discoveries have been to do with Saxon London. Had I been writing this book in the 1960s I would have very little of any substance to say about Saxon London. There was lots of supposition, but almost zero hard evidence. Archaeologists and others were, however, very concerned about the scale of modern development and the gathering pace of destruction. If the archaeological destruction continued unabated, and without adequate recording, questions like 'What happened to London in Saxon times?' stood no chance whatsoever of being answered. As a response to this shocking state of affairs, in 1973 Martin Biddle, Daphne Hudson and Carolyn Heighway produced a thorough but truly frightening assessment of the situation for a new archaeological pressure group known as Rescue.[9]

At the time I bought a copy of *The Future of London's Past* for myself, and it sits beside me as I write. It's a large boxed set consisting of a report with detailed maps and plans. It had a huge impact. Stuffed into the back of my copy is a whole page from the *Sunday Times* of 22 July 1973 which ends with these stark words: 'If the implications of the Rescue report are not followed through, the next survey around 1988 will have a simple title. It will be called The End.' It was powerful stuff, and it did have an effect, although not quite as fast or as well funded as many archaeologists wished. The really big changes happened in the later 1980s, when developer-funding got into its stride. Only then was it possible to ensure that *every* potential archaeological site within the capital could be adequately scrutinised. That was when the smaller pieces of the jigsaw began to fall into place. In urban archaeology it is often the isolated trenches which help to flesh out the bigger picture.

At this point I should say a few words about the way the results of large urban excavations are brought to the public's attention. Generally speaking the big news stories are reported quite rapidly, and well. The excavation of the Roman Forum in London in the 1960s is a good example. More recently the burial of a high-ranking Roman lady, also in London, received a great deal of media attention in 1999. York, under its first Director, Peter Addyman, was the leader in dealing with both the public and the media. The influential and much-imitated Jorvík Viking Centre was archaeology's first successful visitor attraction. Peter also established a system of publishing his more academic reports in a series of volumes known as fascicules, which were intended to be taken together and eventually combined into something altogether larger and more revelatory. The system was set up to avoid some of the huge delays that in the 1970s and eighties were beginning to give urban archaeology a bad name among archaeologists. Most would admit that the fascicule system is not perfect – no such system ever can be – but it does seem to work, and the York fascicules still regularly appear in print.

The situation in London was less rosy. In some respects articles in popular archaeological journals, such as *Current Archaeology*, only made matters worse by whetting our appetites.[10] In their way these were fine, but where was the beef? The answer was that it was hopelessly delayed by a massive logjam caused by too much information, too few staff, and ideals of eventual publication that were quite simply impossible to attain. After the adoption of the new planning regulations of PPG-16 in the 1990s the profession had to take a hard look at the way it published, or more often failed to publish, its results, and this gave rise to shorter academic publications which were backed up by an efficient archive for the handful of scholars who needed to delve deeper. Today, of course, the internet has made archives much more freely available, and web-based files are replacing some of the larger or more obscure reports.

For many years I have been a critic of archaeological reports that make no allowances for the general public. I'm something of an expert in this, as I have written or edited ten pretty obscure ones myself. But in self-defence I have always tried to write shorter, more accessible accounts as well. I am now however convinced that the short 'pop' versions are no real substitute for the Full Monty. As long ago as 1911, the Glastonbury Lake Village excavations were written up in two fat volumes which were both academic and popular. The non-archaeologist reader might require a little effort to get fully to grips with the work, but it can be done – and with some pleasure, because the writing is so good.

The people charged with the writing-up of more recent work in London have learned the lessons of the past, and have produced a series of volumes which give enough detail to satisfy most academics, while still managing to remain accessible to the general reader. These new reports on the archaeology of London (sixteen to date) are absolutely first rate. They are beautifully produced, very well illustrated, with extensive colour, and written in plain English. They have even managed to keep the prices down. Here I shall draw extensively on the general review volume, *The Archaeology of Greater London*, and the principal report on *Middle Saxon London*.[11]

That wake-up call, *The Future of London's Past*, paid special attention to what we knew – or rather did not know – about Anglo-Saxon London. This was a conscious attempt to redress the balance, which hitherto had been very much tilted in favour of Roman Londinium, the walled area to the north of the Thames known even today as the City. From the 1970s the City of London would grow rapidly as one of the world's principal centres of finance and banking – and banks require offices; often these were head offices. Such offices must be large, even palatial, because just like the Roman Forum below them they are expressions of power and the dominance of a new financial elite. Big buildings need big foundations to support them, which in turn cause massive disruption to any buried archaeological remains.

As I have already noted, the main archaeological problem was that the City showed very little solid evidence for any sort of Middle Saxon London. At the time of *The Future of London's Past*, cynics among us attributed this to the fact that the previous generation of archaeologists had been so hell-bent on reaching the juicy layers which held the Roman stuff that they simply missed the very slight traces left by the sort of timber buildings that would have been built in Middle Saxon times. But that was only part of the story. Timber buildings do indeed leave very slight traces, but objects like imported lava querns or chunks of Ipswich Ware are far harder to miss, and such things were not to be found within the area of the Roman walls – at least not in the amounts one would expect for a town.

Eleven years after the publication of *The Future* a very perceptive

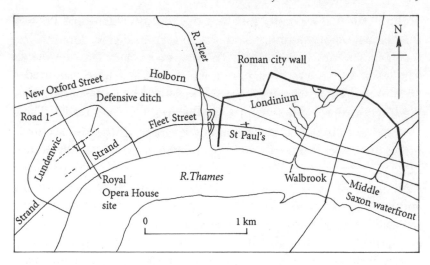

FIG 27   *Middle Saxon London (Lundenwic) and the walled City of Roman London (Londinium). The map shows the position of the Royal Opera House excavations and a main road, known as Road 1, which ran from The Strand to New Oxford Street, both of which were constructed in Roman times. A major defensive ditch was constructed in the earlier ninth century as part of new defensive measures against Viking attacks.*

article was written by Alan Vince of the Museum of London.[12] He worked on pottery, and showed that sherds of distinctively Middle Saxon type, including Ipswich Ware, were only rarely found within the City walls. Other Middle Saxon finds, some of which (a burial for example) had to have been *in situ*, were concentrated outside the walls, along The Strand, an ancient road that approached the City from the west. He then compared the distribution of Middle Saxon finds with that of Late Saxon Wares, which could readily be distinguished because they were tempered by the addition of crushed shells.*

The distribution of Late Saxon shell-tempered pottery showed that the population then seemed to have moved back within the City walls, and Alan Vince argued that this made plenty of sense: the Middle Saxon *wic* now known as Lundenwic was an undefended urban or

---

* Tempering agents like shell or chopped chaff were deliberately added by potters, both to strengthen their vessels and to allow them to dry faster and more evenly before firing.

proto-urban trading centre just west of the City. This would fit with the foundation of Westminster Abbey in its riverside location on what was then Thorney Island in 785. The smart shift back into the walled City was a response to Viking raids, which we know happened in 841, 851 and 871. Vince suggested that the move from Lundenwic back to the City most probably took place in the 870s.

I did not discuss Lundenwic at any length in Chapter 1 because it makes no sense arbitrarily to separate the story of Middle Saxon London from what preceded and followed it. They are all part of the same narrative, and can only be understood with reference to one another.

As a result of Vince's work, attention was sharply focused on the area around The Strand. When it was announced in 1996, after a thankfully long period of gestation during which archaeology managed somehow to struggle its way up the ladder of priorities, that the Royal Opera House was to be massively enlarged and refurbished with lottery cash, there were predictable cries of elitism from the tabloids. But from an entirely selfish point of view I was happy, since the archaeology was to be well cared-for.

The excavations at the Royal Opera site took place between 1989 and 1999, and the full publication appeared just four years later.[13] That in itself was an amazing achievement of organisation and editorial control, and it meant that the results had a huge impact, because they were both immediate and still relevant to academic hot issues, such as the role of *emporia* and 'productive' sites. I won't attempt to summarise all that they revealed, but the highlights are very exciting.

But first, that name Lundenwic. It first appears in laws passed by Kentish kings, when Kent regained control of London from Mercia sometime in the mid to late 670s. In these documents it appears in the form 'Lundenuuic'. Lundenwic is also mentioned in *The Anglo-Saxon Chronicles* for the year 604, but since that document was compiled very much later, this cannot count as the earliest mention of the name. As we have seen, the ending '*wic*' most probably refers to a trading port or centre. When the settlement moved back within the Roman city walls of Londinium in Late Saxon times, it was referred to as 'Lundenburh'. So the three early phases of London were Londinium (Roman), Lundenwic (Middle Saxon) and Lundenburh (Late Saxon).

The old saying that a picture is worth a thousand words most certainly applies to archaeology, where one well-thought-out plan can be worth many pages of descriptive text. The Royal Opera House report has many fine plans showing how the layout of buildings within Lundenwic was modified through time. Their general alignment remained broadly the same, which strongly suggests both that the site was continuously occupied, and that the arrangement of buildings was planned. There were many wells, which have to be maintained open and free from contamination, and this again suggests planning and a degree of social control. The disposal of rubbish in 'middens', or rubbish heaps, which were probably carted away from time to time to be spread on the fields around the settlement, also suggests organisation and indeed delegation.

The buildings were separated by open areas, which could have been small gardens or yards in which various trades such as tanning or smithing were practised. Tanning is a very smelly process, and the pits where the hides were soaked in stale urine were placed well away from the main road and the buildings around it, some of which, being so close to the road itself, may well have been shops.

The main area excavated was crossed by a straight road, known to the archaeologists as Road 1, which probably ran from what is today New Oxford Street, in the north-west, to The Strand, in the south-east. Again, this road provides clear evidence for some form of civic authority. It was certainly not what one might have expected of the time – something muddy and rutted. It had been resurfaced many times, and did not fall into disrepair until the settlement's final, difficult years.

During its most successful and prosperous period in the mid-eighth century, from about 730 to 770, Lundenwic seems to have been far more than a mere trading post or 'proto-urban' settlement. It was undoubtedly a town, and a very successful one at that. Some of the buildings around an alleyway, known as Road 2, clearly formed part of an informal courtyard arrangement where a group of tradesmen shared their skills. One of these must have been an iron smithy, because quantities of slag and furnace lining were found there. A group of wells along a spring line would have provided the workshop with the large amounts of water it needed. After about 770, when the settlement began to decline, rubbish was allowed to accumulate on the alleyway,

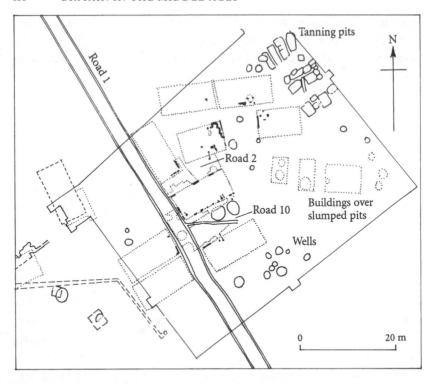

FIG 28 *Middle Saxon structures found in the Royal Opera House excavations. These buildings were in place during the most prosperous phase of Lundenwic's development, between about 730 and 770.*

which suggests that social and civic organisation was beginning to break down. Some of the buildings were clearly domestic houses, because there was abundant evidence for the preparation and consumption of meat and cereals. Weaving certainly took place there too, and a number of imported objects suggest that if the inhabitants were not merchants themselves, then they knew somebody who was.

It would seem that Lundenwic was not defended by walls until some measure of defence was required by the Viking threat. The Venerable Bede, writing around 730, describes London as a major trading centre with Continental Europe, an observation that is borne out by the discovery not only of traded items but of a timber revetted waterfront that has been dated by tree-rings to the year 679, or very soon after. This would suggest that the river was an important part of Lundenwic from the very outset. We also know that Lundenwic would have been served by several churches, which most probably included St Martin in the Fields and St Andrew's, Holborn, and maybe others. Taken together, the evidence for well-maintained streets, consistently aligned buildings, refuse disposal, churches, traded goods and a constructed river frontage all tend to confirm my impression that Lundenwic was indeed a true town.

The Royal Opera House excavations produced abundant evidence for trade with Carolingian Europe in the mid-eighth century. Lundenwic was clearly at the heart of this new, thriving European economy. But all good things must come to an end. The excavations showed that the settlement had roots in the seventh century, flourished in the eighth century, and began to decline after about 770. A large east–west defensive ditch was dug across the northern part of the site in the earlier ninth century. This was an attempt to shrink the outer defences, which hitherto had been overextended. The new, more compact and stronger defences seem to have worked, although by now organisation within the *wic* was beginning to break down. Eventually even the new defences failed when attacked by the Vikings in 871, and Lundenwic succumbed. Settlement then moved east, back within the strengthened Roman walls of the City, to Lundenburh.

Modern excavation is generally speaking so thorough that if it finds nothing, then we can usually conclude that nothing was there. This so-called 'negative evidence' can be very useful. There has been a huge amount of excavation in the City of London in the past thirty years, and so far nobody has yet come across the remains of any immediately post-Roman settlement within the walls of Roman Londinium. After the post-Roman 'Dark Age' hiatus there was sporadic settlement within the walls, and this included the foundation of St Paul's in the year 604. We must conclude that the area occupied by the walled Roman City was entirely abandoned. New evidence suggests that the return to the walled area happened in the mid-ninth century, and the new *burh* of Lundenburh was founded by King Alfred later in the same century.

The discovery and exploration of Middle Saxon Lundenwic has to have been the most important archaeological and historical breakthrough in the nation's capital since the war. But it would be a mistake

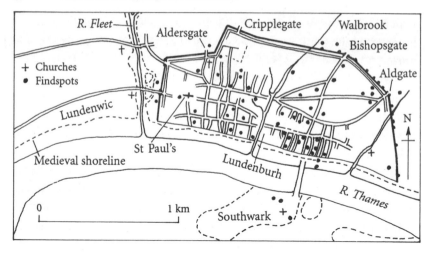

FIG 29   *Map showing the distribution of Late Saxon (late ninth to early eleventh centuries) finds in and around the settlement of Lundenburh, within the old Roman walled City. Lundenburh replaced Middle Saxon Lundenwic, outside the walls, to the west of the Fleet River. It was refounded by King Alfred in 886, when the walls were repaired and rebuilt and a new grid of streets was laid out. Most of the finds are fragments of shelly pottery, characteristic of the Late Saxon period.*

to play down what happened subsequently. Certainly the Late Saxon period was turbulent in London and south-east England, but the city continued to grow and develop nonetheless. Like Winchester, London, or rather Lundenburh, benefited greatly from being refounded by King Alfred as a defended *burh*. As with many other new *burhs*, Lundenburh was subject to extensive replanning, during which it acquired a new grid of streets which were not laid out along Roman antecedents.

It would seem that there were two main areas of settlement within the City, on either side of the Walbrook, the stream which divides the City in half. Recent excavations along Lawrence Lane in the Guildhall have revealed a number of Late Saxon timber buildings arranged side by side along the street frontage. Some of these may well have been shops.[14] Again, it is hard not to see this as truly urban. Perhaps the clearest demonstration of the area occupied in Late Saxon times is still given by Alan Vince's distribution map of shell-tempered pottery, which shows the two settlements alongside their contemporary streets, most of which were probably laid out when Alfred founded the new *burh*.

Lundenburh also possessed a well-built timber river frontage dating to around 970, and there was active trade with Northumbria, the Netherlands, Scandinavia and the Carolingian Empire. Sometime in the late tenth or early eleventh century, London Bridge was rebuilt. The southern end of the bridge was probably defended by a defence work or structure, the 'south work' or Southwark. A major defensive ditch, which may well have been this, was recently excavated. It was dated to the early eleventh century. London was not alone in building a defended river crossing, because it is known that major new bridges were also constructed at this time elsewhere in northern Europe; maybe, as at London, this was to protect their towns from Viking attacks reaching further upstream.

While the story of the two Saxon Londons is very much affected by the Viking presence, the history of York is rather different. Here the Vikings played a more benevolent role, because following that city's swift conquest by the Viking Great Army in the year 866 the city remained at the heart of Danish Britain for some six decades, which is probably why it was treated kindly in the subsequent, late-tenth and early-eleventh century, Viking wars by the Danish King Svein Forkbeard and his son Cnut. The situation in the north and east of England was not the same as that within areas controlled by the West Saxons further south, but that is not to say it was necessarily backward or inferior. Far from it, in fact. York is the classic example of a major city within Viking Britain. As at London, all the major discoveries have been made since the last war. But there has been one important difference.

As we have seen, the recent history of archaeology in London is of a series of large-scale excavations brought about by the expansion of the modern City. In York the situation has been different. The city was known to have had a rich Viking past since at least the nineteenth century, although any details about houses, roads and other structures were largely lacking. The pace of research began to hot up in the 1950s and sixties, but still we lacked anything approaching a large-scale, open-area excavation. People were still in essence looking down holes, in what today we would refer to as 'watching briefs'. All of that was to change in one major large-scale excavation at 16–22 Coppergate. This was 'the Viking Dig', a five-year campaign of excavation from 1976 to 1981. It was a massive operation that produced staggering quantities of material and information. Some 36,000 archaeological contexts revealed over 40,000 individually recorded special or 'small' finds (such as coins and brooches), a quarter of a million pieces of pottery, and five tons of animal bone. The thoroughness of the work was legendary, and involved the sieving of more than eight tons of soil.

After 'the Viking Dig' the pace of development in York either slowed down, or was managed in a way that avoided archaeological destruction. On the surface this would seem to be entirely beneficial, but Dr Richard Hall, who with Peter Addyman is the leading authority on the city's archaeology, plainly has his doubts. He has just edited a major study of Anglo-Scandinavian York in which he makes it clear that 'planning policies are geared principally to the preservation of archaeological deposits *in situ*, notwithstanding that their state of preservation may be deteriorating. Indeed it is salutary to reflect that "the Viking Dig" might never have been undertaken had the present policy framework been in place in the mid-1970s.'[15]

Richard's carefully considered words conceal some very real concerns. The Viking age deposits at York are particularly important because many of them – and those of 'the Viking Dig' were no exception – are waterlogged. As we saw briefly at Yarnton, waterlogged deposits enable fragile organic materials, such as wood, bark, leather and fabrics, to be preserved. But as soon as the water is removed the materials begin to decay. Once restarted, this decay can be very quick indeed – a matter of weeks or months, rather than years.

This is why Richard's statement that some deposits 'may be deteriorating' is so very worrying. I think he can only be talking about one thing. Maisie and I have been actively involved in wetland research all our lives, and we have seen the organic remains of numerous sites vanish before our eyes as soon as the water below the surface began to be pumped out. In most cases this drainage was almost accidental: usually something else was happening nearby that affected the ground water, such as improved land drainage for farming. In other instances the level of ground water was temporarily lowered to allow gravel quarrying to take place. But even a temporary drop in the water table, of maybe a few months, or a year or two at most, is usually enough to do permanent damage to fragile ancient deposits below the ground. The result was always the same: organic remains suffered gravely, or were completely destroyed.

The destruction of waterlogged deposits is a tragedy. It's bad enough when they are excavated first – as excavation is, when all is said and done, no more than methodical destruction. But in the vast majority of instances they are drained without any form of record at all. It can be so frustrating: these unique and fragile vestiges of the distant past survive to our day through some accident of geology or drainage, and then they disappear, in most cases because archaeological warnings are ignored. And why is this? The answer, I'm afraid, is the usual one: money. The excavation of waterlogged archaeological sites is an expensive business. It has to be, because such sites preserve about 90 per cent of everything that was in use at a particular period in the past.

Waterlogged deposits are about far more than mere organic arte-facts. The organic muds and residues found in them hold the clues we need to reconstruct how people lived in the remote past. Happily for us, many British towns and cities were constructed near water. In London it was the Thames, and in York the Ouse. Both are great rivers with extensive floodplains. Both have revealed waterlogged deposits which have completely transformed our knowledge of medieval times. In London, as we will see, the huge revelations were to come from sites along the Thames waterfront. In York it was 'the Viking Dig' which made Jorvík a national name.

Sadly there have been no further big Viking digs in York, because the threat to buried archaeology has been, in theory at least, 'managed'. I know well how hard it is to engineer the artificial raising of ground-water levels, or to prevent seepage from sensitive deposits. I tend to be deeply suspicious of schemes that say they will preserve wet deposits intact and *in situ*. These schemes rarely allow people to monitor their effectiveness. In many instances I suspect (but cannot prove) that they have become an unacknowledged way of achieving destruction by stealth.

Richard Hall is not alone in voicing his concerns. In a paper that

I will discuss very shortly, the environmental specialists at York, Allan Hall and Harry Kenward, whose job it is to analyse samples from waterlogged deposits, complain bitterly that the policy of in-ground preservation has led to a marked decline in the number of waterlogged samples removed from the ground. They point out that it is known that many of these deposits are at risk of drying out in the long term, and describe the failure to collect such material as academically reprehensible. I hope the relevant planning authorities in York will get the message. It could not have been made more clear.

Like Richard Hall too, I would question the currently accepted belief at English Heritage, and within the profession in general, that excavation is only a matter of last resort, to be employed when all else has failed. Of course I believe that we should be careful about what we dig, but we *must* continue to research in this way, because excavation is how archaeologists open new windows on the past. Without the original 'Viking Dig' York's planners would not know what to preserve today – if indeed they are preserving worthwhile remains. Excavation has become a dirty word in certain circles, where people have neither the experience nor the imagination to realise what it can reveal. Peter Addyman's excavations at York did show us, and it is time we remembered what he and his team found there.

If you take a trip through the famous Jorvík Viking Centre in York you will get an excellent impression of life there in the ninth and tenth centuries. Everything, even flies and smells, can be displayed, because waterlogging has preserved the evidence. Pollen grains and seeds show us the plants that grew there. Parasite eggs show us how sanitary (or not) conditions were. Even preserved insects survive. With all this information we can make a very good stab at recreating what it would actually have been like to have lived in Jorvík, even down to the ambient sounds which we take so much for granted in our daily lives. Of course we will never be able to recreate precisely what the people thought, and how they perceived their surroundings, but then we must always have something new to seek. I do, however, believe that one day we will know how the average citizen in early medieval England would have viewed his world. We are just beginning to get inside people's heads by means of a type of study known as 'cognitive archaeology', which has been pioneered by Professor Colin Renfrew and his colleagues at Cambridge.[16] As yet their work is still in its infancy, but the infant seems to be growing rapidly.

The Coppergate dig was where Viking Britain came alive not just for the public, but for archaeologists too. I went there in the later stages, probably in 1981 when I came in from the field to work on the final report of my Fengate excavations. I remember being forcibly struck by the depth of the dig. I was used to finding Bronze Age remains half a metre or so below the surface, but here the archaeologists were working several metres down, surrounded by trench walls that were propped up by heavy steel shoring. The engineering side of the dig was clearly very important – indeed it was a matter of life and death. It was an area that urban archaeologists were to refine so successfully that excavations at places like No. 1 Poultry, in the City of London, were able to take place perfectly safely while construction was happening around and above them. But this kind of potentially dangerous work required levels of expertise, professionalism and discipline that few possessed in the 1960s.

Partly as a result of major digs at York, London and in some of the huge gravel quarries that provided the aggregates required for these developments, archaeologists all over Britain realised that their profession urgently needed to become more professional. Discipline and standards of professional ethics had to be improved. A group of us met in the early 1980s with the intention of founding a self-policing institute for professional field archaeologists. We were elected into office in 1982 as Members of the Institute of Field Archaeologists. Peter Addyman, who was Director of the York Archaeological Trust from 1972 to 2002 and whose name begins with an 'A', was IFA Member No. 1. With only a 'P' to my name, I came in at Number 15.

I cannot pretend that I agree with everything our Institute has achieved in the last thirty years, but it has tried to police the general standards of field archaeology, and it has produced a rigorous Code of Conduct with which I agree absolutely. Sadly, by stressing the importance of professionalism in field archaeology it has unwittingly excluded nearly all amateur involvement, which is something the profession cannot continue to do.

I should add here, while on the subject of archaeological organisations, that the Council for British Archaeology (CBA), which was founded immediately after the war as a response to the problems posed by developing bomb-damaged cities, is very much in favour of public participation at all levels of archaeology – but then I would say that, as I am currently its President. So are the two organisations about to collide? I think not, as there are too many archaeologists who are members of both for that to happen, and besides, our profession has long enjoyed its internal disputes, most of which are amicably resolved over a pint in the pub.

I have often heard it said that the Vikings founded York. They did not. As at London there was an earlier Middle Saxon *wic*, a town-like or proto-urban settlement, known as Eoforwic, which was positioned within the walls of the Roman city of Eboracum. We know a great deal less about Eoforwic than we do of Lundenwic or Hamwic, the Middle Saxon antecedent of Southampton, but there is some environmental and other evidence to suggest that it was less highly developed as a town. Black rats, for example, which when introduced thrive in urban areas, are known to have existed in other *wics*, but were not found in recent excavations at the Fishergate site, which is thought to have been in, or close to, the main settlement of Eoforwic. It also seems to have lacked the sort of built-up streetscapes, to use Richard Hall's phrase, that were found at both Lundenwic and Hamwic.[17]

We do, however, know that Eoforwic was a very significant place to the Northumbrian kings. On the other hand, the distribution of Northumbrian coins suggests that in the later eighth and the ninth centuries the region was becoming increasingly isolated from the developing trading world further south. At present, most informed opinion regards Eoforwic as more a trading centre than a town, but I strongly suspect that that could change if large-scale research began again in York.

I don't want to give the impression that Middle Saxon York was a place of little consequence, because that would be far from the truth. We know for example that Eoforwic contained the cathedral of the Archbishop of the Northumbrians, the Minster, which was founded in AD 627. There are records that the Viking leader Guthfrith, successor to the better-known Halfdan, was buried there in 895 (the Viking-period Minster was not on precisely the same spot as the present Minster). It must also be significant that York was an early strategic objective of the Viking Great Army. It fell to them in 866, very shortly after their arrival in Britain. We do not know whether it was a direct result of this conquest, but at about that time the focus of settlement moved from Fishergate, east of the River Foss, to Coppergate, west of it. The Foss is a tributary of the Ouse, which joins the main river in York.

After the fall of York, and under the leadership and inspiration of Halfdan, warriors settled down in rural estates in the city and the countryside round and about. This policy of settlement and occupation ensured that the Vikings had a firm power base in the region that would provide a source of loyal followers in future military operations. Richard Hall makes the point that Eoforwic was very different in both scale and status to the Jorvík that was recorded in the Domesday Book of 1086. Norman rulers inherited a thriving and fully urban city that had largely grown up under Viking control. It was a major achievement. So much for the background politics; let us now take a brief look at what 'the Viking Dig' produced.

I mentioned earlier that waterlogged deposits could reveal diverse evidence about the past. At York the distinguished specialists in the analysis of plant and insect remains, Allan Hall and Harry Kenward, even headed one of the sections in a recent paper 'An Astonishing Diversity of Evidence'. Writing about the biological remains, they go even further: 'the quality of preservation in many of the deposits has been such that extraordinarily – even bewilderingly – long lists of plant and insect remains have often been compiled from studies of only a kilogramme or two of raw sediment'.[18] This is not the sort of language one expects to read in an academic report on palaeo-environmental remains. But it is very important, because it clearly demonstrates that our reconstructions of life in Viking Jorvík are based on solid information. Just to mention one faunal group, beetles, Harry Kenward and his collaborators were able to identify no fewer than a hundred different species. Many beetles are quite specific about where they choose to live, so they have the potential to tell us a huge amount not just about conditions in Viking York, but also in the countryside around. This brings us to the main point at issue here: how do Hall and Kenward account for such 'bewilderingly' long lists?

Their main conclusion is that the vast majority of the plants were brought to York from outside – for all sorts of purposes, ranging from food and drink to bedstraw, thatch and flooring. Some, like woodland moss, may have arrived attached to wood or wattle, others could have been brought to the city in turves of grass. The insects, on the other hand, probably reflect the local town fauna. Many may originally have been brought to the city, but once there they adapted well to the crowded urban conditions of Viking York, and flourished.

There seems to have been a decline in trade in the ninth century, following the gradual demise of Middle Saxon Eoforwic. Around 900 York's Viking rulers strengthened the Roman walls to the north and west of the rivers Ouse and Foss, to make a smaller but more readily defended city than the Romano-British Eboracum. The site at Copper-gate lies in the area within the confluence of the Ouse to the west and the Foss to the east. We will look at 'the Viking Dig's' setting more closely in Chapter 5, but the most famous discoveries were made on ground that sloped quite sharply down to the River Foss.

The Coppergate dig revealed the remains of a closely packed and perhaps rather squalid town, quite unlike the earlier Roman city. The archaeologist of the Viking period J.D. Richards, quoting Richard Hall, describes Viking York as 'a large compost heap composed of rotting wooden buildings with earth floors covered by decaying vegetation and surrounded by streets and yards filled by pits and middens of organic waste. Organic waste was being dumped at a greater rate than it was being cleared away . . . Nevertheless, whilst no doubt the exterior of the properties was foul and disgusting, their insides may have been tolerably cleanly maintained.'[19]

Four properties, or tenements, were excavated at 16–22 Coppergate. Each one included a rectangular timber building made from posts and woven wattlework. These buildings were thatched and arranged so that their gable ends fronted onto the street, as did at least four of the buildings at the Royal Opera House excavations in London. Behind the buildings their yards contained numerous pits, many of which revealed rich organic remains which showed them to have been used for storage, as latrines or as cesspits. We saw in Lundenwic how crafts played an important part in town life, and Jorvík was no exception to this, because it would appear that the four buildings at Coppergate may have been leased out to craftsmen who were specialists in working iron, copper, lead, silver and gold – plus alloys of these.

Sometime around 975 the wattlework buildings were torn down and replaced by more substantial plank-built structures with sunken floors. On three of the plots the buildings were doubled up, which would suggest that the rebuilding was brought about by the need for more space, either for workshops or for storing traded goods. Finally in the early eleventh century a large warehouse or boatshed was built at the end of the site closest to the river. As in the earliest Viking phase, it would appear that the plank-built structures were used to house craftsmen, including jewellers and woodworkers. But industrial metalworking ceased in this later period, and probably moved towards the urban fringes, away from the most densely populated areas.

So although at times it may have been rather squalid, it is hard to avoid the impression that Viking Jorvík was a thriving, dynamic place in which to have lived. Life there would have been a flurry of activity, with a large variety of crafts and trades being plied. English and foreign ships would regularly arrive and depart from the river port. Even despite the cocktail of organic smells, I would far rather have lived there than in clean, neat and disciplined Roman Eboracum.

PART II

The Middle Ages
(1066–1550)

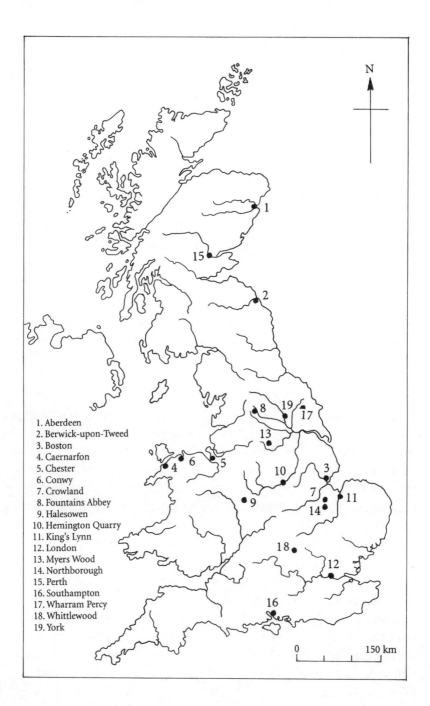

1. Aberdeen
2. Berwick-upon-Tweed
3. Boston
4. Caernarfon
5. Chester
6. Conwy
7. Crowland
8. Fountains Abbey
9. Halesowen
10. Hemington Quarry
11. King's Lynn
12. London
13. Myers Wood
14. Northborough
15. Perth
16. Southampton
17. Wharram Percy
18. Whittlewood
19. York

N

0   150 km

FIG 30   *Principal places mentioned in Part II.*

CHAPTER FIVE

Urban Life in the Middle Ages

THE STORY OF THE MIDDLE AGES has a relatively simple under-lying theme, which helps to explain how people behaved and why they altered their surroundings, both in town and country. But it would be a mistake to suggest that population growth and disease were the only explanations for what happened. People and societies are complex, and are not necessarily predictable. It often takes more than a single cause to have an effect, even if that cause is something as powerful as population.

The first person fully to appreciate the importance of population growth on the stability of society was the eighteenth-century English scholar Thomas Malthus, in his famous *Essay on the Principles of Population* (1798).[1] His thesis was that population will inevitably grow until it outstrips its food sources, then food shortages would lead to an increased death rate, lower fertility, and probably to conflict as well. We now realise that there is more to the analysis of social change than Malthusian pressures alone. Even so, the great man did get it remark-ably right. With Malthus in mind, I find it impossible to view the rapid rise of modern global populations without thinking of potentially dire consequences as well.

The population of Britain, and especially of England, grew steadily from the eleventh to the thirteenth century, when it reached levels, just before the Black Death struck (1348), that were not equalled again until the sixteenth century. I regard this as one of the most important statistics in British history, because the sudden drop in population, following a short pause as society adjusted to the new situation, undoubtedly triggered many fundamental social and economic changes. I will discuss the impact of the various waves of plague on the rural population later, but taken as a whole they probably caused a mortality of round about a third to 45 per cent, which we know was the figure for the populous county of Essex.

I still find it hard to read or think about the Black Death without horror. The first wave of plague, which reached Britain from the Continent in 1348 and raged until the following year, was catastrophic in its effects. Very often historians play down the horror of it all as they analyse its effects and consequences. Sometimes I find such seemingly objective writing cold and heartless; it is almost as if the victims or survivors were not human. Colin Platt's superb book *King Death* is a notable exception. At one point, having been discussing the often-made observation that a degree of economic prosperity frequently followed in the immediate wake of the plague, he adds: 'Call no society happy that loses as many children as ever enter adult life, where death rates rise and life expectations fall, and where the living are beleaguered by the dead.'[2] That says it all. It *is* an emotional subject, even six and a half centuries later. One example will make the point.

Anyone who has visited Ashwell Church, in the beautiful north Hertfordshire village close to which I spent my childhood, will be aware that it possesses some remarkable medieval graffiti, including a fine scratched likeness of old St Paul's Cathedral in London and the complaint of a testy mason: 'The quoins are not jointed aright – I spit at them.' But inscribed inside the wall of the west tower is a Latin verse which captures the horror, fear and guilt felt by survivors in the immediate aftermath of 1349. Translated, it reads:

> 1350 – Miserable, savage, crazed,
> Only the worst of people remain as witnesses,
> And to cap all came a tempest
> With St Maur thundering over the earth.[3]

Were these afflictions the result of direct Malthusian pressures? It's hard to say, but the economic historian M.M. Postan, Colin Platt and others believe that in certain places the rise in population was beginning to fall away anyhow.[4] Food shortages, for example, led to famine in Essex in 1315–17. This would suggest that the most populous parts of the country had either reached or were rapidly approaching the maximum population the resources available could support. What does seem certain is that the plague, which was spread by way of fleas that moved between rats and humans, was far worse in the crowded conditions that then prevailed in towns than it was in the country. Those crowded conditions were the result of general population growth, and perhaps rather surprisingly there does not seem to have been much migration into towns from the countryside – although this was to change after the Black Death.

The Black Death of 1348–49 was not a one-off single event. There were numerous visitations of the pestilence for the next three centuries, starting in 1361. The final outbreaks in Scotland were in 1645–49 and in England 1665–66; the latter was the 'Great Plague' recorded so memorably in his diary by Samuel Pepys, which killed about 56,000 people in London. The plagues caused great towns to shrink and villages to disappear. They also affected the way people regarded themselves and the way they lived their lives. In particular, and perhaps not surprisingly, they affected attitudes to both death and religion. So population and pestilence together helped to change the character of the late Middle Ages. As we will see later, there are good grounds for suggesting that the two to three centuries following the mid-fourteenth century were a period of transition, when the medieval world gradually evolved into the modern world. You could also take the view, as I do, that both were part of essentially the same phenomenon.

Without wishing to oversimplify, the early Middle Ages prior to 1348 were a logical development of what had gone before. The arrival of the Normans in 1066 certainly gave rise to changes in the ruling elite, and they in turn affected the way that ordinary people were governed. But nothing changed fundamentally: nucleated villages thrived, monastic settlements continued to grow, existing *burhs* also continued to develop, and some new ones were founded for the benefit of prosperous landowners. Generally speaking it was business as usual, but under new management. It was also a period of population growth and economic expansion in both town and country.

I shall discuss the impact of the Norman Conquest on British towns when I return to York and my other case-studies shortly, but here I want briefly to consider the effects of the Black Death on the urban landscape. As I have already hinted, it was severe, and led to the phenomenon of 'shrunken towns'.[5] The name suggests that, rather like shrunken heads, the towns contracted, fossilised and stayed that way. Of course there were exceptions, but by and large towns in late medieval Britain were smaller than they had been before the plague. Two examples on the east coast of England will make the point. Both are ports, and can be taken as indicators of the country's general economic health. Grimsby on the Humber and Boston on the Wash are separated by Lindsey, the main land-mass of Lincolnshire, and belong to separate, independent economic and geographical regions.

Grimsby was overcrowded before the Black Death, and is estimated to have lost about 30 per cent of its population in the spring and summer of 1349. More reliable figures are provided by tax statistics, which show a population loss of 40 per cent between 1377 and 1524. So if Grimsby did indeed bounce back after the initial pestilence (and there is no good evidence for such a recovery), it certainly wasn't maintained. The tax figures paint a gloomy picture of the town throughout the late Middle Ages. But if Grimsby was bad, Boston was worse.

On a clear day, if I climbed onto the roof of my barn with my binoculars I could probably just see the tower of Boston Stump, twenty-five kilometres away due north along the Greenwich Meridian. The Stump, the tower of St Botolph's Church, is quite extraordinary, and is described by Pevsner as 'the most prodigious of English parochial steeples'.[6] It is almost ninety metres high, and was clearly positioned to dominate the river, the source of the port's great wealth. It is visible across the flat Fens and the waters of the Wash for well over fifteen kilometres in all directions. I remember seeing it many times when I was working at Seahenge, the Bronze Age timber circle on the north Norfolk coast. It resembled a sharp thorn that had pierced the otherwise unblemished skin of the sea's horizon.

Pevsner points out that the body of St Botolph's Church too is huge, even when judged by the large medieval parish churches of other eastern towns such as Hull, Newcastle and Yarmouth. But the Stump was built throughout the fifteenth century, starting around 1425, and completed about 1515. If Grimsby is anything to go by, this surely would have been a period when the town's population was shrinking. So what was going on?

Boston's population did indeed decline throughout the fifteenth century. This followed a history of rapid growth in the early Middle Ages. The town is not recorded in Domesday, so presumably it did not exist in 1086, but by 1200 it was a major east coast trading port. It was, in other words, a Norman New Town that made good. It expanded rapidly until 1300 and continued to grow throughout the fourteenth century, largely on the proceeds of the wool trade which allowed other towns and cities in the region such as Norwich and Peterborough to flourish. Taking that poll tax assessment of 1377 as a starting point, and finishing with the diocesan household survey of 1563, the town's population fell by a full 50 per cent.

Colin Platt makes the point that Boston's population would probably have recovered from the initial outbreak of plague, which hit the town in 1349, were it not for a succession of later waves of disease. The only way that the town, like Grimsby and many others, could survive was by drawing people in from the surrounding region. If that failed to happen, its collapse would be 'shockingly rapid'. Even London, the most prosperous city in Britain, had to draw heavily upon the population outside. It was immigration that saved Colchester, which only just managed to keep going throughout the fifteenth century, suffering further plague attacks beginning in 1412, 1420, 1426, 1433 and 1463.

To return to the Stump: why was it built when it was? Surely the people had more urgent matters to think about than erecting vast stone towers on the soft, silty soils on the shores of the Wash? That is true, but then people, unlike plants, animals or the stars, do not act in predictable ways – which is why archaeology and history can never lose their fascination. So was the Stump a mark of despair? Was it a case of fiddling while Rome burned? The answer to that is a firm 'no'. Throughout the fifteenth century trade, like the population in general, was in sharp decline, but the power of the town's trading organisations, such as the Corpus Christi Gild, had never been greater. The guilds saw to it that further storeys were added to the Stump as the century progressed. The tower became a symbol of what human organisations could achieve; it was an expression in stone of the stability and protection – insurance by any other word – that institutions could provide their members. But more than that, it was a clear symbol that people's thoughts had turned towards the Church and the supernatural in their pressing need to come to terms with mortality. The presence of King

Death pervaded all aspects of their daily lives. Since I began writing this book I have revisited Boston, and I cannot look up at the Stump without thinking about death and the courage of those men and women who confronted the greatest impostor of them all – and won.

The decline in trade noted in Boston in the fifteenth century continued into the sixteenth, so that by 1524 the town was paying less tax than it had before the onset of plague. Boston may have been exceptional in such a thoroughgoing decline, but its rise had been similarly dramatic. The town may have been less wealthy, but the wealth that was there – and the importance of this should not be underestimated – became concentrated in fewer and fewer hands as time progressed.

Was the story of Boston typical of other successful pre-plague towns? Had I been writing this twenty years ago I would probably have answered 'yes' to that question, simply because historians of late medieval Europe were then interested in finding general patterns. It was fashionable to put forward classificatory schemes that could make sense of what archaeology, to name just one source of new information, was starting to reveal. The highly influential French historian Fernand Braudel liked to do things in threes. His vision of history had three levels of importance, or superficiality, depending on one's viewpoint. At the surface were historical events, below these were the trends and rhythms of history, and below these lay the *longue durée*, the very long-term fundamental trends that differentiate human societies. Like most prehistorians, I tend to inhabit the world of the *longue durée*.[7] Braudel's scheme has been quite successful in making historians and archaeologists reflect on problems of scale and chronology; he has made us think about how our own pet projects might fit into the larger picture, in both time and space.

His thoughts on towns, however, have been rather less successful, perhaps because they were slightly too prescriptive and Gallic for Anglo-Saxon tastes. In 1979 Braudel suggested that towns could be divided into *open* towns, still attached to their agricultural surroundings, *subject* towns, subject to an external authority such as a bishop or king, and *closed* towns, where the inhabitants took power for themselves. He saw the competition among closed towns as the economic engine which had powered European development in the Middle Ages.

But models such as this have failed to find general acceptance, largely because most towns refuse to lie down and be categorised. If this was true twenty years ago it has even more validity today, when the vast amounts of new information produced by urban archaeology defy such simplistic categorisation. One modern approach, pioneered by leading urban archaeologists such as John Schofield, Alan Vince and Martin Carver, actually uses the rapidly accumulating data as the basis for analysis. It is very much a 'bottom-up' rather than 'top-down' approach. In essence this approach treats each town as a unique and complex entity that defies pigeonholes and rigid categorisation. As Schofield puts it: 'Let the data speak; see what it has to say.'[8]

Mindful of the potential dangers, I feel less inclined to draw general conclusions from the story of Boston, but it is true to say that the population of most British towns declined throughout the fourteenth and well into the fifteenth centuries. In some instances the decline was as severe as, if not worse than, that of Boston. Winchester is an example, but here as elsewhere it would be a great mistake to attribute the city's decline to the Black Death alone.[9] As at Boston, where overseas trade was a major influence, other factors applied too. Winchester 'peaked' as a city around 1100, and thereafter lost power and influence to London, its great rival for the role of capital of England in the tenth and eleventh centuries. In the thirteenth century even Boston, itself in decline, overtook Winchester in terms of wealth. We see this decline mirrored in the number of churches that the city could support. In the twelfth century there were fifty-seven. Five were made redundant before 1349 – so the process was under way well prior to the Black Death. By 1400 another nineteen had been lost, and in the century that followed seven more became redundant. Finally twice that number closed before 1600 (of which eleven predated 1500).

We left the story in the previous chapter with the establishment, in the face of military threats, of defensive towns. Most, but not all, of these Saxon and Viking *burhs* were successful, but some succeeded better than others. The city of York was one of the more successful, and continued to thrive in the Middle Ages. The best witness to this must surely be its magnificent Minster, which has to be the most imposing cathedral in Britain.

Every other month I attend a meeting of the Council for British

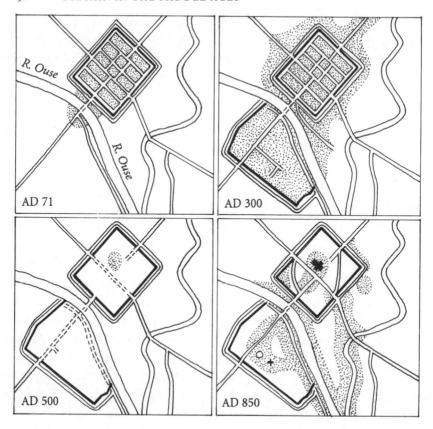

Archaeology, whose headquarters is in York, and I always make a brief diversion to pass close by that stunning building on my way from the station to our offices in the street known as Bootham. I don't know what it is about the Minster's stonework, now that it has had the grime of the railway age washed away, but it produces a soft, warm glow that penetrates through rain and fog. And it's so vast. There's nowhere else quite like it, except perhaps Ely: both are masterpieces that were intended to inspire, and both succeed admirably. Both too remind me that the medieval world was an adjunct, or an accompaniment, to our world. It was most certainly not, unlike the past in L.P. Hartley's *The Go-Between*, a foreign country where people did things differently.

I mentioned in the previous chapter that we would return to York to examine the city in a wider context, and my task has been made

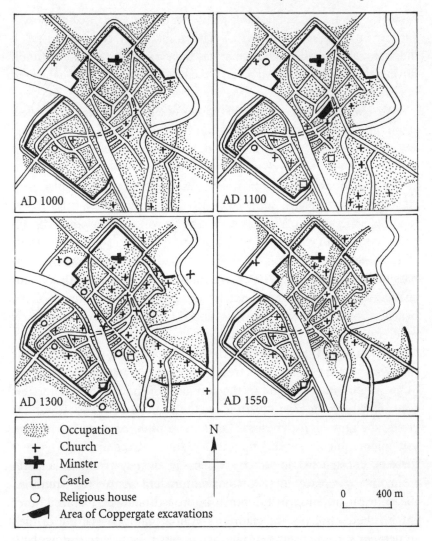

FIG 31 *The development of York, starting with the early Roman fortress of Eboracum (AD 71), which acquired an official civilian settlement known as the Colonia Eboracensis (AD 300). The area seems to have been sparsely settled in post-Roman times (AD 500). The Middle Saxon settlement and trading centre was known as Eoforwic (AD 850). Following the Viking conquest of AD 866 the Anglo-Scandinavian city of Jorvík prospered (AD 1000). After an uprising against the Normans, the city of York prospered and grew through most of the Middle Ages (AD 1100–1300). After about 1450 the city's fortunes declined and the population shrank (AD 1550).*

easier by the recent publication of the results of later medieval excavations in the Coppergate area.[10] The archaeology of medieval York illustrates themes that echo what was happening elsewhere in Britain during the Middle Ages. It is an excellent case-study with which to begin our exploration.

We saw at Colchester that changing town plans can help us understand how a place developed. York has been the subject of much study since the famous 'Viking Dig', and I strongly recommend Richard Hall's recent general narrative guide, which places the most important archaeological and historical discoveries in context. It has a series of very useful town plans, some of which I shall reproduce here. As we saw at Colchester and Winchester, and as we will see at London, certain parts of the main elements of the Roman street plan survived; in most cases these were instances where routes had been fixed by having to pass through gateways in defensive walls. In the case of York a major change was also brought about by the removal downstream of the bridge across the River Ouse. This tended to shift the focus of the early medieval city more to the south and east.

We know that the area was rich in pre-Roman settlements, but the first York was the military fortress known as Eboracum which served as an important early base in the conquest of the north. The fortress controlled both the river crossing and the confluence of two important rivers, the Ouse and the Floss. Then, as so often happened, a civilian settlement quickly sprang up outside the fortified camp. The first fortress, constructed in AD 71, was made entirely from timber, but from AD 107 replacement work and improvements were in stone. As the political situation in the north improved following, among other things, the completion of Hadrian's Wall around AD 133, the civilian settlement spread away from the fort, across the Ouse to the flat land south-west of the river. York thrived throughout the third century, when towns elsewhere in Roman Britain were generally in decline. By the late third century it was made the official capital of northern Britain and the *colonia*, the now-official settlement west of the river, acquired walls. Following the death of his predecessor Constantius in York in AD 306, the new Emperor Constantine proclaimed the toleration of Christianity throughout the Empire, and by AD 314 Eboracum was a bishopric.

In the fourth century decline did set in. Public buildings were abandoned and streets were no longer regularly cleaned. Even so, private houses, especially in the western settlement, continued to be built and occupied even into the early fifth century. I discussed the problems of discovering what happened in fifth- and sixth-century York in *Britain AD*,[11] but while some form of settlement did seem to continue, it is far from clear whether this was actually urban life or something more akin to the 'squatters' camp' that Philip Crummy talked about at Colchester from the same period. Whatever else happened in the Dark Ages, it now seems unlikely that York was entirely abandoned, especially the area around the Minster (where excavations revealed tantalising signs of post-Roman activity).

The earliest evidence for Anglo-Saxon settlement is in the form of cemeteries that were placed some way from the Roman city walls, and it is entirely possible that the built-up areas of the Roman city were avoided quite simply because the masonry and stonework had become dangerous – and besides, the new Anglo-Saxon tradition was to build in wood. By the seventh century the picture becomes more clear, with the emergence of Eoforwic and the construction of a small wooden church on the site of the Minster in 627. A monastery was created in York in the eighth century, and became a centre of learning and scholarship.

The pinning-down of Eoforwic has proved even more problematical than finding Lundenwic. It seems to have been even more informal: essentially a series of ribbon-like settlements running parallel to, and along, the two rivers. But as we have already seen, it was a settlement that boasted royal connections with the kingdom of Northumbria, plus strong ecclesiastical links, and of course long-distance trading connections by way of the river. Richard Hall is in little doubt that many of the archaeological mysteries of Eoforwic could have been settled by now, had York seen as much excavation as London. Sadly that was not to be.

I have already discussed Viking Jorvík in some detail; here I am more interested in its size and general location. Although its archaeological story is still not as clear as we might wish, Middle Saxon Eoforwic was clearly a prime objective for the Viking Great Army which moved rapidly north from East Anglia to capture it in 866. If we compare the plan of Eoforwic in 850 with that of Anglo-Scandinavian Jorvík in 1000, it is clear that the new regime altered the layout of the city considerably. New parts of the old Roman town, such as the area around Coppergate, the scene of 'the Viking Dig', which had lain derelict for centuries, were reoccupied in the later ninth century. Other areas, believed to have been occupied in Middle Saxon times, were abandoned. As we saw previously, new property boundaries were established and the defences were improved. Maybe one reason that inhabitants of Jorvík, Northumbrian English and Scandinavian settlers alike, found their way to, as Richard Hall puts it, a 'mutual toleration', was through the common bond of 'antagonism towards the kings of Wessex'.

In 954 Jorvík fell to Wessex and the city returned to English rule. In 1067–68 it fell to William the Conqueror without a fight, but the following year the townspeople rebelled and were put down ruthlessly – a process which involved the destruction of parts of the city. William stamped his military authority on the city by constructing two castles on mounds on either side of the River Ouse, one of which still carries a mid-thirteenth-century stone keep, known as Clifford's Tower. He demonstrated his moral superiority perhaps even more effectively with the massive reconstruction of the Minster in the 1070s.

After the initial problems posed by the uprising against the Normans, the inhabitants of eleventh- and twelfth-century York gave up violence and the city prospered. It became self-governing, and grew into a major regional centre with trading links over a wide area of northern and Midland England – and indeed overseas too. It received its first royal charter from Henry II sometime between 1155 and 1162.* Despite the depredations of the Black Death, York continued to prosper until about 1475, attracting people from the country round about. It thrived as a major judicial centre and an inland trading port; but its commerce overseas was largely taken over by Hull, with its superior access to the North Sea, after about 1350. The city continued as a major

---

* Royal charters were elaborate documents with grand seals which reflected their importance in medieval times. They assured citizens of their liberties to trade freely, by allowing them to hold regular markets and fairs, collect tolls and elect their own officials. By the time of Henry II charters were a symbol of royal trust, and they also implied some freedom from direct royal authority.

manufacturing centre through most of the Middle Ages, building on a tradition that had begun in Viking times. Its gradual descent from pre-eminence began in the final century of the Middle Ages. After about 1450 other trading towns such as Wakefield and Leeds joined Hull in capturing York's markets, and the population of the city declined.

As I have already noted, excavation in and around the area of the original 'Viking Dig' at 16–22 Coppergate has thrown new light on the lives of ordinary folk in the Middle Ages. Town life is essentially about existing in close proximity to other people without them driving you and your family mad – and vice versa. One way of avoiding friction, if not actually achieving peace and harmony, is to draw lines on the ground that are universally recognised and cannot be crossed. To this end 'burgages', or bounded properties, were established in the early tenth century, and they continued pretty well unaltered for the following millennium. Like most early medieval burgages, those in the Coppergate area were long, thin and rectangular, with one narrow end fronting onto the street. They were clearly surveyed-in, because like many garden allotments today they are laid out in units of one perch, or sixteen feet six inches.

It would be a mistake to imagine that early medieval towns were a sprawl of poor houses dominated by one or two spectacular churches. In fact, close study of the Coppergate area shows that, just like today, even before the thirteenth century certain streets and areas were regarded as more desirable than others. The 'good' streets were often those leading into marketplaces. Many people passed by these properties, so they would have been a good investment for a merchant or shopkeeper; but more than that, high-profile buildings made excellent status symbols for those who wanted to display their wealth and success.

The original dig at 16–22 Coppergate was of course well known for its Viking period discoveries, but in medieval times the site's importance continued, because it provided a good example of the development of four side-by-side tenements, complete with houses, wells and outbuildings, in an area that was a long way from being 'good'. In fact the medieval properties off Coppergate would probably be seen today as more 'bog standard' than 'good'. One reason for this was that the ground sloped quite steeply, was wet and was subject to flooding by the River Floss. It was an area of workshops and poorer housing, but despite that, throughout the Middle Ages the property boundaries were respected. The inhabitants also made efforts to improve their lot, by deliberately raising the ground above the flood level and by improving their buildings.

Before the mid-thirteenth century the buildings at Coppergate were of earthfast construction. In other words, like prehistoric buildings they were constructed around posts that were driven into the ground. These earthfast posts gave the building the rigidity it required while it was being constructed. Once the wattle or plank walls and the roof rafters were in place, the earthfast rigidity became less important, but even then, rotten posts would need to be replaced from time to time – and very often it was simpler to tear the entire structure down and start afresh. Earthfast construction was fundamentally flawed because of the fact that posts driven into the earth will rot off just below the ground, which is where fungi that need air and soil nutrients are most active. It can be a rapid process: earthfast posts on some of our reconstructed buildings at Flag Fen have rotted away within ten years. Posts driven into the ground also draw moisture upwards, because that was how they worked when they were part of a living tree; even when dead, the capillary action of tiny vessels within the wood acts as a sort of microscopic siphon. The result is continual and chronic rising damp.

But around the mid-thirteenth century the inhabitants of Coppergate, and elsewhere in Britain, realised there was a way to sidestep many of these problems. Improvements in carpentry meant that it became possible to prefabricate many components and joints. The result was a new type of building which was constructed around a frame that was braced and rigid in all three dimensions. In some respects this was similar to the change in automotive design which has happened since the war. The old way of building a car was to have a heavy steel chassis onto which was bolted the engine and the bodywork. This provided good horizontal rigidity only. My aged Land-Rover is very much built on this rugged principle, and I am dreading the day when the chassis rusts through. Today cars use the bodywork to provide a much lighter, but rigid frame. The new system requires better design and construction, but it is also a great deal safer, because it provides better all-round protection against impact.

To avoid rising damp, the framework of timber-frame buildings may be raised off the ground on stone pads, as they were at Coppergate. The resulting box-like construction also helps to accommodate the movements in the soil that one finds on wet and heavy land. Such frames are also far better at carrying the extra load imposed by heavier and more fire-resistant roof coverings such as tiles. The inhabitants at Coppergate further realised that they could avoid future problems of subsidence if they spent a little time preparing consolidated foundations before they erected their buildings. From the thirteenth century the Coppergate area improved markedly, and it achieved prosperity in the fourteenth and fifteenth centuries, when there is documentary evidence for merchants building themselves substantial houses in the area. The excavations also provided one fascinating insight into human relations over the past thousand years.

As has been noted, life in towns is largely about maintaining good relations with the people living next door. This means that it is important to be able to chat and pass the time of day, while at the same time retaining a degree of privacy for oneself and one's family. In other words, boundaries need to be porous. High stone walls or towering Leylandii cypress hedges do not promote good neighbourliness. So the actual form that boundaries take matters. This was recognised by the excavators at 16–22 Coppergate: they labelled the four rectangular tenement plots that traversed the site A–D, and recorded the way the boundaries were marked out as time passed.

By and large the boundaries remained remarkably consistent, and did not wander much at all. The actual physical divisions (fence, ditch or path) were all in a sense 'porous', except when a building was constructed right up to the edge of the property, but even that would probably have had windows or doors. It is also entirely possible that in certain instances some form of non-earthfast partition, such as a hurdle, could have been used, but left no archaeological traces. The pattern left by the changing boundary markers shows that the choice was made by the people living in the tenements. It does not appear that any central authority made these decisions. It is also very likely that in instances where the boundaries seem either to have been

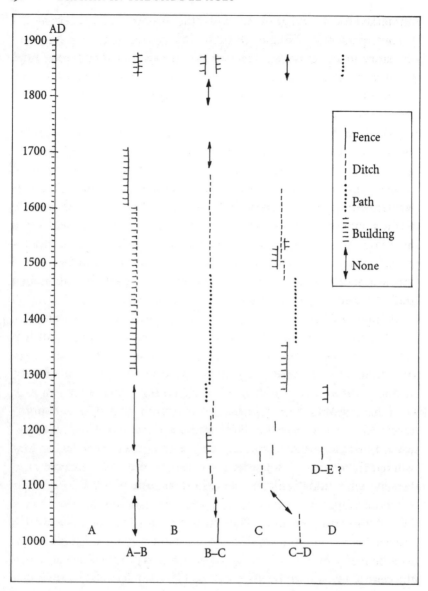

FIG 32 *Excavation at 16–22 Coppergate, York, showed how the physical form of boundary partitions between four tenement plots (A–D) changed through time. This chart also indicates the very slight extent to which the boundaries shifted, especially after the twelfth century.*

unmarked or very lightly marked, the neighbours concerned had become personally close, or related – maybe through marriage. I find the story of the changing Coppergate burgage partitions fascinating, because they mirror how people got on with their neighbours many centuries ago. It's a glimpse of day-to-day life that only archaeology could possibly reveal.

While archaeology can offer unexpected insights such as this into aspects of daily life in the distant past, I would be doing historians a great injustice if I gave the impression that they only wrote about power politics and wars. There have always been historians who have written with rigour and sensitivity about daily life in the past: Nicholas Orme's superb book *Medieval Children*, for instance, vividly shows how youngsters then were just as playful as their modern counter-parts.[12] Documents such as accounts and contracts can be used to throw a huge amount of light on, for example, the medieval building trade. A particularly fine example is *Building in England Down to 1540* (1952) by L.F. Salzman, which details nearly every aspect of the construction business, ranging from cranes, masonry and sources of labour to how that labour force was paid and employed.[13] One might have thought that archaeology could add little. But one would be very wrong.

I have always been fascinated as much by the construction of medieval buildings as by their form and appearance. I well remember when I first came face to face with evidence for how medieval builders worked their magic. I was with a small party from my excavations at Fengate who were being shown around Peterborough Cathedral by our bookkeeper and accountant George Dixon in the early summer of 1972. A fortnight previously I had discovered that George was also an official Cathedral guide, and it was not hard to persuade him to give us a behind-the-scenes tour. We went up into the roof and ascended the central tower, but for me the highlight came when George took us behind the great triple-arcaded Early English west front. This was completed in 1237, and behind it lay concealed the earlier west front. It was unweathered, fresh and intact, just as it had been left by the Norman masons in the later twelfth century. We passed on into the spire of the north-western tower, and there saw the intact thirteenth-century wooden crane which had hoisted the great stones that surrounded us.[14] It consisted of a huge vertical wheel mounted in a timber framework. Rather like the timber scaffold which still sits inside the spire of Salisbury Cathedral, it was as simple to leave it in place as to shift it – and besides, nobody could have known when next it would come in handy.

Church archaeology is an exciting new field that has only really come into its own since about 1980. Today no cathedral or diocese is without an official archaeologist. Gone are the days when a well-intentioned vicar could rip through the complex archaeology of the nave floor while repairing the central heating – or what passed for heating in most churches in the twentieth century. One of the leading authorities on church archaeology is Dr Warwick Rodwell. Warwick wrote the standard introduction, *Church Archaeology*, in 1981, and recently published a magnificent study of Wells Cathedral for English Heritage.[15] If you want to learn just what a great church archaeologist can achieve, get hold of a copy of this stunning book.

One result of this heightened awareness of what lies within and beneath the walls of our ancient churches is that we are beginning to learn a great deal about medieval builders and the way they actually worked. Of course there were accidents and catastrophes aplenty – we should remember that these people were sometimes pushing technology to its very limits – but we now know that they took immense trouble to erect stout scaffolding, as we will see when we examine the construction of the great octagon at Ely in Chapter 7. Good scaffolding was the secret that lay behind all construction projects, great and small.

During the construction and subsequent maintenance of churches and cathedrals, wooden scaffold poles were inserted into so-called putlog holes, which were usually left open to the weather on the outside of churches and domestic buildings, but were plastered over on the interior. The term derives from the putlogs or putlocks, the short horizontal poles that carried the boards of scaffold walkways. Church archaeologists such as Warwick Rodwell have made detailed studies of putlog holes, through which they have been able to work out with considerable precision how some of the best-preserved stone and brick structures were erected. Even the constructional details of that remarkable Saxon tower at Earls Barton have become apparent.[16] Because they are now so closely scrutinised by archaeologists when any new work is undertaken, churches are providing a wealth of new information about the practicalities of erecting medieval buildings. I could easily devote an entire chapter to this fascinating topic, but will confine myself to a few important principles.

First, the scaffolding was made from wooden poles tied together with rope and secured in putlog holes in the wall and in post-holes, or barrels filled with sand, on the ground. This was far from flimsy: I can recall seeing similar timber scaffolding being used during the 1950s in Brussels, where builders were safely working six or seven storeys above ground. When correctly knotted, rope binding tightens in the wet, and timber creaks when it comes under strain. Modern metal scaffold clamps, on the other hand, can slip in the wet or when poorly tightened, and steel poles can buckle without any warning at all. Rodwell points out that medieval walls usually had to be built from two sides simultaneously, and putlog holes could sometimes pass right through the wall to support both internal and external scaffolds.[17] Sometimes the two scaffolds were erected independently, with shorter putlogs and shallower putlog holes. The advantage of this was that the putlog poles could easily be recovered at the end of the job. Long putlogs that passed through the wall were usually sawn off flush with the surface, and in a few instances these can still be found in place.

Today large trucks with revolving hoppers pour ready-mixed concrete into the shuttering of walls and floors. In medieval times the technique of wall building was different, but it also needed huge amounts of lime mortar to bind the masonry facings of the walls together, and to form the rubble core into a solid, load-bearing mass. I remember visiting John Williams' excavations at St Peter's Street, Northampton, in the mid-1970s to see three lime mortar mixers dating to the Middle Saxon period (late seventh or early eighth century).[18] They consisted of a circular, pond-like mixing 'bowl' about three metres in diameter and half a metre deep. The sides of the 'bowl' were formed by woven wattle and mortar, and there was a substantial post at the centre on which pivoted a heavy beam or mixing arm, which extended right across the bowl and was pushed by at least two men (or perhaps horses or oxen) at each end. Six mixing paddles extended from the main arm into the mortar within the bowl. These machines – because that in essence is what they were – were probably used in the construction of a church, and they clearly demonstrate that mortar was required in truly industrial quantities.

One interesting sidelight on medieval building methods is the presence around most churches of a 'constructional layer'. This can be rather mystifying if one doesn't know what to expect when excavating. Essentially it consists of a mass of stone or brick chippings, fragments of tile and numerous drips of cement that fell down from the scaffolding as the walls went up. The 'construction layer' is now almost invariably below the surface, and is thickest near the walls, forming a hard, path-like feature around the building, and tailing off away from the walls. Of course building sites have always been businesslike but generally messy places. For example, the medieval masons' yard at Wells Cathedral has been recovered and was found to contain no less than a metre thickness of stone dust.

Although they were essential to any construction project there is very little direct evidence for carpenters, and the nails, hinges and other fittings they used were produced by blacksmiths working off-site. So the physical evidence for these trades is generally slight. Finally, any modern Health and Safety inspector who happened to visit a building site in the Middle Ages would have had a fit when he saw the area where they worked the lead that was such an important feature of medieval church roofs and windows. Huge amounts were required, and it was all produced on-site. Worse than that, it was melted down in hearths that were set up indoors, often within the church itself. This was because wind and draughts cool the molten lead too quickly, which usually causes cracking. The poisonous fumes that must have poured upwards from the lead-melting hearth or hearths (Rodwell found twenty-four at St Peter's Church, Barton-on-Humber) can only be imagined. Anyone working above them would not have lived for very long.

London was far and away the most important city in Britain in the Middle Ages. In addition to the churches and public buildings found in most large cities of the time, it also included, on Thorney Island at Westminster, the trappings of royal and national government. Powerful people, such as the Bishops of Winchester and Ely, built palaces in London; the capital was also the home of a huge variety of successful monastic foundations and other institutions such as hospitals. But I must concentrate on the general picture, as revealed in a series of town plans, and will only mention specific buildings in passing. I should add that I will cover waterfront archaeology, which has had such a dramatic effect on our understanding of London's development, later, in Chapter 7.

There can be no doubt that power and politics played a large part in the story of London's development. Other factors were important too: England's major arterial roads, which were mostly introduced by the Romans, put London at the hub of a radiating network. The Thames was a major natural route both into and out of Britain, with good access to the Continental mainland. So London was favoured by both geography and infrastructure. Its own history was to play a determining role too. London had emerged as the pre-eminent city of Saxon times, but it was William the Conqueror's decision to be crowned at Westminster which was to have a profound effect on subsequent developments. Doubtless William's choice was influenced by the fact that his defeated predecessor, Harold II, had also been crowned in Edward the Confessor's Abbey at Westminster. Anthropologists would explain this as a conscious act of 'legitimation' on William's part, but whatever the cause, it was an event which put the seal on London's future as the administrative capital of England.

The development of London is a fascinating mixture of political history, ecclesiastical politics and historical economics. If I were to be asked which of these was the most important, I would probably suggest the latter. Positioned where it is, in a natural port and at the hub of a road network, London could not go wrong. Even supreme political power has its limits, and will eventually succumb to the relentless and

FIG 33 *The development of medieval London, starting with the refounding by King Alfred of a new* burh, *known as Lundenburh, within the walled Roman City. London Bridge was rebuilt, partly as a defence against Viking raids, further upstream. From 1066 to 1200 the city grew and prospered. The main new development was the construction of Thames Street, parallel with the river. The period 1200–1350 saw medieval London's greatest development. Even after the Black Death (1350–1500) the city acquired further lanes and alleys, and its merchants grew increasingly prosperous. In times of plague, population levels were maintained by large-scale immigration from outside.*

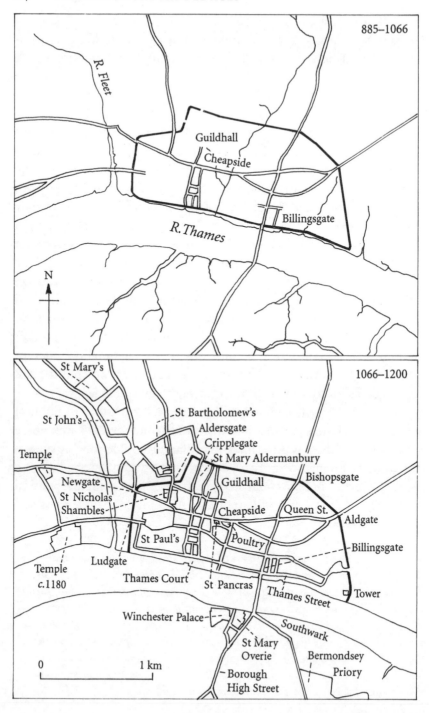

885–1066

Guildhall
Cheapside

R. Fleet

R. Thames

Billingsgate

N

1066–1200

St Mary's

St John's

St Bartholomew's
Aldersgate
Cripplegate
St Mary Aldermanbury

Temple

Bishopsgate

Newgate
St Nicholas
Shambles

Guildhall

Cheapside

Queen St.

Aldgate

Billingsgate

St Paul's

Poultry

Temple
c.1180

Ludgate

Thames Court

St Pancras

Thames Street

Tower

Winchester Palace

Southwark

0   1 km

St Mary
Overie

Bermondsey
Priory

Borough
High Street

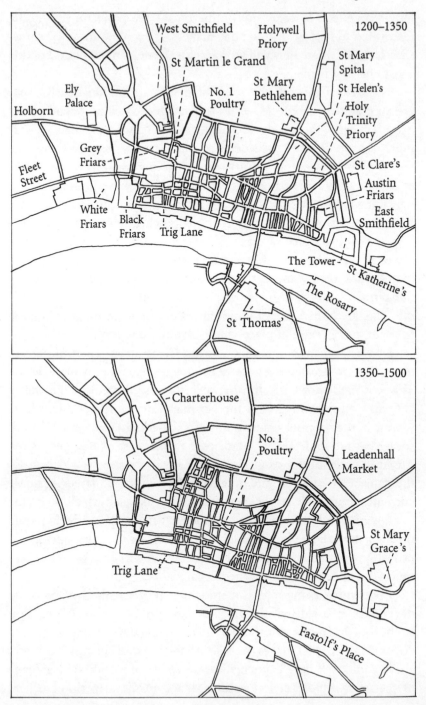

1200–1350

West Smithfield
Holywell Priory
St Martin le Grand
St Mary Spital
St Mary Bethlehem
St Helen's
Ely Palace
No. 1 Poultry
Holy Trinity Priory
Holborn
Grey Friars
St Clare's
Fleet Street
Austin Friars
White Friars
Black Friars
Trig Lane
East Smithfield
The Tower
St Katherine's
The Rosary
St Thomas'

1350–1500

Charterhouse
No. 1 Poultry
Leadenhall Market
St Mary Grace's
Trig Lane
Fastolf's Place

long-term effects of trade and commerce, as once-powerful Winchester discovered to its cost. In the final analysis, if people want to be somewhere, that is where they will go – and for the next millennium London was to be that place.

The town plans tell the story of medieval London clearly. They are an eloquent tribute to what can be achieved when documentary historians and excavating archaeologists collaborate closely. I very much doubt whether such detailed plans could possibly have been produced in the decades prior to that wake-up document, *The Future of London's Past*. Speaking entirely for myself, I have found that this new knowledge about Britain's capital city has transformed the place from a confusing and overblown hotchpotch of streets and districts into something which is explicable – and with which I can identify. Never again will I walk westwards down The Strand without having in the back of my mind the thought that I am now approaching Lundenwic, with the disintegrating walls of Roman Londinium behind me. Thanks to the work of hundreds of urban archaeologists London has acquired a 'sense of place' that is firmly rooted in fact.

I have taken four town plans from Christopher Thomas's recent book *The Archaeology of Medieval London* to illustrate my brief story.[19] The first map shows London between the resettlement of the walled City under King Alfred, and the Norman Conquest of William I. As we saw in the previous chapter, this was the era of Lundenburh, which succeeded the undefended Lundenwic to the west of the Fleet River. Alfred's Lundenburh was given a new network of streets, which is still the subject of research and might well prove to be larger than we currently suppose. It was arranged on a grid-like plan which bore little resemblance to the Roman layout, except where major streets passed through the City walls. Although the new street plan of London was probably on a smaller scale than that at Winchester, the effect was much the same: a Saxon planned town.

I remember being told as a student that archaeology alone could never have revealed that the Norman Conquest happened, because it is the documentary evidence (I include the Bayeux Tapestry as a document here) that makes the case. All the physical changes it brought about could well have happened for other reasons; and besides, many of the most important innovations of the medieval period, such as

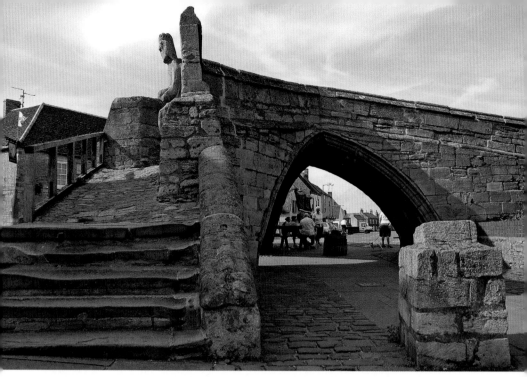

Triangular bridge, Crowland, Lincolnshire. This bridge near the centre of the small town outside Croyland Abbey was built in the later fourteenth century. It consists of three arches arranged at 120° which originally spanned the confluence of two streams. The figure, possibly of Christ, which sits with its back towards the Abbey was probably removed from the west front of the Abbey.

Croyland Abbey's church, St Guthlac's, rises above the small town of Crowland which sits at the end of a long, narrow 'peninsula' of drier ground which reaches far into the Lincolnshire Fens. The river in the foreground is the canalised course of the Welland. In medieval times one of the courses of the Welland passed through Crowland.

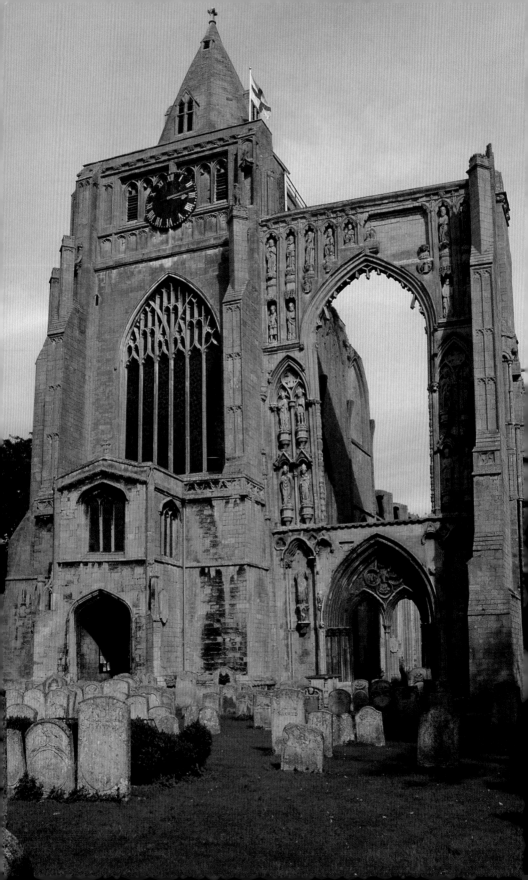

The first of a remarkable series of three medieval bridges across the River Trent was discovered by the late Dr Chris Salisbury in a large gravel pit at Hemington Quarry, Leicestershire. The first to be revealed is shown here. It was found in August 1993, and consisted of a stone-filled pier surrounded by timber. Eventually it was revealed to be one of four piers, which together formed the footings of a fifty-metre-long bridge, constructed around 1240. This, Bridge 3, was the latest bridge of the sequence.

The earliest bridge (1) at Hemington Quarry consisted of trestles and two diamond-shaped timber pier bases, or caissons, which were filled with stone ballast, some of which is still in place here. Tree rings show that the caisson timbers were felled by the year 1097. One caisson is visible directly behind and to the left of the large vertical post in the foreground. The double row of vertical posts belongs to the later phase of Bridge 1, probably dating to the early twelfth century.

Opposite The ruins of St Guthlac's Church, Crowland. This view shows the elaborate west front of this Benedictine house, which was founded in 716 by the Fenland hermit St Guthlac, who reinforced his faith 'in a hideous fen of huge bigness'. The north aisle of the nave is now the parish church. In medieval times this was the parochial aisle – the part of the abbey that was used by the parishioners.

The remains of a possible trestle at Hemington Quarry show how the superstructure of the Norman bridge (1) would have been carried. The two pointed timbers (one lies directly beneath the red-and-white scale) were driven into the riverbed. The large timber would have lain on the riverbed as a base-plate for the two vertical posts which passed through it. The angled brace by the figure (most probably one of a matching pair on the other side of the bridge) would have supported the trestle against the current. When the trestle had been removed it was found to have covered the second caisson of Bridge 1.

A view towards Wharram Percy deserted medieval village, North Yorkshire. The humps and bumps left by the roads, house platforms and other remains of the village are clearly visible in the field beyond the nearest hedge-line. The church is visible to the left of some nineteenth-century cottages, to the centre left.

Wharram Percy. At the foot of the hill in the foreground is the fourteenth-century fishpond, which was reconstructed as part of a recent major research project. The fishpond followed a series of Saxon and early medieval millponds which were also made by damming the Beck. The parish church, St Martin's, mainly dates to the twelfth–fourteenth centuries. It was still roofed in the mid-1950s, and the west face of the tower collapsed in 1959. The building has subsequently been extensively studied, conserved and consolidated.

Church of St Andrew, Northborough, Cambridgeshire. The original church, which occupies the left part of this view, was built in the twelfth and thirteenth centuries. In the early fourteenth century, members of a powerful local family, the Delameres, started work on a major rebuilding which would have given the village one of the largest churches in the county, had it been completed. Building started on the massive south transept, seen here to the right of the picture, with the two polygonal turrets. But then the Black Death intervened and the project was abandoned. The result is a very odd-looking, unbalanced building.

South Gate, King's Lynn, Norfolk. This fine gate through the town walls (which have been demolished on either side of the gatehouse) was constructed around 1520. This view shows the south, or outward-looking, face, which was finished in stone, whereas the north side is mainly of brick. The tall central arch and the large mullioned windows, like the well-finished ashlar masonry, suggest that the gatehouse was built more to impress than to deter visitors to the town.

A view of Ely Cathedral, Cambridgeshire, from the south. The south tower (left), nave and transept (centre) are twelfth-century. The chancel (to the right) is mainly thirteenth-century. The transept, or crossing tower, which is capped by an octagonal timber lantern, can be seen at the centre of the picture.

Opposite The tower of St Botolph's Church, Boston, generally known as The Stump. The vast tower, which is 272 feet high, was positioned to dominate the tidal river, the source of the port's great wealth. It is visible for over ten miles in all directions. It was built throughout the fifteenth century, starting around 1425, and was completed about 1515. The work took place during the worst outbreaks of the Black Death, which effectively reduced the town's population by around a half.

A close-up of the lead-clad timber lantern of Ely Cathedral. The grey lead cladding stands out from the carved limestone pinnacles of the crossing tower. The building of the octagonal lantern followed upon the collapse of the original Norman crossing tower on 22 February 1322. It was immediately rebuilt and enlarged between 1322 and 1328. The timber lantern which crowns it and allows light to flood into the heart of the cathedral was added between 1328 and 1342. It is widely recognised as one of the greatest glories of medieval carpentry.

planned *burhs*, monastic communities and the introduction of the manorial system, actually took place in pre-Norman times. So it might be tempting to suggest that the Norman Conquest was essentially just a 'top-down' affair, that only affected the upper echelons of society – where the changes were indeed dramatic and far-reaching. But that would be a serious error. The presence of the Normans brought an end to struggles between Saxon and Viking. The powerful new monarch, William I, also provided much-needed stability. And perhaps more than any other single factor it is stability that merchants, tradesmen and businesspeople require if they are to prosper.

After an initial Battle of London against the invading Normans, for which there is some archaeological and much historical evidence, the city prospered in the eleventh and twelfth centuries.[20] The earliest domestic buildings of Norman London are like their Saxon and Viking precursors. They were built from timber, wattle and daub, and seem to have been concentrated in areas that were already settled. The major change happens later in the eleventh century, when increasing prosperity led to an expansion into new areas and we see the construction of new stone churches. The first stone houses appear very shortly after this, in the early twelfth century. It is probable that the stonework of most of these buildings was confined to the foundations and cellars. Not surprisingly (as stone has to be brought into London from outside the area), these were the dwellings of richer and more successful people.

The Normans introduced a number of new Continental religious orders, and monastic foundations thrived under their rule. London was to prove a magnet to these religious settlements, and many were founded both within and outside the City walls. There were also several royal palaces, including the large one at Westminster; but the only permanent government institution of the time, the Treasury, remained in Winchester. It was not to move to Westminster until the later twelfth century.

The most important new element of Norman London was the creation of Thames Street, running parallel to the river. This development allowed far better access to the Thames foreshore and the new docks that were then being constructed both to provide the wealth and to furnish the needs of the expanding city. Despite their growing prosperity, however, most Londoners still provided a proportion of their daily requirements close to home. Most households would have kept a few pigs and poultry and have had kitchen gardens. Certainly markets existed and were expanding, but they were nothing like the more integrated and cash-based 'food supply chain', to use business-speak, that came into existence in the thirteenth century.

Southwark, at the southern end of London Bridge, was London's principal suburb.[21] Its main street was Borough High Street, which linked into the existing essentially Roman road network of Kent and the south-east. It was also the site of Winchester Palace, the London base of the still powerful Bishop of Winchester, in whose diocese Southwark lay. Southwark existed to protect the southern approach to London Bridge, which was extensively re-engineered in Norman times, culminating between 1176 and 1209 in the construction of the stone bridge which provided the basis for the famous structure with its shops and houses that survived throughout the Middle Ages and into the nineteenth century, when it was demolished.[22] The new Norman London Bridge was constructed by Peter de Colechurch, whose name deserves better recognition. It was a truly awe-inspiring structure, some 276 metres long and built on nineteen arches with a drawbridge across the central span. Accounts of its width vary, but it was probably around eight metres, with a roadway of half that width to allow for the buildings on either side. The stone used came from Dorset and Kent.

We have seen how the Normans established control of York by constructing two castles. They needed three to do the same job in London, and of these the Tower of London is quite possibly the best-known castle in the world. The Tower is located on the eastern approaches to the City; the other two (Baynards Castle and Mont-fichet's Castle) were to the west. The Tower has acquired many additions over the years, ranging from a huge water-filled moat, an outer curtain wall, and of course a wealth of myths and legends. As a place of awe and horror it has few rivals, and it proves, if anything can, the rule that the truth is stranger and more horrifying than fiction. If the Church is about the ritualisation of eternal life, the Tower has become, through the actions of subsequent rulers, a monument to the rituals of death. But at the core of this terror is one of the most magnificent castles of the early Middle Ages.

The White Tower, the massive square central block of the Tower of London, is one of the largest and most complete Norman keeps in existence. It probably replaced a short-lived wooden structure which had served William's purpose of keeping the populace and any potential usurpers in their place. In a world where the Church and the state were often part of the same power structure, William instructed Gundulf, the Bishop of Rochester, to construct the White Tower in the 1080s. When it was first built, the magnificent new stone castle stood within the City walls, which were demolished to make way for extensive new defences in the thirteenth century. The Tower of London remained a symbol of royal authority throughout the Middle Ages, during which time it acquired a series of major extensions and modifications. It has also been subjected to much archaeological work. I visited the site of a major trench through the now filled-in moat in the mid-1990s. The site supervisor who showed me around was very excited, because of course the deposits were very wet, and all sorts of environmental evidence was preserved in them. Samples of this sort are important, because they give us information about ordinary life in and around the Tower, whereas historical sources tend, by their very nature, to favour the important people who either ran, or were imprisoned within, the great fortress.

Archaeology tends not to be about the Great and the Good, and in this book I have generally tried to stay clear of their works in favour of more ordinary buildings, land- and townscapes. London is, however, a capital, and it possesses or possessed three of the most remarkable structures of medieval Britain, so I have had to bend my usual rule in this instance. We have glimpsed two, the Tower and London Bridge, but there is a third which many consider to be equally extraordinary. For some reason it has stayed out of the limelight, maybe because it is dwarfed by its neighbours, Pugin's great Houses of Parliament (1840) and that masterpiece of the medieval mason, Westminster Abbey. The building in question is Westminster Hall.

The Great Hall, as it was originally known, was built on reclaimed or reinforced marshy ground near the north-east shore of Thorney Island by William Rufus, the second son of William the Conqueror, in 1097. It still seems vast, and it must have appeared truly colossal in Norman times: its internal dimensions are 73 x 20.5 metres, which made it the largest stone hall north of the Alps. Today it is the largest medieval hall surviving in Europe. The enormous roof could not have been supported on a single span, and the original was probably held up by two parallel rows of pillars or posts. To our eyes it would have been a strange mix of the down-to-earth and the lavish, with an earthen floor and a raised dais for the throne at the south end, which would have been approached along the central aisle, between two rows of roof supports.

Near the end of the fourteenth century (probably between 1394 and 1400) the original Norman hall was substantially refurbished and a magnificent single-span oak hammer-beam roof was added by the master carpenter Hugh Herland. R.W. Brunskill, a leading authority on medieval timber construction, describes hammer-beam construction as 'the most extravagant and the least probable of the ways of achieving a long span with short pieces of timber'.[23] Westminster Hall has the largest single-span roof in the medieval world. It was an extraordinary feat of engineering that required the walls to be raised by a metre and a half and reinforced by external flying buttresses. Access to the hall was now through a grand ceremonial entranceway, flanked by towers, in the north end. Like the hall it served, this entranceway was plainly designed to impress. You entered from the main public yard, where crowds gathered on state occasions, and were confronted by the vast space with carved angels on the hammer-beams and the relieving arch-braces of the roof soaring high above it. To describe this breathtaking achievement as being 'designed to impress', as I have just done, is wholly to miss the point. As I found when I looked above me at Ely, words fail in the presence of such genius.

Christopher Thomas sees the twelfth century as the time when the capital was made.[24] By that time there were no other cities that could have been possible contenders. The population of London at the beginning of the century was around 20,000, and only a hundred years later it was double that. Recently politicians have decided that London requires a strong leader. The Normans knew this too, and the first mayor, Henry Fitz Ailwyn, was inaugurated in 1189. The mayor was to become a symbol of the capital and a powerful supporter of the merchant class. London, by now by far the largest port in Britain, had come of age.

If the developments of the twelfth century were remarkable they were, if anything, outstripped by what happened in the subsequent 150 or so years between 1200 and 1350. By now the main grid of streets had been established, but the rapidly rising population led to the creation of a large subsidiary network of small lanes and alleys. If the population was 40,000 by 1200, it had probably reached something in the order of 80–100,000 by 1300. London was probably now more than double the size of its three or four closest rivals in Britain. Reproduction was not the only means by which population growth was achieved. Immigration from outside, a process that became so important after the impact of the plagues in the mid-fourteenth century, had begun well before that. It has been suggested that throughout the twelfth and thirteenth centuries London was already attracting people living within a radius of about sixty-four kilometres from the city. By comparison, most other prosperous towns and cities drew on a population living within only thirty-two kilometres.[25]

Like all other amateur medievalists I get much pleasure from looking at churches. I usually make a point of arriving armed with the relevant volume of the great Nikolaus Pevsner's *Buildings of England* series (currently being revised and enlarged to a very high standard). With Pevsner's help I then mentally deconstruct the building, noting the clues he points out with such admirable clarity. For me it's something of a game – a sort of historical crossword puzzle. Most medieval masons worked from a set of accepted conventions or mental templates, and while many parish churches reveal splendid digressions and excesses, they can sometimes be rather predictable. When there are surprises they tend to be charming rather than revelatory.

Maybe that is why I get even more pleasure from ambling my way through the streets of Britain's older towns and cities on the lookout for medieval domestic or non-ecclesiastical buildings, seeking more of those revelatory moments. My pleasure is complete when the buildings are pubs or inns and they reveal their hidden glories as I lift a pint to my lips and glance up at a sumptuously carved medieval ceiling. Never will I forget the Lion at Buckden in old Huntingdonshire. The ceiling there was breathtaking. Pevsner reckons that it dates to around 1500; it features beautifully carved oak beams that surround a large central boss depicting the Agnus Dei.

The thing about medieval domestic and public structures is that they are so splendidly unpredictable. Unlike the great churches, they are also constructed on a human scale. I was most forcibly struck by this recently when I visited the important medieval pilgrimage destination at Little Walsingham, in Norfolk. Admittedly most of the ecclesiastical buildings had been swept away in the Dissolution of the Monasteries, but the original town square was still there, pretty well intact. I visited in the off-season and had the town almost to myself, and could imagine what the place would have been like when thronged with pilgrims and hawkers selling cheap religious tat – which was still on sale in souvenir shops, but at grossly inflated prices.

Anyone interested in medieval buildings cannot be without two recently published and lavishly illustrated books which manage to combine excellent scholarship with lively text: John Schofield's *Medieval London Houses* and Anthony Quiney's *Town Houses of Medieval Britain*.[26] Reading John Schofield's account it is clear that some of the constructional developments we noted at York were also happening in London. Structurally speaking, one of the biggest changes was the move from earthfast construction to timber-framing, which in London probably happened by the thirteenth century.[27] Schofield suggests that the earliest timber-framed houses were based around long, thin vertical panels. In the fourteenth century the panels were rectangular, and the structure was strengthened by wooden trusses placed at regular intervals. Solid framing in square panels became more usual in the fifteenth and sixteenth centuries.

While timber was still the main material used for domestic structures, from the twelfth century stone was used for grander buildings. As I noted earlier, London does not possess a good source of building stone, so most of the new stone buildings of the thirteenth century were built from material quarried in the south-east: chalk rubble was used for foundations and for infilling the central cavities of walls. Other more readily available sources of stone, such as greensand and ragstone, were used for exterior facings; only the most upmarket builders could afford fine stone, such as Purbeck marble from Dorset. All of this points to the existence of long-term trading networks, good communications and of course a ready supply of money and/or credit. After 1212 thatch was banned because it was a fire hazard, and was replaced by tiles or shingles. The floors of most ordinary houses were of beaten or rammed earth, covered with fresh straw. Higher-status buildings had wooden floors, and one or two important churches and public buildings had floors tiled in decorated 'Westminster' tiles, which may still be seen in the Chapter House at Westminster Abbey – one of the finest medieval tiled floors in Britain.

I have mentioned the importance of waterfront archaeology several times in passing. London has had its share of such sites, and they are important, but not just for what they can reveal about medieval docks and quays. Almost by definition they usually reveal extensive waterlogged deposits, where preservation is superb. Very often too the construction of a timber water frontage will also require that the ground behind the timber wall is filled in and consolidated to provide a stable working surface for the men unloading the various vessels. At London these so-called back-filled deposits often comprised anything the builders could lay their hands on that was cheap and freely available. So large amounts of domestic refuse found their way into the watery ground. As a result of post-war excavation we now know a huge amount about the ordinary, day-to-day aspects of medieval houses. One might suppose that cheap locks and padlocks were a relatively modern invention, but no, they occur plentifully in the back-filled rubbish layers. From the mid-thirteenth century most households would have possessed a wooden chest or coffer for their valuables. These were usually bound with metal straps and reinforcements, which occur with increasing frequency through the Middle Ages. The growing popularity of such furniture is a good indicator of general prosperity.

Like many people, I am intrigued by the introduction of glass windows into ordinary houses. It may be stating the obvious, but glass retains heat while admitting light, and its introduction into domestic architecture would have transformed day-to-day life, especially in winter. So far the evidence suggests that glass was first introduced into high-status London houses from the late thirteenth century. As time passed its use spread to other, less grand buildings, but for a long time glazed windows would have been seen as a symbol of success or prestige. The climate in Britain can be both wet and cold, and windows as a result have tended to be rather small. It was not until just after the Middle Ages that it became fashionable to have enormous windows, perhaps best illustrated at Hardwick Hall, built in the late sixteenth century by that extraordinary Tudor figure Bess of Hardwick, Countess of Shrewsbury.[28] Her great creation, Hardwick Hall ('more glass than wall'), is my favourite English stately home, but perched on the top of a hill, and with such huge areas of glass, it must have been impossibly cold in winter. It is a fine illustration of what even the grandest of people were prepared to endure to advertise their social status.

If window light was restricted for most Londoners in the Middle Ages, one way around the problem was to use lamps, which were of course a major fire risk. Hanging oil lamps, made from pottery, were the main form of lighting in the earlier Middle Ages, but these were replaced from the fourteenth century by lamp-holders made of glass. Iron, lead or pewter candleholders appear from the thirteenth century, and these could be highly decorated.

Impressions gained at school can stay with one for life. Like most people, I have tended to think of cities in the Middle Ages as being grossly unhygienic, with muddy roads awash with the excrement that was constantly being thrown from upstairs windows by wizened hags whose toothless mouths screamed 'Gardyloo!' as they consigned another potful of ordure to the four winds. These early impressions are constantly being reinforced both by Hollywood and by costume dramas on television, which portray city life in the Middle Ages as little short of suicidally squalid. Certainly places like Viking York were rather ramshackle when compared for example with the Roman fortress at Eboracum, but ramshackle is not the same as chaotic. As we have seen, houses were located within clearly defined tenements; streets were kept clean and were maintained in good order, and the fact that people continued to live there suggests that sources of acceptable drinking water must have been available too.

Medieval people were not stupid, and they could see that the population of London was constantly growing. They realised well before the catastrophe of the Black Death that public health was an important issue. Indeed, the prosperity of the City depended upon the maintenance of a healthy population. That is doubtless why we see the foundation of charitable hospitals, including St Bartholomew's, from the late eleventh and twelfth centuries onwards. Quite quickly these grew into large, well organised institutions, one of which, the priory and hospital of St Mary Spital at Bishopsgate, north of the City walls, has been extensively excavated and fully documented in the first of the fine series of Museum of London Archaeology Service monographs I referred to earlier.[29]

Today we take a supply of clean water for granted, and we know that it is essential for the maintenance of good public health. Before recent excavations at the site known as No. 1 Poultry, in the heart of the walled City, we had no idea of the efforts and resources that the citizens of London were prepared to expend in order to guarantee a clean water supply. These excavations were probably the largest and most complex yet undertaken in any British city. They began on 3 July 1995 and finished almost a year later, on 9 June 1996, as the new buildings were themselves finished. It was a major excavation that was completed on time and to budget. In many respects it came to symbolise the modern approach to archaeology, which places great emphasis on tight management and professional standards of budgetary control. Sadly, given problems of on-site health and safety, and a host of interlinking and all-important deadlines, there is almost no room in urban archaeology today for amateurism, be it never so enthusiastic.

The work at No. 1 Poultry took place within and below buildings that were going up around them.[30] It revealed a wealth of information, including at least fifty-four Roman and thirty-seven later buildings. One of the most spectacular discoveries was of an intact, underground, stone-built fountain house. This was a long, rectangular building with a vaulted roof which provided access to water for the inhabitants of London and was reached by a flight of stairs from the surface, near the modern street of Cheapside. The water was conducted to the fountain house through lead pipes from the River Tyburn, three kilometres to the west (at the point where Oxford Street crossed it). The water supply was first established around 1236–45, and the building revealed at No. 1 Poultry dated to a phase of reconstruction in 1286.

If medieval towns were not as squalid as we once believed, another myth which I have retained since my schooldays is that monasteries were always located in tranquil and sometimes inaccessible rural locations. After all, the idea lying behind monasticism was to escape the hurly-burly of daily life with all its cares, to seek deeper, mystical meaning through discipline, abstinence and meditation. The Celtic tradition was to do this in isolation, with monks living in solitary cells. The Roman and Catholic approach tended to follow eastern Mediterranean traditions of disciplined but communal living. Both approaches sought seclusion from the ordinary day-to-day world. Then, in the early thirteenth century the traditions of medieval monasticism were greatly enriched by the sudden and dramatic rise of the friars.

The friars or brothers (from the Latin word *fratres*) belonged to the mendicant, or begging, orders that included the Franciscans, Dominicans, Carmelites and Augustinians. Their view of the monastic life was very different to what had gone before. They believed that their support should come from the population in which they lived, so their communities were often located in towns and cities. They took vows of poverty and preferred to engage with, rather than retreat from, the secular world. In their religious life they were evangelical and they placed great emphasis on learning, both in their own communities and in the emerging universities. It seems likely that the emergence of the friars may have been a response to the rising importance of towns and the need to provide education and spiritual support to their populations.

The rise of the friaries was both fast and dramatic. To give some idea of what was happening in London in the thirteenth century, early friaries were established near the Tower (the Crutched Friars) and west of Bishopsgate (Augustinians); Carmelite or White Friars founded a house west of the Fleet River in 1241. The two largest houses were the Franciscans, or Grey Friars, who established their house near Newgate within the City walls in 1239, and the Dominicans, or Black Friars, who built their house on the site of the demolished Montfichet's Castle and Baynards Tower, in the south-west corner of the City, in 1275.

Medieval London, with all its palaces, monasteries, hospitals, friaries and public buildings, reached its peak in the early years of the fourteenth century, by which time it was almost four times as large as any other city in Britain. It was by no stretch of the imagination an egalitarian community. There were huge disparities of wealth and living standards. The richest and most influential people lived in stone buildings which we would instantly recognise as large and comfortable houses, but the poorest lived in humble, earth-floored, timber-framed buildings that had a life expectancy of thirty or forty years – if, that is, they were not destroyed by fire in the meantime. The city had acquired numerous new lanes and alleys, which were to prove disastrous when the Black Death first appeared in London, at Stepney in December 1348. By the time the first wave of disease had abated a year later, up to one third of the population had been exterminated.

I don't want to dwell on the undoubted horrors of the Black Death, because I am more concerned here with the growth, or rather survival, of the city of London. The way the population coped is, however, very interesting. For a start, there is little evidence to suggest that all social life disintegrated, and that the usual patterns of decent behaviour were abandoned in the face of widespread death and horror. Three emergency burial grounds were designated, one at East and two at West Smithfield. All have received some archaeological attention, but most information came from extensive excavations at the East Smithfield cemetery in 1987, where 753 of 2,400 skeletons were unearthed. There were two types of burial at East Smithfield: conventional single graves, and long straight trenches in which bodies were arranged side by side, in places up to five deep. The point to make is that these burials were arranged with some care. The grisly Hollywood image of deep black pits filled with the putrefying remains of bodies, into which new victims were pitched higgledy-piggledy from rickety carts, seems altogether wide of the mark. The archaeological evidence also suggests that the estimated number of plague victims in the three recognised cemeteries (around 10,000) may have been very much smaller than the total number of deaths (around 50,000) that most historians and other authorities would accept. Whatever its cause, this is a statistical discrepancy that one day will have to be sorted out.

A religious person would affirm that faith overcomes death. The evidence from fourteenth- and fifteenth-century London, however, suggests that wealth was what defeated its effects. In other words, the process of immigration continued unabated because people were still attracted to the prosperity of the city. We know today, with our epidemiological knowledge of the plague and how it spreads, that the move from country to city was potentially risky. It is hard for us to know why people wanted to migrate to London. But the fact is that they did – and probably for all sorts of reasons. For a start, migration had already become an established process, City merchants required new staff, there was a general shortage of labour because of plague, and there was also a strong desire to break free of the feudal ties that had affected so many rural people. All of these factors probably played a part in individual decision-making processes. Above all, London, then as now, was the place where you stood the best chance of improving your life. Ultimately the move to London, both before and after 1348, was motivated by personal ambition.

It was probably the great wealth of London that allowed it to weather the first, terrible impact of the disease. It continued to be the most important port in the country, and although its population did not recover to pre-Black Death levels until just after the medieval period, its wealth had reached and exceeded those levels by the fifteenth century – half a century or so after 1348. Christopher Thomas points to one important conclusion from these statistics: more money and fewer people meant that the average wealth was higher, and some individuals were considerably wealthier.[31] These people were also becoming better organised, into guilds; markets were developing and the cash economy continued to grow apace. These social and economic developments meant that London acquired a series of fine new stone buildings. While all this was going on, more land was being reclaimed from the river, and the city's port facilities continued to be improved. Throughout the Middle Ages London was a stable place in which to live. There do not seem to have been religious tensions there in the fifteenth century, although of course there were to be massive changes in the sixteenth, with the Reformation and the Dissolution of the Monasteries.

In London, as in many other important medieval cities such as York, deposits of the later Middle Ages are generally less environmentally and archaeologically informative than those from earlier periods. This is partly due to the fact that, being raised on a build-up of earlier layers, they are often dry or only partially waterlogged, which leads to inferior preservation. Modern buildings have very deep foundations, but even Victorian houses and offices in London frequently had basements and cellars which reached into and destroyed later medieval levels. But it is clear that London continued to develop after 1348, although the pace of change was slower than previously. New housing was required for the new immigrants, and the increased wealth of the population led to the construction of larger houses, some of which were positioned in bigger plots formed by the amalgamation of neighbouring tenements. The increasing prosperity led to the construction of additional lanes and alleys, but not on the same scale as before 1300. It would seem that the effects of the waves of plague were felt most keenly in the suburbs, where late medieval development was considerably slower.

Southwark, however, was an exception. The town at the south end of London Bridge continued to develop, and new stone buildings were constructed. One reason why Southwark appeared to go against the general trend was that it had long enjoyed the status of an independent borough in its own right. In the Middle Ages its government was separate from that of London, which may help to explain why in the late sixteenth century it was the site of three theatres: the Globe, the Rose and one further upstream, opposite Blackfriars, the Swan.[32]

London was a commercial centre, which meant that goods of all sorts and descriptions were traded there. Some of these goods came from overseas, but many were locally produced or, like wool and cloth, were taken to refurbished markets such as that at the Westminster 'woolstaple' from further afield in Britain. In the later Middle Ages the increasing volume, organisation and sophistication of trade, which was mostly based around a cash economy, led to the development of new and improved markets. One of the most important of these was established in 1493 by the Corporation of London.

Leadenhall Market was a model of its kind and consisted of four stone-built ranges of buildings around an open courtyard. The building stone came from Reigate and Caen, in Normandy. With such purpose-built structures we have come a long way from the open marketplaces of rural Britain. The size, scale and status of the building must reflect the importance in which markets were held in the later Middle Ages. The plan and elevation of this market have been reconstructed from excavation and documentary sources.[33] It had an arcaded ground floor which rather resembled a monastic cloister. This open area was for a public or common market which would have sold day-to-day items such as eggs, poultry, vegetables, cheese, grain, etc.

The first and second storeys were used to house grain, which was carried to the ground in sacks by way of spiral staircases at the four corners of the building. Grain was a valuable commodity in the Middle Ages, and this arrangement would have kept the corn dry and relatively free from vermin. The windows were shuttered, not glazed.

As we saw at Boston after 1348, organisations of merchants, trades and professions grew in importance, reflecting their increasing influence in society at large. In London the scale of this expansion matched the city's wealth. Some forty new company halls were constructed, and the Guildhall was completely rebuilt between 1411 and 1430. That building still stands today.

I have to say I find it hard to tear myself away from medieval London. The modern city has a character of its own, but very little of the medieval city survived the Great Fire of 1666 and then the Blitz. Developers in the nineteenth and twentieth centuries almost completed the process. I do believe, however, that there is more to a place than its buildings alone, and that some of the enterprise and flair that characterised London in the Middle Ages may still be found not just in the alleys and markets of the East End or Portobello Road, but in the offices of the great merchant banks and the Stock Exchange. I am convinced that something of the medieval attitude still lives on in Britain's capital city.

My disinclination, or inability, to leave London has meant that I have largely ignored other important places such as Bristol, Norwich, Canterbury and Lincoln. But as I said in the Introduction, this is not a textbook, and I am not attempting here to offer a balanced and comprehensive view of medieval Britain. Instead I am trying to capture a flavour of its spirit, as revealed by my own experience of archaeology. So I make only a half-hearted apology for having dwelt for so long in Winchester, York and London, where urban archaeology was born and

FIG 34 *Plan and elevation of Leadenhall Market, established by the Corporation of London in 1493. This purpose-built market building was arranged around an open courtyard. The ground floor was a public market selling daily provisions such as vegetables, eggs, etc. The two storeys above were for storing grain, which was brought to the ground in sacks carried down four spiral staircases, one at each corner. The windows were shuttered, not glazed.*

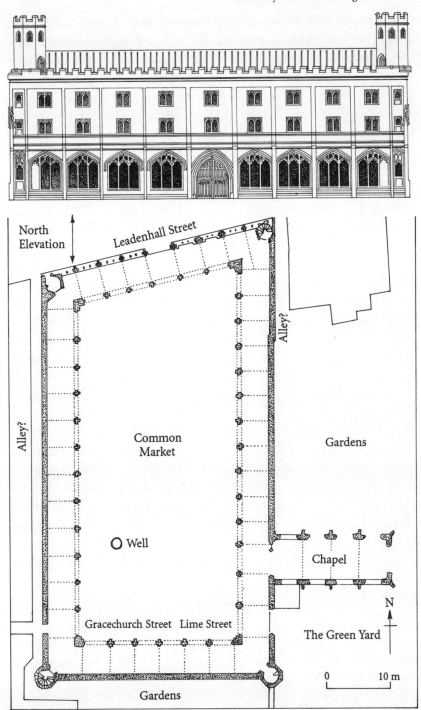

grew up. But even now I have not finished. In Chapter 7 I will return to the port of London, and will also visit Southampton, another of the places where urban archaeologists made their mark in the two decades after the war.

CHAPTER SIX

Rural Life in the Middle Ages

URBAN ARCHAEOLOGY has made astonishing progress in the last four decades, and if anything the pace of this work is still increasing. But what about research into rural Britain in the Middle Ages? Has that also been successful? The answer to that is a clear yes, but with a huge *caveat*: the money available for research has been much harder to acquire, which has meant that research programmes have tended to be smaller in scale; but to make up for this they have generally been longer in duration and very well thought-out. The impact of commercial archaeology has been considerable, but not as dramatic as in towns, where for obvious reasons work tends to be focused within smaller areas. The simple fact that towns are geographically restricted also means that research into documentary sources can be better coordinated and the results of the various digs can be linked with the common body of documentary research, to provide the bones of a developing narrative. It's much harder to do this, even with the aid of computers, in the far-flung world of the medieval countryside. The budgets of commercial projects are also very tight, which may make it difficult to do as much documentary research as some rural projects might require if, like Shapwick, say, they are to come alive and make sense. Clearly there are huge problems to overcome, but even so progress has been remarkable.

Readers of *Britain AD* will be aware that I have long been an admirer of the great landscape historian W.G. Hoskins and his remarkable book *The Making of the English Landscape*. This was first published in 1955, and it helped launch a new wave of interest in landscape studies. Much to Hoskins's credit he treated townscapes and rural landscapes as being equally important and closely related. Another leading landscape historian of the day, Maurice Beresford, had published his seminal book on the recently recognised phenomenon of deserted medieval villages, *The Lost Villages of England*, the previous year. Together, the impact of these two books was immense.

In the 1940s Hoskins and Beresford, working in Leicestershire and Warwickshire respectively, realised that the humps and bumps that were visible in many grass fields were in fact the remains of deserted medieval villages (DMVs). This simple observation was to have profound consequences, because it soon became clear that DMVs were to be found in their thousands in a huge swathe of central and eastern England, running from Northumberland in the north-east down to Dorset and Somerset in the south. In 1954 the known number of DMVs was 1,353; by 1968 the figure had risen to 2,263. I can't give a precise current figure, because most research is now carried out at a regional level and deserted villages are no longer arbitrarily distinguished from shrunken villages, but it is likely to be even larger. The main point to note, however, is that the general or overall distribution of DMVs remains much the same.

We have already seen that the processes of settlement nucleation and manorialisation were well under way in Later Saxon times and continued into the Middle Ages, giving rise to the system of farming and land management known as the Open Field or 'champion' System. This is the exemplar, the classic medieval rural arrangement that was taught at school and which I believed to have been universal throughout the British Isles until I learned better at university. Now I realise that it was a regional adaptation to a particular set of soils and circumstances. That is not to underestimate its great success and its huge contribution not just to the medieval economy but to the coherence of rural societies, which were united by the need to work the land together. We were given a hint of the geographical extent of landscapes that were based around nucleated settlements in the distribution of DMVs, but this picture has recently been confirmed and supported by a very important study which came at the problem from a rather different direction.

For six years I was a member of AMAC, the Ancient Monuments Advisory Committee of English Heritage. Our job was to provide independent advice to English Heritage about aspects of archaeology in its day-to-day work. The work was varied: at one meeting we would

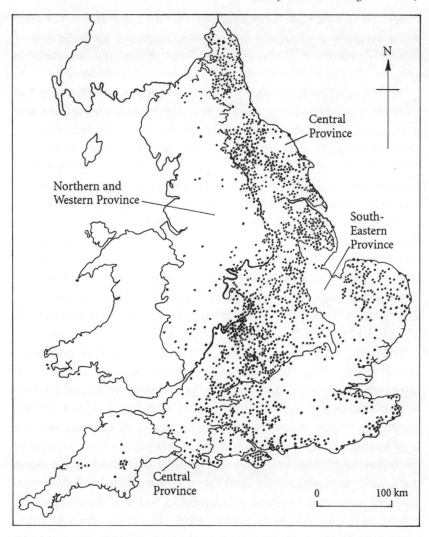

FIG 35 *Locations of deserted medieval villages in England. This map is based on the number of sites that were known in 1968, and is taken from a pioneering book,* Deserted Medieval Villages, *edited by Maurice Beresford and John Hurst.*[1] *Superimposed on the medieval settlement pattern are the boundaries between the three provinces of England as they were defined in a study by Roberts and Wrathmell (2000) of settlement nucleation in the mid-nineteenth century.*

consider the future of Stonehenge, at another we would argue with equal vehemence about the impact of a proposed septic tank on a filled-in castle moat. It was great fun, very challenging, and brought one face to face with the academic and political realities of running something as complex as a national archaeological service. It also had its perks, one of which was the distribution to committee members of heavily discounted books and publications.

I well remember one meeting when, after an excellent buffet lunch, I was handed a copy of an archaeological atlas. It was larger than the average road atlas, and wouldn't even begin to fit into my briefcase. I almost left it behind, because I had another meeting to attend and didn't want too many things to cart around with me. At the end of the day the train back north was delayed, so I glanced at the atlas. At first I was unimpressed. It was based on a study of mid-nineteenth-century rural settlements patterns in England, and I thought it could have little or no relevance to anything any earlier. How wrong I was. The book, *An Atlas of Rural Settlement in England* by Brian Roberts and Stuart Wrathmell, proved to be not just a fascinating read, but a truly original piece of archaeological research. Essentially it used the nineteenth-century data on settlement nucleation as a basis for drawing comparisons with other periods. Areas of the country with long-lived boundaries between different types of farming, administration or whatever were traced back through time. The emphasis was on long-term trends and landscape characterisation.

Roberts and Wrathmell were able to differentiate three rural settlement provinces, which they could demonstrate had significance that extended at least as far back as Later Saxon times, and quite possibly even earlier. The Central Province broadly coincides with the distribution of DMVs and nucleated settlements. Here, to paraphrase Roberts and Wrathmell, villages and hamlets were supported by distinctive communally organised fields. By way of contrast, settlements in the provinces on either side (the Northern and Western Province and the South-Eastern Province) had their own characteristics, but were generally less nucleated. Here the open fields were more restricted and the arable fields more enclosed; these landscapes also involved larger areas of common grazing and unimproved pastureland. Woodland was also a major feature.

As we have seen, the landscapes of the Central Province are sometimes described as 'champion', a word which derives from the Eliza-
bethan term 'champaine' (from the French *champ*, a field), which was
used to describe arable land.[2] The landscapes of the two other provinces are sometimes described as 'woodland' landscapes (a somewhat
misleading term, as woodland was not always of major importance).
Wales and Scotland would probably fall broadly within the Northern
and Western Province. Here I will deal with the Central Province first,
and will start with the obvious question: what caused the wholesale
abandonment of villages and settlements across such a huge swathe of
the countryside? Was there a single, simple explanation, such as the
Black Death, or was it more complex than that?

It was soon realised that the explanation lay not so much in the
deserted villages themselves as in the landscapes around them. Later
it also became apparent that the phenomenon of deserted villages
could not be studied in isolation; it was part of a broader picture
which included successful villages, surviving villages and villages that
had shrunk or had shifted. As time passed it was also realised that it
was necessary to look beyond villages to other forms of settlement
within the rural scene, such as monastic sites and isolated farmsteads.

As it turned out, DMVs were to prove an academically rewarding
red herring, because it was realised that in order to understand the
problem of desertion or shrinkage, attention must be focused on
their setting: the landscape. You could not explain changes in rural
settlement without also explaining how farms worked, why the economy developed, and how this in turn was affected by purely social
factors such as the influence of landlords, the Church, taxation, etc.
In other words, any study of the decline and demise of villages should
also take into account the reasons why they came into existence in
the first place. It's a much overused word, but the approach to the
problem had to be holistic. In order to explain why medieval rural life
changed so profoundly, that way of life itself needed to be better
understood.

This new holistic approach to the study of the English medieval
landscape has implications that apply to the rest of Britain, and indeed elsewhere. I have already mentioned the important book by
Carenza Lewis, Patrick Mitchell-Fox and Christopher Dyer, in which

it was suggested that nucleation was part of a new economic system in which villages were created as institutional communities that were equipped to cope with a new and productive agrarian system.[3] The important point to note here is that many, if not most, of these nucleated villages were already in existence at the time of the Norman Conquest. As a system it was up and running by the beginning of the Middle Ages, which was the period in which it both flourished and declined.

I shall discuss the way nucleated villages and the Open Field system operated shortly, containing the story we left off in Chapter 3. But before that I must make a few general points. First, although it can be very useful, the clear and simple distinction between town and country is probably misleading when applied to medieval Britain. The fact is that people in the towns depended on those living in the country for their food and drink, thatch, wool and other raw materials, just as rural communities depended on urban markets to sell their surplus goods and livestock. Even the great city of London depended on its hinterland not just for food and materials but, as we have already seen, for that all-important resource, labour.

The historian Charles Phythian-Adams, Professor of Local History at Leicester University, has shown that it is also probably a mistake to assume that the arrangement of administrative units such as counties or hundreds reflected the way that people actually organised their lives.[4] Other factors, such as rural market networks, were more important to them. In the Fens, an area I am familiar with myself, people in those wetlands that had been successfully drained had regional links which crossed county boundaries via the natural communication routes up and along the river valleys that extend into the Fenland basin. In other areas, such as the middle and upper Thames Valley, where as we saw in Chapter 1 production began so early, the wool trade depended on market centres whose arrangement ignored administrative geography. Phythian-Adams argues that many towns were positioned on the boundary between different farming regions, such as arable and pastoral, where they encouraged trade between producers from the two regions. Again, the location of these market towns was determined by their position within the farmed, rather than the administrative, landscape.

I began the previous chapter with some thoughts on the impact of the Black Death on urban life after the mid-fourteenth century, and concluded that discussion with the observation that in the early Middle Ages (i.e. 1066–1348) it was essentially 'business as usual'. I went on to say that in rural areas of England there were changes in the make-up of the ruling classes and in the way that ordinary people were governed. Certainly much did remain as it had been before: manorial courts and nucleated villages remained, and in certain places the process of nucleation continued after the Norman Conquest. But although the fundamental system of rural governance remained substantially the same, the people doing the governing changed. Land ownership was concentrated in the hands of a small Norman aristocracy who ruled their estates by way of the manorial system that had been established, in places, up to two centuries earlier.[5]

While the fundamentals of the system may have remained more or less constant, the Norman Conquest caused big changes which are recorded in that most remarkable document of 1086, the Domesday Book. So far I have mentioned Domesday in passing and without any explanation, but here I must pause and discuss it briefly, because although it is a historical document, it is so detailed and usually so accurate that it can often be used as a direct check on archaeological evidence. Written in Latin, it is invaluable to both archaeologists and historians alike, and England's history would be very much poorer if it had not survived. The book is a report on a great survey which was commissioned by William the Conqueror in Gloucester over Christmas in 1085. It was named Domesday, in the words of the Treasurer of England in the twelfth century, Richard fitzNigel, 'not because it passes judgement on any doubtful points raised, but because it is not permissible to contradict its decisions, any more than it will be those of the Last Judgement' (or Day of Doom).[6]

Domesday records the number of hides of land in each English county, and assesses the size and value of acreage and livestock possessed by each individual landowner. The survey is arranged by tenurial arrangements rather than territory, and lists more than 13,000 *vills*, which in Domesday are the smallest unit of local administration. A *vill* was an area of land rather than a settlement, and could sometimes contain several small hamlets; it should not be confused with the word 'village', which derives from it.[7] It is still not entirely clear whether Domesday was compiled for purposes to do with the collection of taxes, or whether it was a tenurial survey to record landholdings and the names of the people who owned them. The five bound volumes of the Great and Little Domesday,* currently housed at London's Public Record Office, are a vast resource which has proved very well suited to computer analysis, which is starting to reveal much new information about the economic history of Norman times.

Domesday shows that just twenty years after the Conquest, a mere 8 per cent of land in England was owned by people with English names. The rest belonged to Normans, the Crown or the Church, and of these the Crown had the largest single estate, amounting to about 17 per cent of the available land.

As we saw in the previous chapter, the post-Conquest period was a time of display: in most cities there were magnificent new castles and cathedrals. In the country we find new manors in which the new elites indulged in conspicuous consumption which was done not only for its own sake, but also to impress tenants and others dining in the large new halls. In rural areas this consumption was largely funded from rents. Farming tenants found the money to pay these rents by growing cash crops which were sold at urban markets. The landowners probably also owned and organised the markets themselves – so they were winners both ways.

From the late twelfth to the fourteenth centuries we see the population rise, and with it the growth of markets.[8] This in turn led to an increasing use of cash. Many markets were in towns, but some were in villages, usually as part of fairs, where it was not unusual to find a wide range of goods offered for sale. As a rule it was landowners (including ecclesiastical or monastic landowners) who sought permission to establish new markets. To give an idea of the scale of this increase, some 2,800 new markets were established between 1200 and 1500 in England alone. From about the fourteenth century we see the emergence of interdependent regional economies, a process that became more important in the fifteenth century, following the Black

---

* The Domesday Book was never fully completed. It was left in two volumes: Great Domesday, which contains most of the information gathered; and Little Domesday, containing the records for Essex, Norfolk and Suffolk, which were the last to be compiled.

Death. We are still uncertain to what extent rural peasant families had access to urban markets, but again this probably improved after the mid-fourteenth century.

When I was at school I learned that life in Europe in the Middle Ages was governed by the so-called Feudal System. This acquired its name from the Latin word *feudum*, which refers to property held by a tenant in return for service. As its name implies, it is all about reciprocal rights and obligations. The terms and conditions of the system varied widely across Britain, essentially from one landowner to another. As we have seen, in southern Britain it became established as part of the process of nucleation and manorialisation, and was not introduced by the Normans. The trouble with a term like 'the Feudal System' is that definite article, *the*. The truth is that there was no one system, and the term is probably best avoided. At the risk of seeming to split hairs, I prefer to use the noun 'feudalism' when I discuss that particular aspect of society – which is what I plan to do now.

Rural society in the early Middle Ages was based on reciprocal obligations. As the population grew from the eleventh to the fourteenth centuries, rents continued to pour in and landowners became ever more prosperous. By the same token, those towards the foot of the social tree found their bargaining position becoming weaker. Labour, in other words, was becoming cheaper. Viewed from the perspective of a landowner, it was a buyer's market, and they possessed the cash with which to drive hard bargains. The landlord/labourer balance was dramatically altered by the Black Death. Again from the point of view of somebody buying in labour, it now became a seller's market. One might suppose that the changes brought about by such a sudden and catastrophic population decline would have been instantaneous, but in fact they took some time to happen, because feudalism was not a simple market arrangement. It involved a variety of other social ties, obligations and institutions, and these took time to change. There were also other and unforeseen consequences of the plague.

Bubonic plague is horribly selective. It tends to be most fatal to the old and the very young. Cruelly, people in the prime of life stood a better chance of surviving, but their children and babies died. Colin Platt cites the example of Halesowen, a large village with a manor in the West Midlands owned by the 'white canons' of the impossibly-named

Premonstratensian order.* He makes the point that the survival and prosperity of rural communities such as this depend on the work of a young labour force, and suggests that *who* dies might be as important as *how many*.[9] The 1349 death rate at Halesowen for men of twenty and over was 40–46 per cent, and that for all women was about 42 per cent. Plague fatality rates rose from about 20 per cent of young adults to about 60 per cent of the elderly. Almost all the survivors were in their twenties or thirties. This most probably explains why villages like Halesowen appeared to bounce back so quickly: 82 per cent of landholdings vacated by plague victims were being worked by new tenants within the year. Some 42 per cent of the new tenants were sons and daughters of the dead. Platt points out that this gave the new generation an opportunity to rise at once into the privileged tenant class: 'In a society previously characterised . . . by overabundant labour, by soil exhaustion and by declining productivity, the time had come for Malthusian checks.'[10]

It's hard to imagine how people coped with such tragedy and instability. One minute death and destruction were everywhere, in the next there were hitherto undreamed-of opportunities for self-advancement. The new young tenants at Halesowen took advantage of their improved status. In the following two decades they raised a fresh generation of children to replace those who had died in the first impact of the plague. Then the plague struck again in 1361, 1369 and 1375, and that new generation was largely wiped out. The result was that the population in the parish became increasingly elderly. They found it harder to reproduce themselves. It was a process that led to stagnation and decline by the end of the fourteenth century. By now, at Halesowen and in many rural areas, vacant plots of land did not find ready takers. The whole basis of feudalism, especially in the more intensively farmed champion arable landscapes of the Midlands, was starting to creak.

It was not just these fertile regions that felt the effects of the plague in the latter years of the century. We will see shortly that the champion landscapes of the English Midlands and the Central Province were a specialised adaptation to heavy soils that are best worked cooperatively.

---

* Their name comes from Prémontré, the place in north-west France where they were founded in 1120 by St Norbert.

It is no wonder that their local populations felt the later effects of the Black Death. But other, less intensively farmed regions fared little better. They too were vulnerable. Colin Platt cites the example of the tiny hamlets at Bilsdale, in north-east Yorkshire. Anyone who knows the area will appreciate that it can be bleak, especially in winter – and the weather prior to 1348 had been dire. These hamlets were located in small clearances in the surrounding woodland, known as assarts. Assart fields were good for a few seasons, but the essential nutrients in their soil soon leached out once the tree roots had rotted away. The Black Death must have been the last straw, and the Bilsdale hamlets were soon abandoned.

In the previous chapter I mentioned the paradoxical case of the Boston Stump. But there are also instances of churches where building operations were brought to a sudden halt by the onset of the Black Death, and never resumed. I cannot resist mentioning an example that I used to drive past for many years when taking my team to our excavations of prehistoric sites in the gravel pits at Maxey and Etton. These sites were in the lower Welland Valley, a few miles north of Peterborough, and the building in question is the little parish church of Northborough. Even today it has a strangely unbalanced appearance. The reason for this is a very grand south transept, which dwarfs the rest of the church. At first I assumed that this transept was just an example of Victorian insensitivity. But the more I looked, the more I became convinced that the stonework could not be nineteenth-century. It had all the appearance of ancient masonry. My next thought was that it might be a part of what seemed to be the ruins of an abbey just a few yards up the road. I even remember looking Northborough up in the Royal Commission survey of Peterborough, which I kept with me in the Land-Rover, but it was just outside the area they surveyed. Sadly I did not have the time to research any further, because the Etton dig finished in 1987 and my mind had to turn to the writing of the report.

Then, about five years ago, our small contracting company was commissioned to do an archaeological watching brief because the vicar of Northborough needed to lay a cable through the churchyard. Most of the route followed by the cable had already been disturbed and all we found were a few bones, including one or two human ones – as one is bound to find in most ancient churchyards. All in all it was a remarkably unexciting dig, and I was preparing to break off for lunch when a churchwarden appeared at my elbow and asked if I would like to have a look in the church. I jumped at his offer. One reason I was so keen to look inside was that I was still curious about why it seemed so unbalanced. It was also quite unlike many of the churches in the area, which are classic eastern 'wool churches' – magnificent buildings built from the profits of the wool trade in the early Middle Ages. The medieval churches in the nearby villages of Maxey and Glinton are particularly fine, and Glinton has a superb stone spire, visible for miles around. But the little church at Northborough is not so grand. For a start, it doesn't possess a tower to house its bells, which hang in a simple bellcote above the roof.[11]

As I was taken round I learned that in the early Middle Ages the powerful Norman family in the area was the Delameres. They had very grand ideas indeed. First they rebuilt their manor in the latest taste, and it was this that I had mistaken for an abbey.* They then embarked on the wholesale rebuilding of the small Norman parish church, which they intended to be as huge as their social ambitions. But they had overstretched themselves, and when the Black Death struck the rebuilding came to an abrupt stop, with only the south transept completed. This was a mortuary transept which contains an ossuary, complete with bones that are still visible within it. So that is the explanation for why the transept is so out of scale to the rest of the building. I confess I have grown attached to the church. Yes, it is odd and unbalanced, but it is also a fine monument to the folly of human ambition.

Although Northborough is a startling example of how the Black Death affected buildings in the mid-fourteenth century, it is not unique. Colin Platt mentions others, of which the half-completed parish church at Ashbourne in Derbyshire is among the strangest. But given the extreme severity of its other effects, the Black Death did not cause as much disruption to construction projects as one might have expected. In part this may have been a reflection of the sort of altered religious priorities we saw in the case of the Boston Stump, but there

---

* While we were digging at Maxey the manor of the Delameres was sold, and it became a restaurant which featured a gleaming replica suit of armour (of the wrong period) in its magnificent fourteenth-century gatehouse.

was also a short period of bounce-back in the aftermath of the first wave of disease, which allowed most projects either to be completed or at least finished off to acceptable standards. That is why churches like Northborough and Ashbourne are not more common.

Earlier I complained, perhaps unfairly, that some historians have tended to treat the aftermath of the Black Death rather coldly. But the fact remains, as at Halesowen, that some of the changes brought about by the catastrophe were beneficial to the survivors, who in truth needed all the help they could muster. Some of these changes, as we saw in the previous chapter, were already afoot before the plague struck, but as land that belonged to the dead was redistributed, fewer families had to live at the subsistence level. Perhaps even more significantly, the greater availability of land meant that enterprising peasants could put together more rational, less dispersed and larger holdings which began, as Paul Stamper has noted, to take on the characteristics of the modern farm.[12]

The countryside in the later Middle Ages became more diverse. Regional differences arose and town/country relationships varied from one place to another. The regional variation reflected the fact that people appreciated the special qualities of their particular landscapes, which they were able to exploit. Sometimes the differences could be quite subtle. For example, as a farmer I have long been irritated by academic colleagues who sometimes fail to understand that there is more to pasture and grazing than mere grass. The quality of grazing can vary from field to field, and can be better or worse at different times of the year and in wet or dry conditions. I still retain older pastures of native grasses, but most modern farmers have replaced their old grass fields, many times, with modern ryegrass leys which tend to iron out such subtleties. But in the past they mattered, which is why certain regions were better for producing, say, milk for cheese, than others. Hence the phrase 'as different as chalk and cheese'. Good milk for making cheese tends to be produced on clay soils: although not a medieval cheese, Stilton, for example, is traditionally produced on the heavy lands of Leicestershire and Rutland.

So far I have painted rural areas as a sort of labour 'pool' for great cities such as London. This may have been the case in some instances, but in others the country had its own appeal: following depopulation caused by successive waves of plague, rural housing improved and more good land became available. This would have been attractive to many town families, and could well have contributed to the decline in the population of certain towns. Regional economic factors, as we saw in the case of York and Hull, played an important role in rural areas too, because towns provided the markets that formed the basis of regional economies.

I had my own rather dog-eared copy of Maurice Beresford's *The Lost Villages of England* as a student, when I was trying to decide on the sort of archaeology I would specialise in for the second part of my degree. It was, and is, a superb book, but I was somewhat put off by the sheer completeness of it all. I can recall thinking that if we knew so much, what was there left to discover, and how long would it take for a young person to acquire all this knowledge before he could start making an original contribution himself? So, if anything, it put me off medieval archaeology. I went on to specialise in prehistory, and my copy of the book must have vanished somewhere, because I spent quite a long time combing my shelves for it when I was drawing material together for the present project. In frustration I went on the internet and bought another copy, a modern reprint with an excellent new Introduction by the historian Professor Christopher Dyer, who has done so much to pioneer what I have termed the 'holistic' approach to the medieval countryside.[13]

Beresford and W.G. Hoskins were trained as historians, but both also possessed a good eye for the landscape. Both too realised the importance of regional studies, in which documentary evidence could be linked to what was out there in the actual landscape. It was not surprising therefore that in the 1950s attention began to shift towards archaeology, as opposed to history pure and simple. Given that regionalism and local specialisation were such features of the later Middle Ages, this is probably the moment to move from the general to the particular. In the world of medieval rural archaeology that can mean only one thing: Wharram Percy in North Yorkshire, surely the most famous DMV of them all.

I have long been an admirer of the Wharram Percy project, and not just for its extraordinary longevity: no less than forty years, from 1950 to 1990. I admire it principally because it pioneered the teamwork approach to archaeology. Before the war archaeology was invariably done by great men such as Mortimer Wheeler or (more rarely) women, such as Dorothy Garrod. They were the figureheads, and although they relied on good teamwork to achieve their results, their collaborators rarely took centre stage. Even after the war most archaeological excavations tended to be organised on quasi-military lines, with more than a hint of a distinction between officers and 'other ranks'.

I well remember excavating a nameless but profoundly cold, exposed and unpleasant site in Essex just before and after Christmas 1966. There were just three of us working at the time: the director, her principal assistant and myself. I was there because I needed the money to pay off my huge college bar bill, and the assistant was a pal who was doing me a favour. Even so, during breaks in excavation my college friend and the director had their cups of tea in the director's hut, whereas I had to make do in the diggers' shed, accompanied by dozens of spades, picks and shovels. I can't say that the experience scarred me for life, but it was instructive none the less, and I vowed I would never run a dig on those lines if I ever became a professional archaeologist.

As I have said, Maurice Beresford was a historian, and he started the Wharram Percy project in 1950, but he was neither a born nor a trained field archaeologist. Two years later the site was visited by a young Cambridge postgraduate student of medieval pottery, John Hurst. He was appalled by Beresford's archaeological techniques, or lack of them, but impressed by the thought and the research lying behind the project. Beresford recognised his own technical shortcomings, and asked Hurst to take over the running of the excavations.* Thus was born a partnership that was to have a profound effect on the subsequent course of medieval archaeology.

Anyone who worked on projects funded by the Inspectorate of Ancient Monuments, an antecedent of English Heritage, would one day be visited by John Hurst, who was their Assistant Chief Inspector.

---

* Beresford was not shy of admitting that his excavation techniques were weak, but they served their purpose. Above all they showed that the buildings of the deserted village were of more than a single period, and that the archaeological remains were complex. The photograph demonstrating this point (of excavations in 1952, before Hurst joined) could also be used to show how *not* to lay out an archaeological trench. See Maurice Beresford and John Hurst, *Wharram Percy Deserted Medieval Village* (English Heritage and B.T. Batsford Books, London, 1990), p.30.

I remember him as a quiet and very affable man; he was also a shrewd judge of an archaeological project, and I never took his visits for granted. I wanted to show that we were up to the mark. He retired in 1987. Like everyone else in the archaeological world I was shattered by the news that he had been assaulted in the street and murdered on 29 April 2003 in the village of Great Casterton, just north of Stamford, Rutland. He was seventy-five. I have never been able to pass the spot where he was attacked without thinking about him. It would be tempting to devote several pages to Wharram Percy, if only in memory of John, but I think it would be a mistake, because he and Beresford have written a popular and well illustrated account of their work, which requires a whole volume to do it justice.[14] So I shall say a few brief words, and then look at a more recent project that is taking the type of research begun at Wharram Percy into new territory.

John Hurst introduced the then new techniques of open area excavation to Wharram. He also introduced meticulous recording methods, where everything was noted down in three dimensions. Several years were spent excavating just two houses. At first it was thought that these buildings had been flimsy and insubstantial, and would have required frequent rebuilding. Then in the 1980s it was realised that the seemingly fragile walls were only used to fill-in the spaces between curved vertical beams known as crucks. These curved crucks reached from the floor to the roof. Far from being flimsy, the cruck-built longhouses of the early Middle Ages were substantial and well-built structures that could stand for upwards of two centuries. Sizeable barns were also constructed using crucks.

Crucks were often made from the trunks of black poplar (*Populus nigra*), a massive native tree which has largely vanished from the English landscape, but which grows in a tall, gentle curve as a way of coping with the prevailing wind.[15] I have to admit that I am something of a black poplar obsessive, and have planted eighty around our farm. Not only do they encourage poplar hawk moths and other insects, but even in a light breeze their leaves make a relaxing rustling sound, rather like water beneath a punt as one drifts lazily along. They also grow extremely fast, and have delightful catkins in early spring: red on the male and green on the female trees.

Longhouses were a popular style of building right across rural

FIG 36   *An artist's reconstruction of a cruck-built tithe barn at the deserted medieval village of Wharram Percy, Yorkshire. This barn burnt down in 1553, and the reconstruction is based on the lower walls and foundations. Tithe barns were used to store payments in kind to the Church. Crucks were the long, curving beams that reached from the floor to the apex of the roof.*

Britain in the early Middle Ages, but they began to be replaced by other types of building in the later Middle Ages. Farms of the courtyard pattern, perhaps more familiar to us today, start to replace longhouses and barns from the fourteenth century. But there was no hard and fast rule: sometimes courtyard structures could themselves be cruck-built and resemble a group of small longhouses. If there was a general tendency it was that regional diversity was to become increasingly important in the later Middle Ages. Some trends were, however, consistent. We saw in York and London that stone construction began to be used from the early twelfth and thirteenth centuries. Something similar was happening in the countryside too. Here timber was also being replaced by stonework, if only for the lowest two or three courses. Country builders, like their cousins in town, realised the importance of rising damp and sound foundations. Paul Stamper has suggested that the trend towards stone was a result of the decline in timber supplies as more and more land was put aside for arable. Christopher Dyer believes it was connected with the rise in importance of professional carpenters in the thirteenth century, a fact that can be documented in written sources. Personally, I tend to favour the 'common sense' view that anyone who has ever built a structure with damp footings will soon make a big effort to try something better. Quite possibly all three of us are right, and various factors conspired together to effect the widespread change.

Another trend visible in both town and country in the earlier Middle Ages was towards better-defined property boundaries. These were known as tofts when they surrounded houses; small garden plots were known as garths and the smallholding of land attached to each toft was termed a croft. We saw how fixed and long-lasting these boundaries were in the otherwise quite informal urban settlement at York. The measures were made necessary by the increasing population of the twelfth and thirteenth centuries, and became particularly evident in the later thirteenth and fourteenth centuries.[16] The boundaries took the form of fences, walls, ditches, banks and hedges. In forested areas ditches and banks were generally used. At the beginning of the Middle Ages, outside the main fields and settlements in many districts woodland, heath and moor were allowed to remain 'open' and unenclosed – available to all communities in the region. But as pressure on resources, such as rough grazing and forest products, rose, even these remoter areas were parcelled up between the communities that used them. This represents the final partitioning of the British countryside.

We have seen that there is no simple, one-size-fits-all explanation for the abandonment of DMVs, but in many instances the population decline, and the consequent social effects, following the devastating initial impact and successive waves of plague, certainly played an important part. We should not forget either that in many places the high levels of urban and rural population by the start of that fateful fourteenth century were already causing the system to creak. And it was the people towards the bottom of society who felt the pain the most. Work was scarce and poorly paid, and feudalism was not particularly kind to those individuals whose obligations were repaid by work.

Around 1300, many people were less well-off than they would have been a century before. As we saw earlier, in certain places food and other essential supplies were in short supply. Everything seemed set for the catastrophe that eventually struck in 1348. The effects of successive waves of plague were made worse by the success of the earlier medieval economy, which allowed such prosperity to develop. Viewed from a modern perspective, however, the terrible slaughter did ultimately have several social benefits. Greater individual freedom, combined with the loosening of many of the restrictive bonds of feudalism, did promote flexibility and allow success to be rewarded. The result was the diverse, regionalised economy of the fifteenth and sixteenth centuries. But it was a process that had losers as well as winners. We saw how York conceded ground to places like Hull. Some towns almost vanished off the map. Others prospered. Something similar was happening in the countryside. To understand these changes we must work on a case-by-case basis. Broad-brush generalities won't work.

It would seem that Wharram Percy ultimately fell victim to the widespread depopulation of the English Midlands in the fifteenth century. Wharram was abandoned shortly after 1500, following a century of steady decline. This view of what happened differs a great deal from the simple idea of collapse and rapid abandonment following a devastating attack of disease that wiped out the entire population. Instead, what we see is a period of population decline that ultimately led to a countryside that was better suited not just to a somewhat smaller population, but to an economy that was developing distinctive regional identities. These changes were helped by the fact that in the years after 1348 it became easier for people to move between town and country. In an environment where labour now had greater intrinsic value, rural landlords were unable to tie people down so effectively, and of course the economic incentives for workers to move were far greater than they had ever been.

So the economic and social changes that mark what some have seen as the transformation of the Middle Ages had roots that extended back before 1348. The dreadful plagues tipped the balance, but change was probably bound to happen sooner or later. We can also see the archaeological impact of these underlying processes in a recent survey of twelve parishes in the heart of the English Midlands, in an area of the so-called 'champion' country of manors, nucleated villages and Open Fields. This is the archetypical rural landscape of the Middle Ages – the sort of thing we learned about at school, where we were taught that rural life in the Middle Ages was fixed and unchanging, held together (tied down might be a better way of describing it) by the unbending obligations of the feudal system. But what really happened?

In Chapter 3 we saw how the process of nucleation began at Shapwick in Somerset, a parish that was affected by monastic landowners. In a moment I will return there to see how things went in the full Middle Ages. But now I want to turn to another, and much larger, survey, where field and documentary evidence is coming together to paint a coherent picture of change and development. Both types of survey show that the landscapes of what Roberts and Wrathmell termed the Central Province were often in a state of flux in the Middle Ages. They were not as rigidly confined within a feudal corset as one was taught at school.

The Whittlewood survey covers no fewer than twelve parishes in the heart of the Midland champion landscape on the Buckinghamshire–Northamptonshire border.[17] Its director is Professor Chris Dyer, who modestly describes himself as 'a social and economic historian with archaeological interests'. Like most people active in the field he worked at Wharram Percy, but the scale of his Whittlewood survey is much larger. So it has to make full use of computers and modern satellite-based surveying techniques such as GPS (Global Positioning Systems). The underlying approach is also different, and reflects the fact that the Whittlewood project began in 1990 and is currently receiving at least adequate funding (something which could not always be said for Wharram).

The big difference between Wharram and Whittlewood is that the earlier project was based around a site – indeed, what was to become *the* site: the deserted village of Wharram Percy. Chris Dyer's approach is altogether different. His 'site' is the landscape itself – all one hundred square kilometres of it. There is an irony in this new approach. I have heard it said that Whittlewood is not pioneering new techniques, such as open area excavation, in quite the same way that Wharram did. That is grossly unfair, because there is far more to good field archaeology than mere technique. Besides, I believe that at Whittlewood they are developing new ways of working and of thinking. Today we are learning about nanotechnology – the science of the tiny – and Whittlewood is doing its bit here. Instead of open areas, the team work in very small trenches, sometimes just a metre square. These recall the 'shovel-pit testing' employed at Shapwick. As the villages around Whittlewood are not deserted these trenches often have to be placed in people's back gardens – hence their size. The trick is to combine results from these micro-digs with the broader picture, and that requires much skill and expertise.

The Whittlewood survey is led by research questions which have to be addressed over a very large area. This requires the active co-operation of the general public living in the region. So the survey has to get people involved, whether they are initially keen to help or not, and everyone has to be 'on side'. The aim is to give local people a sense of ownership: it's their project too, and not something entirely imposed on them from outside. This is a very real challenge. As I have just noted, field archaeology has to be about more than mere technique: of course we will always need pioneering projects like Wharram to develop approaches such as open area excavation, but we also need a rather different type of pioneer to invent a new style of community-based archaeology that's appropriate for the twenty-first century, when people want, indeed in some cases *demand*, to be involved. Today more and more people are taking an interest in their surroundings and in family and local history. The challenge to archaeologists is to channel this enthusiasm into worthwhile long-term research. I find it pleasing to think that the teams at Whittlewood and Shapwick which are trying to discover the truth about communal land management in the Middle Ages are doing so by reinventing communal archaeology in the twenty-first century. As I see it, they are pioneers in every sense of the word.

The Whittlewood project draws no chronological lines, so prehistoric and Romano-British remains are recorded with the same care. So far preliminary results suggest that the landscape was farmed, including arable, in pre-Roman and Roman times, but reverted to woodland in the early medieval period. It seems likely that the reversion to woodland may have been deliberate, because the area is known to have been an important royal hunting forest in the twelfth century. Such forests were sometimes little more than clever schemes to raise money for the Treasury by way of fines, levies and taxes for poaching, illegal pasture or tree-felling. The arrangement was not popular with the people who lived and farmed in the area.

The political situation was further clouded by the presence of another institutional body, the Church. Here the picture seems to have been complex indeed, with a series of Saxon minsters which gave rise to a number of local parish churches. The question the team are currently trying to address is the extent to which the hierarchy of local and regional Church politics affected life in the parishes. It all sounds rather messy, and far from straightforward – rather like modern life, it would seem. And that's the crux of the matter. Life has never been straightforward, and archaeological research should be structured to reflect that fact.

Whittlewood is showing us that the sort of simple economic models we have used to explain phenomena such as village nucleation, shrinkage and desertion are probably wide of the mark. There may be a core of truth somewhere there, but the complexities are such that it becomes almost impossible to apply such general rules to specific cases. And today people want to learn about the specifics of the places where they live. You cannot fob them off with blanket explanations such as 'You live in the Northern and Western Province, and therefore your village was part of the so-called woodland economy, where settlement was widely dispersed and very little land was held in common.' Whittlewood is showing that in reality the situation was far more complicated than that, even in the heart of the seemingly straightforward Central Province. Chris Dyer explains: 'There are so many variables, you end up with a really complex system. People tend to think that woodland equals dispersal, for instance, but we are seeing nuc-leated settlements and woodland together. In other places, without much woodland, we see dispersal – not so much a single village as a string of hamlets within easy walking distance. Nor is there any grand plan, no single "planning moment". Our evidence shows that villages are gradual accretions, and that some villages can change their form quite radically.'[18]

Factors such as the sort of local politics that involved landowners and the Church probably helped to determine why certain communi-ties, even within the generally nucleated settlements of the Central Province, decided to remain as they were: enclosed and dispersed. Others followed the course of nucleation, manorialisation and the Open Field system. We saw that Shapwick, on the south-western fringes of the Central Province in Somerset, was persuaded to nucleate in the mid-tenth century, probably under the influence of the powerful St Dunstan of Glastonbury Abbey. What happened then? Did the new system collapse or prosper?

The evidence suggests that it prospered. A new manor was con-structed at the head of the village, probably some time in the tenth century. In the twelfth century it was surrounded by an impressive flat-bottomed moat. Like many medieval moats it may have served a defensive purpose, but this was probably less significant than its role as a status symbol. It marked the manor as somewhere altogether special, at the top of the local feudal tree. Just outside the moat was the great tithe barn of Glastonbury Abbey, where the in-kind ecclesiastical taxes of corn were stored. This complex of stone buildings would have dominated the village in every sense.

Mick Aston and Chris Gerrard have estimated the village popu-lation at Shapwick. In the centuries prior to the Black Death it rose from about 158 people in 1086 (Domesday) to 282 in 1327. Then it fell sharply (interestingly just prior to the plague) to 110 in 1340, rising to just 145 by 1387.[19] Excavations have confirmed that the decrease in population was accompanied by the abandonment and combination of certain housing plots in the village. So at Shapwick the village adapted to the new situation, and was never abandoned. As we saw at Whittlewood, however, it was never a straightforward picture: the population decreased prior to the Black Death, and of course the presence of Glastonbury Abbey, the great and powerful landowner, was always a complicating political factor. Then, in the sixteenth century, drainage of the nearby marshes added a further level of complexity. The situation changed yet again in November 1539 when Glastonbury Abbey was suppressed and the estate at Shapwick fell into private ownership.

Given such a changing history, it would be hard to support the traditional position that the centuries of the Middle Ages were tranquil, largely due to the continuance of feudal ties and obligations. In reality life in the countryside may often have been stable, but that stability concealed underlying complexity. There were local political agreements, purely social obligations, and of course economic arrangements, and these all changed from one area to another and from generation to generation – rather like life in our own, avowedly changing times.

I want now briefly to consider why and how the communal, nucleated settlements of the champion landscapes ended. In the process we will begin to understand why the two provinces on either side of the Central Province developed in the way they did. Many people have written about this, but a recent book, *Shaping Medieval Landscapes*, by the distinguished landscape historian and archaeologist Tom Williamson, has made some suggestions that seem actually to make sense from a farming perspective.[20]

Sometimes it can be exasperating to read theoretical explanations for agrarian change that are made by economic historians who wouldn't know what to do with a field of hay were it presented to them on a plate. Tom does. He keeps sheep, and he understands how the farming landscape works. He has realised the simple truth that whatever the prevailing political situation might be, the farm is always part of a complex system; that what happens in summer must support the farm through the winter, and that soil fertility must be maintained at all costs. It is not generally appreciated that grass is a crop, just like any other cereal, and even long-established pasture can rapidly deteriorate if it is abused. Such neglected grass produces very poor hay, which is relevant to our current theme. Incidentally, today the proliferation of incompetent equestrian or 'horsiculture' holdings throughout rural Britain shows what happens when grass is grossly overgrazed: it dies, and is soon replaced by weeds such as dock and poisonous ragwort which distributes its seeds on the wind. In an ideal world I would forcibly make the people responsible read Tom's excellent book to learn what might happen if they do not change their ways.

Tom's arguments are complex, and I am aware that I run a grave risk of oversimplifying them, but he sets out to address the question of why specialised, nucleated 'champion' landscapes developed on the clay lands of Northants in the Central Province, but not on the clays of Kent/Essex or the peaty soils of north Norfolk in the South-eastern Province. By and large he stays clear of what one might term 'macro-economic' arguments, although he recognises that population growth in the centuries prior to 1300 played a role in the development of Open Field cooperative farming, as did the subsequent decline in population following the successive waves of plague. He points out in a refreshingly forceful manner that the decisions to nucleate settlements and operate Open Field systems were the outcome of what he terms rational adjustments to complex environmental circumstances made by farmers and managers living in a real world, structured by the rhythms of the seasons and the demands of the soil. Sometimes these demands could be hard to ignore.

The successful operation of an Open Field system requires land to lie fallow and to be recharged and renewed by grazing animals on it or by spreading manure across it. Incidentally, manure is not the same as dung, or animal faeces. Muck is a mixture of dung and straw bedding, but it is chemically 'hot' and needs to be reduced to manure before it can be spread on the land. Manure is produced in an external muck-heap, which must rot down or compost for at least four to six months, during which process it gives off heat and steam. Manure can be made by gathering up muck from the fields, as horse-keepers ought to do (because horse dung is very 'hot', and kills off grass if allowed to remain on the ground), but is usually made by clearing out buildings or open crew yards where animals have been kept over winter. The clearing-out process aerates the muck and speeds up the composting process.

The medieval way of dealing with 'hot' dung was to turn animals out on the open fields after harvest. One of the fields would be fallow and available to livestock all the time. The dung breaks down quickly enough in the open air. Another way of adding nitrogen (an essential part of plant fertility) to the soil was by growing peas or beans, which have little colonies of nitrogen-fixing bacteria in their root systems. So the usual crop rotation of Open Fields in the English Midlands was cereals, followed by peas or beans, and then fallow. Most villages in the Midlands operated two or three large open fields, but this pattern varied considerably across the country.

Tom Williamson was interested in why champion farming never developed on the clay soils of north Norfolk, whereas it thrived on what seemed to be closely similar terrain in nearby Northamptonshire and parts of Cambridgeshire. When he came to examine the two soils, as any farmer would routinely do, he found that the Norfolk clay land was deficient in copper. Pigs require enormous quantities of copper (I sadly recall finding a dead ewe that had broken into my feed store and eaten her fill of copper-rich pig pellets, which can be poisonous to ruminants). Sheep and cattle also need copper, but less of it than pigs. The point is that copper has to be present in the hay or grazing. It is hard to supplement naturally. Today we use techniques such as bolus guns, which shoot a capsule into the animal's gullet.

In the past even quite a slight copper deficiency would have been a problem: afflicted lambs are born with a condition known as 'sway back', where they have trouble maintaining balance and standing upright. In most instances 'sway back' lambs die within a day or two of birth. Worse still, hay made from grass grown on land with a copper deficiency is also low in copper, which means that animals housed over winter and given such fodder rarely thrive. Weaker animals may well die. With poor-quality hay there would be no animals (whether they were housed over winter or were left out in the open) to provide manure or to graze the open fields. Without animal manure sustained arable farming in large open fields would not work. So on the copper-deficient soils of north Norfolk the farming system remained less intensive, and was based around individual holdings of land. A system such as this, where many fewer animals are kept per acre, is far more sustainable: grazing is under less pressure, and although they will not grow fat, stock stand a better chance of surviving the winter in fields where there is some shelter and occasional forage.

Champion farming in the English Midlands was an intensive system, and even by modern standards it was something of an ecological nightmare: there were no hedges, fields were vast and woodland was confined to the fringes. The heavy soil was only in a fit condition to plough for a very brief 'window', usually in May. If you tried to plough the land when it was too dry it set like concrete; too wet and it turned to porridge. If you got it right it ploughed very well, but it paid to use large ploughs with sizeable teams of oxen, or even better, horses. Similarly, harvest was a time of communal effort. These teams of men and animals were the product of local cooperation and agreement, a process that was mediated through the manorial system, or via major landowners and of course agents of the Church, in places like Shapwick. In short, there were good, practical reasons why it paid people to work the land of the Central Province together.

Williamson acknowledges that the practicalities of farming were not the only factors at play here. Like anyone else, farmers are social people, and they respond to local customs, practice and history. So if one travelled through a stretch of countryside where land conditions gradually began to favour champion over woodland styles of farming, one probably would not find a gradual transition. Instead there would be a sharp distinction, where one set of communities had gone one way, and another the other. This sort of 'clumping' effect is often observed, and probably reflects local preferences rather than a series of objective agrarian decisions.

The Open Field system thrived in the years prior to the fourteenth century, but then declined quite rapidly. It is not hard to see why: it was based on communal effort, and when labour became more scarce it was harder to organise. People also changed their attitudes towards the land and their role within farming. From the fifteenth century the great open fields of the Central Province began to be enclosed on an increasing scale. This change in attitude reflected the growth of what we would now recognise as a capitalist, market-based economy. In such circumstances individual holdings of land allowed farmers to develop what we would today describe as niche markets. By 1400 the process of regional specialisation was under way, and just as collective farms failed to thrive in post-Communist Russia, largely because they were too inflexible, so the great Open Field communities became increasingly parcelled up into individual enclosures – even during the sixteenth century, when general population levels in England began to increase. By then it was too late to turn back the clock. Irreversible processes had begun.

I come now to the final part of this chapter, in which I look at a region outside the 'classic' champion landscape of the Central Province. My examination of the certainties I expected to find in the Central Province has revealed instead variety, regional distinctiveness and unpredictability. Indeed, one of the reasons I wanted to write this book was to visit areas of study outside my own immediate field of expertise where I could find, if not certainties, then an archaeological world that didn't continually challenge all of one's fondly held beliefs. But it would appear that my researches so far have revealed that medieval archaeologists are as fond of slaughtering sacred cows as are the most radical of my fellow prehistorians. Now surely we must be approaching more predictable territory? For a start, most research into medieval rural landscapes has been into Open Field systems and the champion landscapes. And as a general rule, where there is research, there is controversy.

So what happens if one strays into the Northern and Western Province? Surely here we know more or less what we are going to find: the different regions escaped the population pressures of the eleventh and twelfth centuries; most rural communities existed in patterns of settlement and farming systems that changed little through time. Essentially these should prove to be conservative landscapes. I might also expect to discover that there were relatively few towns to complicate town–country relations, because the major changes of the pre-Industrial Revolution had yet to happen. But by coincidence Nick Higham, a friend and colleague at Manchester University, has just published a regional survey of the north-west in the Middle Ages, and he has shown that all my preconceptions are flawed – profoundly flawed.[21] Indeed, his revelations turn one's view not just of his region, but of the period itself, upside down.

I have always had an interest in the north-west because of the region's close relationship with Ireland in the Neolithic and Bronze Ages. If pottery of those periods is anything to go by, there was regular communication across the Irish Sea in the third millennium BC, but until recently I knew little or nothing about the region after the Roman period, when of course the great walled city of Chester flourished. My interest was rekindled when I received an invitation to take part in a live televised excavation in a suburb of Roman Chester known as Heronbridge. Previous excavations had revealed a Roman dock where goods were loaded and unloaded from ships on the river. Today the site sits within a large and well maintained rural estate, with stout oak trees and pheasants everywhere. Alongside the grass fields that conceal the hidden Romano-British roadside suburb, the River Dee wends its tranquil way to the sea a few miles further downstream. I have worked in few places that were more restful.

The Roman remains were most remarkable, and showed the area to have been very prosperous even in the later years of the fourth century, when similar industrial suburbs elsewhere in Roman Britain were in sharp decline. However, my interest was well and truly aroused when I learned about a large, crescent-shaped earthwork that had quite clearly been imposed on top of the abandoned Romano-British buildings. Part of this bank had been excavated, and a war cemetery was discovered there. The bodies, probably of soldiers, had been horribly mutilated, with deep cuts into the bone of skulls and limbs. The archaeological evidence shows that these burials were placed in the ground in the earlier seventh century, and the best candidate for a battle has to be the well-attested Battle of Chester, which took place in AD 613. In this conflict King Æthelfrith of Northumbria defeated the combined Welsh forces of Gwynedd and Powys, and the earthwork was probably constructed by Æthelfrith to consolidate his victory and to receive supplies and reinforcements by way of the river.

The discovery of the precise site of a known late Dark Age battle is, I believe, unique. But it also illustrates both why Nick Higham considers the area a frontier, and what happened in the region after the Roman period. Essentially it reverted to something approaching an underpopulated wilderness – the conventional, but usually mistaken, view of Dark Age northern Britain. It seems likely that the initial reversion to scrub and underpopulation may well have been the result of conflict and frontier lawlessness of the sort we saw at Heronbridge – but we don't know for certain.

Nick Higham's study is a classic landscape history of the post-1974 counties of Lancashire, Merseyside, Greater Manchester and Cheshire in the medieval period. It's a detailed piece of work, rich in maps and other supporting evidence. Essentially the landscape consists of upland, the western Pennines and Peak District, and lower-lying, flatter and more fertile river valley land along the principal rivers, the Ribble, the Mersey and the Dee, which marks the southern limit of the study area. But this seeming simplicity conceals a huge diversity of landscape sub-types, of which the extensive lowland mosses (very acid sphagnum moss bogs, largely fed by rainwater) are the best-known. Mosses provided peat for both fuel and grazing, and they were partially drained on a piecemeal basis throughout the medieval period. Even so, large expanses existed in Victorian times, and a few fragments have survived until today. I should add here that peat-based grazing is extremely poor in copper.

It used to be believed that the clearance of the lowland landscape in the north-west, as elsewhere, was essentially a post-Roman phenomenon, but now there is abundant evidence from pollen analysis and archaeology that trees were being cleared to make way for grazing from at least the Bronze Age (say 1000 BC). The process continued throughout the Iron Age and into the Roman period, during which the major towns, with civilian settlements attached to a military camp, were established at Chester, Manchester, Lancaster and Northwich. There were also other Roman towns such as Nantwich and Middlewich, both of which owed their prosperity to rock-salt, which we now know was being extracted in the Iron Age too.

Between the Roman period and the eleventh century we hit something of an archaeological dark age, largely because pottery – surely the archaeologist's greatest friend – either ceases to survive, or to be made and used. So we must fall back on radiocarbon dates and pollen analysis, a technique that is particularly useful in the north-west, where generally acid soil conditions mean that pollen grains survive well. The pollen data suggest that woodland did indeed increase after the Roman period, in the fifth and sixth centuries, but there is also evidence that crops (cereals and flax) were still being grown. So the area was not abandoned entirely. Higham suggests that in the second part of the first millennium AD woodland cover was indeed extensive, but there was substantial clearing too. During this time the major Roman settlements were also being reoccupied and new centres were being established. Many Roman roads continued in use and new routes were appearing.

Towards the end of the first millennium AD, we encounter the Vikings. It used to be believed that the Viking presence here was little short of a major mass-migration, an idea that is supported by numerous Norse place-names and findspots of Viking material, including the famous Cuerdale hoard which we discussed in Chapter 1. However, Higham points out that the pollen evidence does not show the massive expansion of woodland clearance one might expect from such a large influx of new people. This would tend to suggest that much of the supposed new Viking 'presence' was due to the adoption of fresh ideas and culture, as much as to ethnic change. If there was indeed a huge invasion then there must also have been a huge exodus from the area, because if anything the pollen record shows that in fact less land was farmed in Viking times and immediately thereafter. But after that there was a very big change indeed.

As Higham describes it, the period from 1086 to 1349 witnessed perhaps the most far-reaching changes to the landscape of the north-west between the Ice Age and the Industrial Revolution.[22] These changes are still poorly understood, but there was a huge population expansion, and many new tracts of the landscape were occupied. By the end of the period the rural settlement pattern was much as it is today. Although in theory the north-west was well outside the area of champion landscapes and there were still large expanses of woodland, particularly on the higher ground, the bare bones of the manorial system had already been established in the Later Saxon period. It was now time to put flesh on those bones – which is what happened, and quite rapidly. Specialised upland cattle-farming settlements came into existence, known as vaccaries (from the Latin word *vaccus*, a cow). There was also increased pressure to clear woodland for grazing, which meant that what little was left was exploited more thoroughly, through more intensive coppicing and pollarding of trees. So although it is fair to describe this as an overall 'woodland' landscape – and the population it supported was much smaller than that of, say, the champion lands of the Central Province – it had changed almost beyond recognition from what it had been in the tenth century.

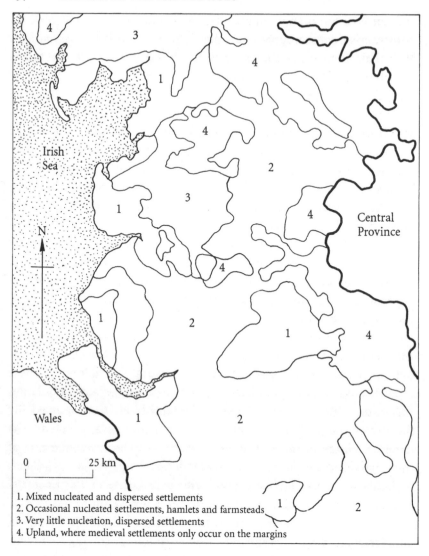

Irish
Sea

N

Wales

0   25 km

1. Mixed nucleated and dispersed settlements
2. Occasional nucleated settlements, hamlets and farmsteads
3. Very little nucleation, dispersed settlements
4. Upland, where medieval settlements only occur on the margins

Central
Province

FIG 37   *North-western England in the Middle Ages.*

I've already mentioned that the manorial system was in existence, but the Open Field system that came into being differed from that of the Midland champion landscapes in many important respects. Generally there was just a single Open Field, and in some cases individual enclosed holdings continued, albeit farmed cooperatively under the influence of the manor. The systems that evolved were suited to the constraints imposed by the landscape, which was probably more varied than that of any other part of England. This variety is reflected by the distribution of the various landscapes that were mapped (largely using data derived somewhat later) by Roberts and Wrathmell for their *Medieval Atlas*. A glance at this map shows that nucleated settlements, which tended to be found on the better-quality land, played an important role in the development of these supposedly woodland landscapes. But here, as elsewhere in medieval Britain, the distinction was by no means clear-cut.

The landscapes of the earlier Middle Ages in the north-west were affected by the population changes of the fourteenth and later centuries, but there does not appear to have been any decline either in the rural population or the region's economy prior to 1348, as we noted in one or two instances in southern Britain. This is somewhat surprising, given the rapidity of growth and expansion in the years 1086–1349 and the fact that the region is not particularly fertile when compared to other areas of Britain. This in turn would suggest that the medieval farmers essentially 'got it right', and did not exploit their land in a manner that was to prove unsustainable.

After the impact of the plague, population did indeed decline, and this is best seen in certain towns, of which Chester is probably the most important. In the countryside there is little or no evidence for deserted villages, but there are signs that peasant workers removed their labour from those directly owned manorial farms known as *demesnes* – a tendency that can be observed over much of Britain. As a result these farms declined from the later thirteenth century. After 1540, and for the next two centuries, we begin to see the first hints of altogether greater changes. Large areas of the landscape were reorganised into regularly-laid-out rectangular fields of pasture, which were intended to produce the milk needed for the growing cheese industry. This was part of the widespread process of regional economic specialisation. By now too, many large lowland mosses were under serious attack from drainage.

In 1540 manufacturing was just beginning. Higham quotes the great antiquarian John Leland, who wrote that Manchester men were buying Irish yarn at the port of Liverpool, and that canal (brown) coal was being mined near Wigan and sea coal off Bolton; he further noted that several towns were prospering, especially Warrington.[23] These are all names that would feature prominently in the much later Industrial Revolution, which inclines one to question just how rapid that 'revolution' – if such it was – had actually been. It is hard to avoid the conclusion that the seeds of this, the greatest change that first Britain and later the rest of the world would ever experience, had started to germinate in the late medieval period.

CHAPTER SEVEN

Trade, Industry and Security

IN THIS CHAPTER I want to address some of the topics that we take for granted nowadays and that were also of central importance to medieval society, most especially to urban medieval society. I have already painted a picture of trade in Middle Saxon times, and in this chapter we will see what subsequently developed from this. So far I have not paid much attention to castles and town walls. This does not reflect any lack of interest in them, but I felt that more progress had recently been made in other aspects of medieval archaeology, and that most people interested in the past would have some knowledge of the subject, if only from reading the excellent guide books one can buy at places like Caernarfon, Castle Rising or the Tower of London, to name but three.

One reason I like archaeology so much is that it has traditionally addressed what one might term the humdrum aspects of life: what people ate, how they disposed of their rubbish and how they made their tools and implements. Maybe this 'bottom-up' approach prevented some archaeologists from raising their expectations. Their thoughts, like their eyes, were rooted in their trenches. But that is, I believe, changing. Today we are less afraid to paint on a larger canvas. Archaeologists in the first half of the twentieth century were generally wary about speculating on the broader implications of their discoveries, but since the 1960s we have grown in confidence as the realisation has dawned on us that our work has a cumulative value; that when the results from relatively unexciting, routine projects are combined the picture they reveal can sometimes be startling. Further, being based on a large body of independently derived data, such a picture can be both credible and convincing. A good case in point is what John and Bryony Coles have termed 'the wetland revolution'.[1]

The 'wetland revolution' of the two Coleses is essentially a rural phenomenon, and most of the sites and projects included within it across the world are prehistoric. But it has indeed proved to be something of a revolution, because of the quality and quantity of the information the various new wetland sites have revealed. Before wetland archaeology received this recent publicity, prehistorians were content to work with the driest of finds, sites and objects: usually just pottery, stone, faint traces in the soil of long-vanished posts, and so forth. Once the preservative qualities of waterlogged conditions had been fully understood – and this was the process that the trumpeting of the wetland revolution from the academic rooftops helped to promote – people began to seek out wetter areas to 'flesh out', as it were, their more conventional dryland projects.

If the importance of wetland archaeology came to prehistory relatively late, the altogether younger subject of urban archaeology acquired it almost from the outset. Many of the earliest excavations in London had waterlogged levels, as of course did the well-known 'Viking Dig' at Coppergate, York. There are numerous other examples, including Wood Quay in Dublin, Dorestad in Holland, Bergen and Trondheim in Norway, and dozens more. One reason for this is that Roman and early medieval towns were often located near water, because ships had improved and both trade and raiding were such important aspects of life that it was worthwhile to construct complex docks and waterfronts. So waterfront archaeology was soon seen to be an integral part of urban archaeology, and not something apart, different and somehow difficult to acquire for those archaeologists who had grown up working on dry sites. In prehistory there is still, sadly, a clear distinction between 'wet' and 'dry' archaeologists, and I have to say I have recently seen many promising wet rural sites butchered by dryland archaeologists, simply out of ignorance and inexperience. I do not believe that such things would happen in most towns, because the proper recording of timber and the sampling of wetland deposits is an integral part of the 'culture' of urban archaeology.

It would be fair to say that waterfront archaeology has transformed our understanding of urban life in medieval Europe, quite simply because the docks were at a town's heart. They were why it was there in the first place. As Brian Hobley wrote in the Introduction to what is still a very useful overview of the subject, waterfront archaeology can provide graphic evidence of – and suggest reasons for – a town's origins, growth and decline.[2] I have already discussed the roles of those Middle Saxon trading centres, the *wics* and the *emporia*, and I will now turn my attention to two medieval centres that had both once been *wics*, but which had then developed into important ports. I will start with Southampton and then return to what was by far the greatest port in medieval Britain, London.

Medieval Southampton was the subject of three major excavation projects before Colin Platt directed work there between 1966 and 1969. He was then assigned the task, with Richard Coleman-Smith, of editing the three earlier projects and his own work together, which he did with great success in a two-volume report that I consider to be one of the best archaeological reports produced in Britain since the war.[3]

Apart from being the subject of such a fine report, one reason I wanted to look at medieval Southampton is the completeness of the picture provided both by written records and the findings of archaeology. Colin Platt was not able to draw upon the rich information that might have come from the excavation of a waterlogged waterfront, largely because the medieval waterfront was deeply buried beneath the modern road which now runs along what were originally the waterside town walls to the south and west. Even without such an important source of data, the report gives a remarkably vivid impression of a regional trading centre and its many contacts overseas in the later Middle Ages.

Today Southampton is part of a rather ill-defined coastal conurbation that includes Eastleigh, Fareham, Portsmouth and Havant, all linked together by stationary traffic on the M27. Hidden within the plethora of modern docks and warehouses it is possible to trace the outline of the medieval town by following the unusually well preserved remains of the walls.

Medieval Southampton was placed on the south-western corner of a peninsula formed by the confluence of the Rivers Test and Itchen at the point where they flowed into Southampton Water. It was bounded by a fine set of defensive walls, which entirely surrounded the town, even on the two sides that overlooked Southampton Water. On the landward side the two lengths of wall were further reinforced by a deep external ditch. Within the walled area was the castle, in a well secured area. Outside the town walls was a large area of common fields with suburbs clustering closer to the walls. The site of the Saxon trading centre or *wic* known as Hamwic was on the eastern side of the peninsula, about half a kilometre distant. The town was served by two quays, West Quay and West Hithe to the west, and Town Quay to the south. Both were positioned close to gates through the walls into the town.

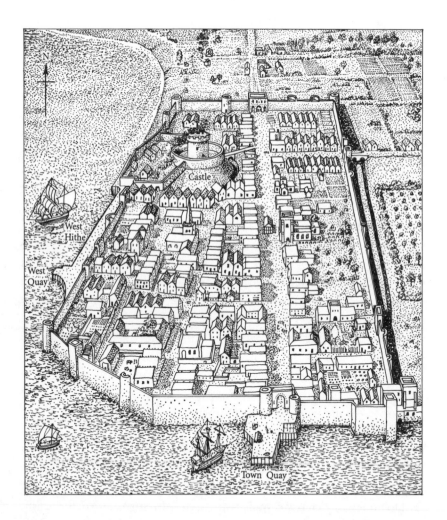

FIG 38 *The walled town of Southampton as it might have appeared in the later Middle Ages.*

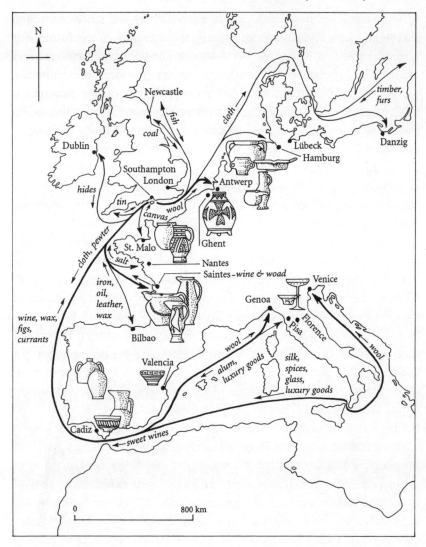

FIG 39 *Southampton's overseas trade from the twelfth to the fifteenth centuries, also showing the sources of the main imported types of glass and pottery. The principal English commodities exported in exchange were wool and cloth.*

Documentary evidence points to trade with France in wine; with Spain in oil, iron and wine; with Normandy in linen and canvas; with the Baltic in timber; with Ireland in hides; with the Low Countries in haberdashery and household goods; with Italy in silk, spices and dyes; and finally with the Bay of Bourgneuf, at the mouth of the Loire near Nantes, in salt. All of these items were traded for English wool and cloth.[4] The excavations revealed an interesting diversity of imported pottery and glass which complements well the picture of trade given by the documentary sources.[5] It would appear that the trade in foreign pottery was essentially in one direction only. Even in England, locally-produced Southampton wares were mostly confined to an area within about thirty miles of the town. Less exotic imported items, such as household goods, iron and fish, were confined to a similar-sized area, but wines were traded inland as far as Oxford, and dyestuffs, probably from Italy, reached as far north as Coventry and Leicester.

A point worth making here is the regularity of this trade. We are not talking about intermittent visits of itinerant maritime peddlers, but of a proper mercantile marine. It would be a great mistake to confuse the sort of trade that was taking place in Southampton and London in the Middle Ages with the sporadic visits of trading vessels from the eastern Mediterranean to small ports in Devon and Cornwall that we know took place in the fifth to seventh centuries, following the collapse of Roman rule.[6] Any possible confusion may come from my perhaps rather misleading use of the term 'trade'. There is archaeological trade, which I have just described. Such 'trade' is often represented by two or three sherds of imported pottery. Then there is what one might term real trade, where the imports occur in significant numbers, indicating regular, if not actually scheduled, contacts. Sometimes one can come across direct archaeological evidence to suggest that trade was indeed part of a routine contractual arrangement. My wife Maisie was recently involved in excavations at the port of Boston, Lincolnshire, which had recovered half a notched tally stick which she had to write up. Naturally she referred to the bible of medieval wooden artefacts, *Wood and Woodworking in Anglo-Scandinavian and Medieval York*, by Carole Morris, which revealed a fascinating story.[7]

Tally sticks formed an essential part of day-to-day medieval business transactions, and many of the words associated with the way they were used still form an essential part of modern English. The word 'tally' itself has passed into the language as a term for keeping score. It derives from the Latin *talea*, meaning a rod or stick.

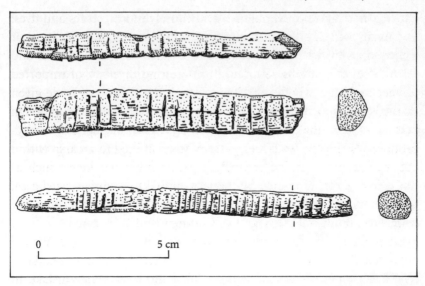

FIG 40   *Two tally sticks from the excavations at medieval York. Tally sticks were used to record and make commercial transactions. They were split or broken, and the parties to the deal kept a portion each. The examples here probably represent small local deals rather than major, long-distance arrangements, and date to the mid–late fourteenth century (two views, above) and the mid–late thirteenth century (below).*

At first glance the use of notched sticks sounds crude, but actually it was far from that. The notches were carved by hand and represented either a sum of money or a count of, say, bundles of hides taken aboard a ship as cargo. The stick was then split in two by inserting a tool and twisting it. This caused an irregular split which left a broad butt-end (known as the stock) and a smaller piece (the foil) that could only be matched with the grain and notches of its original stock. The stock would be given to the person who paid for the cargo as a receipt. Despite the fact that the system was recognised across Europe, it was only the English Exchequer that formalised it, ultimately giving rise to the Stock Exchange, where wooden stocks themselves were traded, sometimes in advance of the arrival of the cargoes that they represented; in effect this was what we would understand today as a futures market. Many medieval tallies still survive in the Public Records

Office, dated between the twelfth and the early nineteenth centuries. The word 'foil' survives in modern English as the retained remnant of a cheque or invoice: the counterfoil.

Most of the tally sticks found in Britain were probably for smaller private transactions made after the main cargo had landed. The earliest examples, from Milk Street in London, date from Later Saxon times, and tallies from the Middle Ages have been found at London, King's Lynn, Southampton and York. At any one time there were probably hundreds, if not thousands, of tallies in circulation, and their comparative rarity can be explained by the fact that they were made of wood, which soon rots down if dropped on the ground. As with most of the tallies from England, the largest collection, of some six hundred (from Bergen, dating to the period 1130–1350), comes from waterlogged deposits.

That mention of waterlogging is an entirely uncontrived link to our next topic, the Thames waterfront in London, where as at Southampton and other ports in medieval Britain we will be talking about 'real' trade, but on an altogether larger scale. As we saw earlier, no other city in Britain could compete with the sheer trading muscle of medieval London. It was in a class of its own. Big ports demand good docks and unloading facilities, and that is what a series of excavations in the mid-1970s along the north shore of the river, just south of Thames Street, revealed.

Just as Peter Addyman and Richard Hall are the names we think of whenever York is mentioned, Gustav Milne is the person who will always be linked with the London waterfront. Although we had both spent our professional lives working with waterlogged deposits, it's a sad fact that the worlds of rural prehistory and urban archaeology generally remain resolutely separate.[8] But sometimes, very rarely, they coincide, which is how I came to meet Gus.

A few years ago *Time Team* had made arrangements to investigate a prehistoric pile-built causeway that appeared to run across the Thames quite close to Vauxhall Bridge, in the heart of London.[9] Within the piles were votive offerings of Middle Bronze Age metalwork. Gus was there because of his detailed knowledge of the river and its history. I was there because the site looked like a clone of my own one at Flag Fen in Peterborough. I was immediately impressed by Gus. His knowledge was huge, but he didn't flaunt it. I suppose you could say he had an air of understated authority. I knew about his work, because Maisie had bought most of his publications, as she has always held that wetland archaeology and ancient woodworking know no chronological boundaries. He has written much, and has played a major role in setting medieval London within its wider European contexts.[10] As a field archaeologist I admire him because he has done most of his significant work intensively, in major excavations of relatively short duration – rather like the Coppergate dig in York. In each instance the excavations have had an influence on the subject that far outweighs the actual time spent in digging. Maybe it takes a prehistorian to appreciate that Gus has made one of the largest individual contributions to British archaeology of anyone.

When I was a boy my father had an office in the City, and an antique maiden aunt had a flat in Chelsea that overlooked the river. On visits to London I well remember the excitement of watching as tugs towing strings of barges dropped their funnels to pass under the Albert Bridge. In those days there was no equivalent of the Chelsea Embankment when one went further downstream towards Thames Street, the Norman period riverside road we encountered in Chapter 5. One was denied a clear view of the river by numerous warehouses, many of which, even in the 1950s, were already dilapidated.

The major medieval discoveries along the London waterfront were made in the 1970s, eighties and nineties, during the period of rapid commercial development whose start more or less coincided with the publication of *The Future of London's Past* in 1973. Some work had taken place on the edge of the Thames in the 1960s, but here I want to concentrate on what happened later.

It's not often that the position of an archaeological site threatened by development actually leaves traces on the cityscape. Usually one looks up at some huge glass office block while one's guide confidently asserts that this was 'the site of the Roman Forum', or whatever. It might well have been, but now it is so plainly the site of something altogether more dominant – and horrible – that what had been there previously seems almost to have been erased, the change is so complete and all-enveloping. I hate it when today I drive through Fengate, the scene of my first major excavations in the 1970s, and see the faceless, steel-clad warehouses and cloned 'retail outlets' that now clutter the fringes of suburban Peterborough. They do much more than merely conceal the places where my team and I spent many happy and rewarding summers excavating Bronze Age landscapes. Somehow the contrast provided by their shiny, strident presence seems to deny the gentler existence of what had been there previously. But the sites of the series of excavations that took place along the course of Thames Street are now marked by what Gus has described as a pedestrian-friendly pathway that opens up new riverside vistas for visitors to the historic city, while providing a haven of relative peace in which office workers can enjoy a summer lunch break.[11] I think that's quite a fitting memorial.

For a quarter of a century, following the release of *The Future of London's Past*, the newly established Department of Urban Archaeology of the Museum of London made the waterfront south of Thames Street their principal research priority – and it paid off handsomely. They proved beyond all doubt that this ground had been made up with a progressive series of timber and masonry revetment walls that dated from the tenth to the fifteenth centuries. Their excavations revealed literally tonnes of finds, most of which came from the material that had been back-filled behind the new revetments to provide hard standing along the dockside. Having been dumped at known intervals, which could be precisely dated by using coins and tree-ring dates of timbers from the revetment walls, these deposits have provided a breathtaking collection – a series of massive, dated time-capsules – of objects from daily life throughout the Middle Ages. Furthermore, as most of the deposits were waterlogged, the survival of wood, leather and other organic materials has been excellent. In a way which would have been inconceivable just thirty-five years ago, we can now date, for example, medieval shoes and footwear with the precision that was once reserved for pottery.

The excavations at Trig Lane, which runs into Thames Street from the direction of St Paul's, took place over three seasons in 1974–76. The principal report was completed with amazing rapidity in 1980, and was published soon after.[12] It had an enormous impact at the time. Few archaeologists had seen so much heavy-duty medieval timber and carpentry before. We knew that English carpenters were some of the finest in Europe, thanks to such achievements as the wooden scaffold still within the spire of Salisbury Cathedral, the great octagonal lantern above the transept at Ely Cathedral and the hammer-beam roof of Westminster Hall, but it was fascinating to see what they could produce when faced with a more utilitarian challenge. If the test of good engineering is not to over-engineer, but to produce cost-effective solutions to specific problems, then they seem to have succeeded admirably. I won't attempt to give a phase-by-phase breakdown of the various revetments encountered during the excavations, but the sequence revealed was very detailed: the site was in active use between the late thirteenth and mid-fifteenth centuries, during which Gus Milne was able to distinguish six distinct periods, of which the three main ones (III–V) could be subdivided into four to six phases of rebuilding, replacement and major repair. The report includes detailed analysis of the different joints used in the carpentry of the different waterside revetments.

Whenever I write a book like this, one of the hardest decisions I have to make concerns illustrations. So far I have gone for the general picture, hence my use of maps and town plans. But in this instance I want to show two things. First, just how proficient was the carpentry employed at Trig Lane, and second, how well it was excavated, recorded and published. So I have decided to dive into the depths of the report and extract two illustrations of woodworking in period V (*c.*1380–*c.*1440). The first is of a new revetment (in Milne's terms Group 11) which was constructed around 1380 and marked a fresh advance of the waterfront into the river. The small rectangular structure at the front of the main revetment wall was probably constructed to support a watertank. The second illustration shows two of the main supporting timbers, or staves, revealing the extraordinary complexity of the male joints cut in their lower ends. These were secured within female sockets in the timber base plate, which was in turn secured into the ground by a series of closely set earthfast posts.* The back braces, which both prevented the revetment from buckling outwards when the interior was filled with rubble and soil, and helped to displace pressure on the wall at high tide, were particularly well conceived. They evolved from

---

* The word 'plate' is used to refer to a timber, usually at the top or bottom of a wall, into which the timbers of the wall (and the roof) slotted.

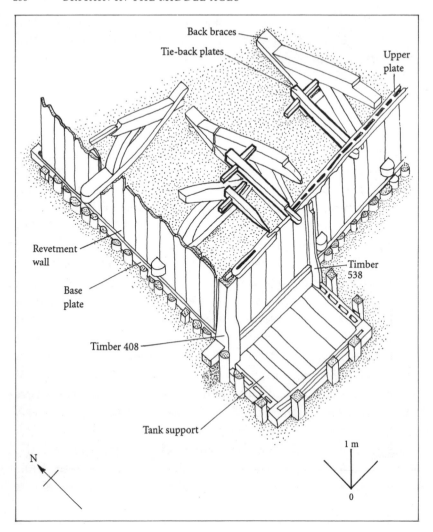

FIG 41   *The riverside revetment at Trig Lane, London, about 1380, as revealed in the excavations of 1974–76. The planks of the revetment wall are fixed into a base plate using mortise and tenon joints. Similar joints secure the upper ends of the planks to an upper plate which also has mortise holes cut in it for a second storey, which has not survived. The back of the revetment wall is secured by heavy back braces and lighter tie-back plates. The small rectangular structure at the front was built to support a water tank.*

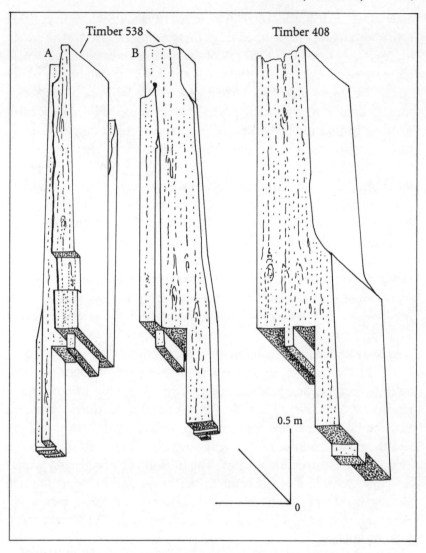

FIG 42 *Two of the main upright timbers or staves that supported the revetment wall at Trig Lane, London (c.1380). Timber 538 is shown in two views, from the east (A) and west (B). The drawing shows the complex arrangement of tenons which fitted into mortises cut in the base plate. The extended feet of the two staves were mortised into the timbers surrounding the smaller platform to the south-west of the main revetment wall.*

a series of back braces of slightly different design which supported earlier revetments. It is interesting that the upper parts of the back braces clearly reach above the top of the existing revetment wall, which quite strongly suggests that there was another storey above the upper plate. The upper plate was further secured by tie-back plates which were secured into position by posts driven into the soil and back-filled material behind the revetment. The suggestion of an upper storey is further supported by the presence of mortises in the top face of that upper plate; presumably these were cut to hold the planks of the upper-storey revetment. Unfortunately these timbers did not survive.

The research at Trig Lane into the details of timber constructional techniques gave added impetus to what was then developing into a sub-discipline: the archaeological study of carpentry. The late Cecil Hewitt, whom I briefly mentioned in the Introduction, took the analysis of certain joints, in particular the scarf joint, to new heights. Scarfs occur where two timbers are joined end to end by an obliquely-cut overlapping joint, which was notched and pegged into position by a seemingly endless succession of evolving pegs and tenons.

If Cecil came across a scarf in a medieval roof in southern England, he once told me, he could sometimes date it to within half, or even a quarter of, a century. I mention that he could do this in southern England because we now appreciate that different parts of the country had their own traditions of carpentry which did not necessarily abide by the same constructional 'rules'. The titles of two of the many papers he wrote give a hint of the complexities he revelled in: 'Scarf Jointing During the Later Thirteenth and Fourteenth Centuries and a Reappraisal of the Origin of Spurred Tenons', and 'The Notched Lap Joint in England'.[13]

Hewitt's crowning achievement was *English Historic Carpentry* (1980),which placed the achievements of English carpenters at the very peak of medieval constructional woodworkers.[14] Today we would consider these men both structural engineers and architects. I find it strange that their achievements have not received the recognition they deserve, especially when I stand beneath the octagon in the transept of Ely Cathedral and stare up at the massive carved trunks of eight gilded oak trees, which seem to hover high above, suspended not by faith or medieval alchemy, but by the good, solid and inspired carpentry of Master Carpenter William of Hurle, who was paid £8 *per annum* between 1328 and 1342.[15] That's the equivalent of about £10,000 a year today. Genius can sometimes be bought quite cheaply.

The planning and construction of polygonal buildings was very much a feature of English medieval architecture. The best-known examples are undoubtedly the chapter houses – where the members of monastic communities met, mainly to discuss the day-to-day management of the monastery and its estates – which accompanied many of the great abbeys. These large open spaces still impress today, but their roofing provided carpenters with some of their greatest challenges. The chapter house at York Minster is extraordinary, with a spire roof soaring above a timber vault. But the greatest example of such carpentry is the octagonal lantern at Ely, which Cecil Hewitt describes as 'without question, the supreme achievement of the English medieval period in polygonally planned timber construction'.

When one visits Ely, one's attention is inevitably drawn upwards to those eight massive oak trees that form the lantern itself. But it could not have been constructed without the timber framework – in effect one of the largest domes in the medieval world – that supports it. The carpentry of this supporting vault is superbly simple in concept but complex in execution, and we know that it was built in close conjunction with the masons who designed and erected the stonework. Masons and carpenters even used the same huge scaffold to bridge the enormous distances. It is only when one looks at the different angles and planes of the various timbers comprising the vault that one realises how superb, for example, was the complex joinery of the central octagonal ring-beam.

Before I leave the topic of woodworking and waterfronts, I would like to return to some of the general themes with which we began this discussion. It would be hard to overestimate the importance of what the excavations along Thames Street revealed. Gus Milne talked in terms of tonnes of artefacts. In addition, the Museum of London now has records of no fewer than a hundred waterside revetments. It would be a mistake to assume that the techniques of carpentry employed were specific to the riverfront alone. For example, when timber framing for domestic buildings grew in popularity, as we saw in Chapter 5,

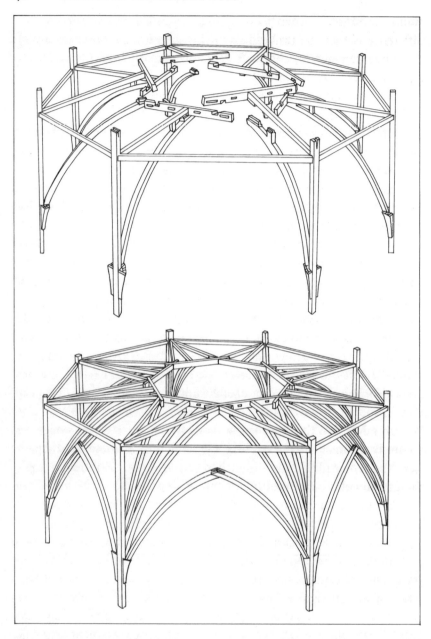

FIG 43   *Two views of the timber framework of the octagonal roof of the transept of Ely Cathedral. The design and supervision was by Master Carpenter William of Hurle, who worked on the construction from 1328 to 1342. The upper*

similar techniques began to be employed on the waterfront; the big difference is that the timbers along the waterfront can be accurately dated by tree-rings. So observations at places like Trig Lane have direct relevance even further inland.[16]

The usual pattern in archaeology is for pottery to be used to date a given set of deposits. But the dumped back-filled material behind the different phases of revetment along the Thames riverfront could be dated far more precisely by the tree-rings of their particular retaining revetment. So timber was giving very precise dates to pottery – which in turn could be used to date other sites both in London and outside. The archaeological 'knock-on effects' of what was revealed along the Thames foreshore are being felt to this day.

I mentioned that many of the finds from the waterfront were organic, and as they were simply swept up when soil was needed for back-filling a new stretch of revetment, they represent an entirely random sample of what was being used by ordinary people at any particular time. Very often in archaeology one is at a loss to decide whether or not certain articles are representative of what people were actually using at a given time. I'm put in mind of those wonderful clothed bodies found in waterlogged oak coffins in Denmark: were these people wearing the everyday apparel of the Bronze Age, or were they in special clothes made to accompany them to the Next World?[17] We can never know. But we can in London, where the huge variety of relatively ordinary bits and pieces leaves one in no doubt that these were the remains of daily life in the Middle Ages. The picture these things paint can be extraordinarily vivid.

Gus Milne describes how the rings, belts, buckles and buttons found in the back-filled material along the waterfront provide graphic evidence for the gradual introduction of mass-production in the medieval market. As he puts it, there was clearly as big a demand for the cheap and cheerful as for the higher-quality stuff. Never before has a series of British excavations revealed so much about footwear in the

drawing shows the construction of the basic framework of the vault, with the complex inner sill beam exploded to show the joints. The central void is filled by an octagonal 'lantern' (not shown here) which allows light to enter the heart of the cathedral.

Middle Ages. Before 1200 everyone wore shoes fastened by drawstrings; fashion was not an issue. Then, quite soon after 1350 we find a huge variety of shoe types. Some were simply slip-on, others were front-laced or side-laced, buckled or latchet.* There is also a bewildering variety of decoration, shapes and styles, ranging from solid-soled pattens, generally worn as overshoes, to elegant 'Poulaines' with long, pointed toes that were usually padded with moss. As time passed different styles of shoes came and went, as did the manner in which they were finished and decorated. Thanks to a superb report on this footwear it is now possible to date medieval shoes in London and elsewhere with considerable precision.[18]

The finds from the London waterfront also illustrate the increasing control and influence of the Guilds. Large numbers of ordinary domestic knives found their way into the back-filled deposits behind the revetment walls, and over a hundred of these carry cutlers' marks; of these, just one could be dated to the thirteenth century; the rest were all fourteenth-century. The variety of finds from the London waterfront is truly extraordinary. All of medieval life is represented, from tiny buttons to large timbers taken from derelict or disused ships. Gus Milne reckons that over thirty ships and boats are represented, some of which probably derived from overseas.

Let me leave the last word on the London waterfront to Gus Milne. Writing about the enduring legacy of the excavations, and the finds recovered from them, he notes that 'Here is a window into the economic, technological and social history of medieval England that is as tangible as it is profound.'[19] That tangible quality is what makes archaeology real to so many people: one can go to the Museum of London and actually see the items that the archaeologists removed from the ground. No picture in a book can ever replace the experience of seeing something, be it never so humble, in the flesh – and of course if one goes down into the reserve collections, there are literally tonnes of items to choose from.

We are drawing towards the end of this book, but I have so far merely touched upon two topics that form the core of most discussions of medieval archaeology, because they survive to this day in the form

---

* A triangular leather thong that is threaded through a pair of holes for fastening.

of superb buildings and romantic ruins. I refer of course to abbeys and castles. I shall have a little more to say about abbeys in the final chapter, but here I must apologise for having treated castles with such apparent indifference. I have to admit that over the years I have suffered aversion therapy when it comes to castles. Inevitably one attends lectures, seminars and conferences as part of an active archaeological career, and castles tend to pop up quite frequently. For me, the trouble has been that after one or two stunning introductory slides, most lecturers then slip into an exhaustive discussion of defences and the details of their subsequent development. I suppose the general trends are fairly interesting: how rectangular keeps, such as the Tower of London, were replaced by rounded towers, such as Clifford's Tower in York, as these were stronger and did not have sharp corners that could be undermined. But even so, this sort of information hardly grabs me by the throat. It is interesting, certainly, but not fascinating, and to me the details of castle defences are, at best, dull.

So as this is a book about my own exploration of medieval archaeology, I decided I would have to give castles a miss. Then, just as I was completing the final draft of the manuscript I spotted a new book in the lists of Windgather Press, a relatively young publishing house that is publishing a superb series of books on medieval and landscape archaeology. Its title accurately describes what is inside: *Castles in Context*.[20] It's a superb book that everyone interested in medieval archaeology should read, because it describes why castles were built and how they were used by the people living in the area. It blows away the cobwebs that still surround medieval siege warfare. It's a book about the uses of power and how a large and spectacular building can attract attention over the centuries, simply by its presence.

The principal debate surrounding castles has to do with their central role. This boils down to a simple question: were they primarily intended to be military structures, or symbols of power, influence and prestige? This is a debate with which I am quite familiar, because Iron Age hillforts have been discussed in these terms for at least thirty years, and still there is no consensus among prehistorians – although most would agree that a simple, or sole, military or symbolic role seems unlikely. Hitherto the usual approach to British castles has been to see them as military structures with defences that evolved to meet new threats, such as the introduction of gunpowder. Their positioning within the landscape has tended to be analysed in terms of strategic military considerations alone. Windsor Castle, for example, was seen to control an important crossing point of the Thames. While such factors undoubtedly played a part – even a major part – the visually striking location of so many castles, such as Alnwick, Dover, Windsor, Scarborough or Conwy, is surely about more than mere tactical advantage. Such locations are commanding in every sense of the word. Many castles, too, were built to look beautiful: the graceful banded masonry and polygonal towers of Caernarfon being a prime example. These buildings, like Durham or Lincoln Cathedrals, were deliberately positioned in the landscape to impress.

The evidence for actual combat is still quite rare in Iron Age hillforts, but as Robert Liddiard points out in *Castles in Context* they were capable of both offence and defence. As offensive structures they were important logistically and as bases for mounting raids and attacks. On longer marches, large forces could be housed within the outer walls of castles along the route. Castles are, however, most often seen in the popular imagination as defensive structures, designed to resist set-piece sieges. Medieval sieges are nearly always portrayed as prolonged and bloody, which indeed they could be. But extended sieges were time consuming and costly to both sides, in men and materials. Consequently a series of military conventions were developed that were aimed at sidestepping or avoiding them. One such convention has been termed 'conditional respite', where the besieging commander agreed to lift the siege for a fixed period while a beleaguered garrison petitioned its lord for aid.[21] There were many other recognised formalities to siege warfare, most of which were intended to resolve the matter one way or another without excessive bloodshed or expense.

I mentioned that certain castles were clearly sited to impress the viewer. Sometimes the landscape itself was modified to make the castle look better. The stunning situation of Leeds Castle in Kent is made the more splendid by a late-thirteenth-century-designed landscape that was also laid out to look magnificent from within the building itself. Other designed landscapes that surrounded castles were intended to be agriculturally productive, or more often to be fine places for hunting. These were as much about lordly recreation as anything else; in essence they were parks.

It's important not to look at castles merely as fortifications or isolated structures, because many clues as to how they were actually used can be seen in their immediate surroundings. The two main entrances to the Iron Age hillfort at Maiden Castle in Dorset consist of a complex labyrinth of ditches, banks and ramparts. In theory such complexity was intended to slow down and baffle attacking forces, which undoubtedly it would have done. But even today, as one passes through these entranceworks one is struck by their sheer scale. The route into the fortress was clearly intended not just to repel attackers, but to impress visitors.

Robert Liddiard has reconstructed the journey of approach into Ruthlin Castle, Denbighshire, as it might have been in the fourteenth century.[22] As the visitor draws closer, the castle dominates everything. Approaching the town the traveller passes the gallows, the symbol of the lordly family, the de Greys, as dispensers of royal justice. Entering the marketplace, with its pillory, the route passes the houses of the richest citizens outside the gate. After a journey through the deer park, fishponds and orchards, the castle is then entered through the main gatehouse, which gives onto a courtyard, and towers with commanding views of the surrounding landscape. In essence this is a theatrical experience designed to impress even casual visitors with the power and importance of the de Greys. Many of the factors that affect the way we now regard castles also apply to walled settlements, with which they are often closely associated.

There have been many references in this book to town and city walls. Most of us either take them for granted, or are ignorant of their presence. Every time I take a train from King's Lynn, my preferred route to London, I have to drive to the station through the magnificent South Gate in the town walls, which now stands in rather sad isolation, as the walls on either side have been demolished. As elsewhere in Britain the original course of the walls is reflected in the layout of the streets, but in Lynn we are fortunate to have good stretches of wall surviving, though in a rather vestigial state. One of the better stretches now incorporates a pub, the Hob in the Well, which is an excellent reason to pay it a visit.

At Lynn there is nothing remotely comparable to, say, the magnificent walls at York, Caernarfon, Chester or Conwy. Even so, it is possible to learn a great deal about the town's walls simply by studying them closely. The great South Gate, for example, must have been designed by someone with as good a knowledge of church as of military architecture, which might suggest that it was constructed as much to impress as to defend. Similarly, a close examination of the stone used in the surviving stretches of wall shows that in certain places rocks were used that simply do not occur in Britain, but are relatively commonplace in the Baltic. Presumably they were taken to Norfolk as ships' ballast in the days when Lynn was a leading port and a member of the Hanseatic League,* that extraordinary northern medieval precursor to the Common Market which at its height boasted two hundred towns as members. It was founded in the thirteenth century and survived in places until the seventeenth.

King's Lynn was one of the most prosperous British ports outside London during the Middle Ages, having access to ten counties up the River Great Ouse. It was known as 'the Warehouse of the Wash', and if any place needed walls to defend its wealth, then Lynn did. The walls were built and added to in the light of specific perceived threats, such as civil war in the mid-twelfth and thirteenth centuries and fear of French invasion in the mid-fourteenth. We will discuss the significance of this later, but these threats can hardly be seen as either constant or immediate; the best way to describe them would be 'low-level'.

Until very recently, I had the notion that town walls in medieval times were restricted to certain of the great cities or to a few border areas, where massive fortifications came to resemble castles more than communities.[23] Most people will be aware of the impressive fortifications which were built along the Welsh Marches by King Edward I in the late thirteenth century. These were intended to symbolise to the recently defeated Welsh the military might of England. They look very impressive indeed, but were they actually constructed to sustain serious and prolonged attack – and were such attacks a constant reality? Their very survival in such good condition suggests a possible answer. These are questions which I will touch on shortly. At this stage all I wish to

---

* The term derives from the German word *hanse*, meaning a guild or company.

point out is that Edward's campaign of massive military enhancement along the Welsh borders was taking place in the heart of Britain, where people still had to go about their daily lives.

Edward, who was a very able ruler, took an unusually close personal interest in his castles along the Welsh border. He appreciated the fact that ordinary life had to continue. Indeed, it was not in his financial interest to stop it. So he built a series of planned defended towns which were twinned with the royal castles at Aberystwyth, Caernarfon, Conwy, Flint and Rhuddlan. These new defended towns, whose grid layout of streets was planned, are known to historians as 'bastides' after closely similar new towns in France that probably inspired them. Edward did not just concentrate on the Welsh borders, and built bastides elsewhere, at places like Berwick-upon-Tweed, Kingston-upon-Hull and New Winchelsea.[24]

I mention this information to show that the subject of town walls is extremely complex, and cannot readily be separated from other issues such as castles. Like castles, each walled town should be seen within its regional and historical context. Sometimes the foundation of a walled town may be part of a wider political or military process, like, for example the Alfredan *burhs* or Scottish burghs, the Edwardian bastides along the Welsh borders, or coastal towns protected against cross-Channel raiding like New Winchelsea. Nevertheless their subsequent histories will largely be determined by local factors, and walled towns, like urban archaeology in general, are probably best approached on a case-by-case basis. In the past the tendency was to view them, like castles, as being almost entirely defensive. Today we realise that just like their prehistoric forebears the hillforts, medieval walled towns were also important symbols of power and authority. The analysis of precisely what power, or powers, might have motivated such works – be it aristocratic, royal, ecclesiastical, mercantile or merely local – must reflect the individual histories of the places concerned. All we can say at this stage is that such analyses are never likely to be straightforward.

A recent survey of walled towns in Britain has drawn attention to their quantity and extraordinary diversity.[25] The authors, Oliver Creighton and Robert Higham, point out that the great majority of towns in medieval Britain were undefended, but even so, the numbers with walls are still large. There are also some surprises. Although such an exercise is fraught with difficulties, they estimate that of some 640 towns (boroughs as opposed to *burhs*) in England, just 211 were defended. In Wales, the proportion was 91:55. A higher proportion of towns in England were defended in the tenth century than at any other time. At this period there were relatively few towns in Wales, where the settlement pattern was essentially rural. Most Welsh towns came into existence, often through plantation, after the Norman Conquest, when they were provided with walls from the outset.

Given the long history of conflict between Scotland and England, one might expect many towns north of the border to be defended, but in fact only about 5 per cent of Scottish towns (burghs*) were walled before the fifteenth century. This might seem strange, given that we know that the taking and retaking of burghs was a feature of the Scottish Wars of Independence. It would be wrong to suppose that Scottish towns were somehow less significant than their counterparts south of the border. Scotland did indeed have a largely rural economy, but as I have already noted in passing, thanks to top-quality excavations at places like Aberdeen and Perth, it is now appreciated that towns north of the border played a far more important role than was once believed. There were many of them, too. I counted seventy-six on a recently published map of burghs that appeared in the records before 1430.[26] As one might expect, most were on the southern and the eastern coastal lowlands. These places were towns in every sense of the word, and the local communities would have had much to lose if they fell into enemy hands. Yet still the vast majority were undefended.

Creighton and Higham suggest that the relative rarity of walled towns in both Scotland and England along the borders (Edward's coastal port at Berwick perhaps being the exception that proves the rule) reflects the fact that defences were not necessarily constructed in times of conflict.† They may have been built for other reasons, to do with the expression of power and feudal aristocratic authority, but – and this is important – in the light of a *lower* level of threat, as we saw

---

* Traditionally founded by David I (1124–53), Scottish burghs were distinct from their English equivalents, the boroughs. They were more uniform in their laws and customs, and until the Act of Union in 1707 they had a more unified voice in national politics.

† English examples of undefended towns close to the Scottish borders include Hexham and Morpeth.

along the Welsh borders. The contrast between the situation along the Welsh Marches and the Scottish borders is most striking, and this seems a convincing, if counter-intuitive, argument to explain it.[27]

The suggestion made by Creighton and Higham is bound to cause controversy, because people are wedded to the simplistic notion that major defences equate with all-out warfare. I and other prehistorians have been ridiculed as 'Merrie Englanders' for suggesting that Iron Age hillforts were built more to display power and control than to provide secure military defence – and nothing else. I would not deny for one moment that hillforts could indeed have been used as places of refuge and as forts in times of conflict, but the fact remains that the vast bulk of the population were living in undefended settlements in the open countryside around the forts. Furthermore, convincing war cemeteries are either rare or absent in the many hillforts that have been excavated, but bodies with sword cuts are known elsewhere, in both the Bronze and Iron Ages.[28] So fighting certainly happened – but not in the obvious places. Sadly, shortly before I wrote this, terrorists exploded bombs on London buses and the Underground, but not in defended places such as Chelsea Barracks or the concrete bunkers beneath the Ministry of Defence.

Creighton and Higham's argument is best supported by the approach to town walls adopted by the authorities of the medieval Church. The authors suggest that a relatively small proportion of towns founded by ecclesiastical lords were defended. But the few that were are very instructive. At Beverley, Glasgow and St Andrews the towns were given stone gateways, but no walls; at other places, such as Bury St Edmunds, Salisbury and Wells, initiatives to build complete circuits just 'fizzled out'; smaller ecclesiastical boroughs, such as Farnham, were marked out by earthworks that served as boundary markers, but were never meant to resist attack. A gateway says all sorts of things to the traveller: he is made aware that he is arriving somewhere special, and that the authorities running the place must be special too. Maybe something similar was in the minds of the people who built the South Gate at King's Lynn, which we know was a prosperous mercantile town, noted for its civic pride.

I want now to take a brief look at what today we would refer to as medieval infrastructure. Imports have to be distributed, and the wool and cloth exported from Britain had to reach ports somehow. Roads were also needed to bring food and other provisions to the many towns. But surely medieval roads were a mess? Indeed, one of the most enduring symbols of medieval muddle and incompetence concerns the state of the roads. I remember at school learning how the Romans built those fabulous paved roads that ran across the countryside as straight as a die. The entire enterprise exuded the sort of military efficiency we were being brought up to admire. Subsequently I have learned that many Roman roads were actually crooked, and the civil (as opposed to military) ones were not always very well constructed. Even so, the pictures we were shown of hapless medieval peasants vainly attempting to drive overloaded wagons through mud up to the axles have persisted. But what were medieval roads actually like? Were they really that atrocious?

The first answer is that many medieval roads were in fact Roman. We saw in Chapter 1 that the trading networks of southern England in Middle Saxon times were largely based around Roman roads, which must have been kept in some sort of repair, or they couldn't have been used. Very often Roman roads form part of the foundations of modern roads – and very good foundations they make, too. The modern road that ran through that Roman settlement at Heronbridge just outside Chester was following the line of Watling Street on its way into Chester from the south. Sometimes the modern road veered slightly off the Roman alignment, and then it was possible to dig through the turf and reveal the edges of the Roman road, but mostly the Roman layers remained hidden beneath tarmac.

I came across the Roman Fen Causeway on many occasions. This was a military road constructed in the mid-first century AD, quite possibly as part of the suppression of Boudica's revolt of AD 60 and 61. Usually one found scraps of Romano-British pottery, and maybe the odd coin. But at one time I was excavating at a place where the road had been used in medieval times as the drive to a stone-built house or hunting lodge on the very edge of the fen. As a result there was lots of pottery, but none of it was Roman. Instead, what I found was the usual later medieval green-glazed stuff that is so common in the area. It was hard to tell whether the road had actually been resurfaced in medieval times, because its surface had been scratched by modern ploughing, but I'm pretty certain that it had been, as there was a large amount of gravel lying around the place, and this was all mixed up with green glazed pottery. To be frank, I don't really think this an issue: if you are using a road regularly, then you make sure you keep it in working order, especially if, as in this case, good supplies of fresh gravel could be found two or three hundred metres to the east.

Paul Stamper also finds it hard to accept the 'quagmire' view of medieval roads in Britain.[29] He points to the fact that documents make many references to the regular and frequent movement of royal and aristocratic households from one manor to another. He gives the example of Edward I and his large retinue, who managed to travel on average thirty-two kilometres a day when on the move. He notes that water transport would have been used for most large or bulky loads, just as in Roman and post-medieval times, but he also quotes the example of the large Lincolnshire limestone industry, which moved most of its stone by road. So it must have been feasible.

Numerous urban excavations have shown what happens if roads are abandoned. As we saw in Lundenwic in the Middle Saxon period, when alleyways were abandoned rubbish soon accumulated on them, rendering them useless. Similarly in Colchester, immediately after Roman rule the walled area was largely abandoned, and some of the Roman roads were soon covered with soil and vegetation. I have witnessed the process myself: a track that was once used by tractors and other farm traffic was diverted, and just twenty years later the old route, which had been consolidated every winter with chalk rubble and hardcore, now supports sturdy young trees of beech and holly. You certainly couldn't drive even a powerful modern tractor along it without several hours' work with a chainsaw. Roads have to be maintained if they are to stay in use. There may well have been many quagmires in wet winters in the less accessible and more remote parts of the country, but the people who constructed Britain's towns and cathedrals would have been perfectly capable of maintaining the most regularly used roads in good working order. To suggest otherwise is slightly insulting.

Many medieval stone bridges are still of course in use, having been repaired, enlarged and resurfaced many times subsequently. I regularly use two: one takes the road from Huntingdon to Godmanchester across the River Great Ouse, the other takes the old Great North Road across the River Nene at Wansford. My favourite, however, is the strange triangular bridge in the small Fenland town of Crowland. Crowland, or Croyland, was the site of one of the great Fenland abbeys (founded by St Guthlac around 716), and its ruins still dominate the small, higgledy-piggledy town around it. Originally the bridge crossed the place where three streams came together. According to Pevsner it was built in the fourteenth century, although a similar bridge is also mentioned in 943.[30] This was just the sort of spot where one would expect myths and tales to accumulate, which may explain the presence of a strange sitting stone statue with a smooth, featureless and ghostly face which still gives me the creeps when I walk past on a winter's evening. Pevsner suggests that the statue may actually be of Christ, and was probably taken from a gable end of the abbey after the Dissolution. Sadly the three streams, like most of Crowland's water-ways, have long since been filled in, rendering the bridge stranded and pointless. Even so, it still has a powerful presence. One day the local authorities might have the imagination to restore the waterways and turn this small and characterful Fenland town into what it was in medieval times: a pocket-sized Venice. It would certainly be a great, and possibly profitable, improvement.

The medieval bridges that still survive are built from stone, but it seems most unlikely that this was always the case. We know that medieval carpenters were masters of their craft, and we also know that the Romano-British were capable of building bridges from both stone and timber.[31] Given the fact that many of the skills of masonry were lost in Saxon times, it seems highly probable that most earlier medieval bridges were built from wood. It is harder to achieve the very large spans of a stone bridge using timber trestles, but there is almost no limit to what can be bridged if sufficient timbers are used – here I am put in mind of those truly staggering nineteenth-century railway bridges that crossed, or rather filled, mountain gorges in western North America. But what is the evidence for early timber bridges in Britain? This is where Chris Salisbury, the dedicatee of this book, enters the picture.

Maisie and I knew Chris for maybe twenty-five years. He was a regular visitor to Flag Fen and our other sites. His first visit was on a weekend when we were working in a gravel quarry in the Welland Valley just north of Peterborough, and he seemed so knowledgeable that we assumed he was a fellow professional. In those days we worked in the evenings and on weekends, because we had no statutory rights whatsoever. If a gravel company wanted to wipe out a site they could, and would, do so. Most of the good ones would provide notice of their intentions, but they didn't have to. This meant that we relied very heavily on the goodwill of the companies, and also made it necessary to keep a pool of local volunteers handy in case some emergency arose. That was why we would regularly open our excavations to local people on weekends. It was a two-way process. They got to see what was happening on their doorstep, and we got to meet them and spot the people who were genuinely interested. I'm glad to say that several of the people we met at such open days went on to join the profession.

One might have thought that when the government introduced the planning requirement (PPG-16) to consider archaeology in any new development, all our problems would be over. That was in 1989. But all existing Planning Consents were exempt, because such legislation can never be retroactive – which is quite reasonable. Many gravel quarries operate on a long-term basis, and acquire their Planning Consents well in advance. If they did not, they would have to close down operations and make their staff redundant every time the quarry moved onto fresh land. In some parts of England, and one thinks immediately of the Thames and Trent gravels, consents were very long-lived. Consequently old-style, pre-PPG-16, voluntary arrangements continued, with funding provided by sources other than the gravel companies. Gill Hey's recent project at Yarnton, near Oxford, which we discussed in Chapter 1, was a case in point: it was funded by English Heritage, just as we used to be in the 1970s and eighties.

After several visits to each other's sites I learned that Chris Salisbury's doctorate was in medicine, and not archaeology. In fact he was a full-time GP, and did his archaeology in his spare moments. He maintained close links with all the gravel companies working in the Trent Valley, and although he operated alone and from home, he would regularly visit the professional teams working in the area and inform them of his latest discoveries. He made some remarkable finds. I once visited a quarry near Shardlow in Derbyshire where he had discovered a Bronze Age logboat that had sunk because it had been overloaded with large rocks. I took a photo of him leaning on the boat and jotting something down in the small notebook he always carried with him.*

Chris was particularly adept at finding fish weirs, the rows of posts or stakes that were used to channel fish into nets or woven traps. These seem to have been more frequently employed on the Trent than elsewhere, but one cannot tell whether this is a reflection of ancient reality or of Chris's assiduity. Personally I suspect the latter. Chris's work on fish weirs showed the extent to which people exploited rivers for food from pre-Roman times right through the medieval period and later. It was a very serious, almost industrial, business and would have provided people with the sources of protein and oils which they needed to take them through the months of winter. Chris retired from medicine in 1992 and started his second career as a full-time archaeologist. Sadly he died in 2004. But he left us with one final discovery, for which he will always be remembered: aside from the roof of Lincoln Cathedral, it remains the largest medieval timber structure in eastern England. I am talking here about the wooden bridge that once carried the medieval road from London to Derby across the Trent.

It may sound obvious, but timber bridges do not survive well when they fall out of use. Frequently they are destroyed, or cannibalised for a new one. Failing that they rot and disintegrate, or simply wash away in the winter floods. The modern Trent crossing of the A6 Derby road today is by Cavendish Bridge, about 1.3 kilometres upstream of Hemington quarry, near Castle Donington in Leicestershire. This quarry is one of those operations that was granted its Planning Consent before 1989, but fortunately the company running it was very cooperative, and Chris was able to make regular visits in his new capacity as freelance roving archaeologist. His four-wheel drive was a mobile archaeological rapid response unit, equipped with everything one would need for a dig, from surveying equipment and shovels to hot tea.

The Hemington find is extremely important because it revealed

---

* It appears in *Britain BC*, between pages 272 and 273.

how difficult it must have been to maintain an important river crossing in use. Chris discovered the remains of no fewer than three wooden bridges across an old course of the River Trent, which it turned out had been built in quick succession over just two centuries. If anything can, this surely proves how seriously medieval people took their roads. Chris found the timbers of the first bridge in August 1993, on one of his regular visits to the quarry. Realising that he had discovered more than he could deal with on his own, he contacted the Leicester Archaeological Unit, who mounted a rescue dig, funded by the county council.[32]

It turned out that the first bridge at Hemington was also the latest. The timbers Chris had found were parts of two angular but boat-shaped piers that would have supported the bridge superstructure. The two piers on the northern side of the river were made from stone whose chamfered, ashlar* blocks were held together with iron cramps sealed with lead. Above the stone piers were masonry columns that would have supported the timbers of the bridge proper. The four piers together formed a major bridge, some fifty metres long. Tree-ring dates suggest that it was built in the 1230s.

As work on the thirteenth-century bridge was drawing to a close the team came across the timbers of the second bridge, which was entirely built from timber and dated to Norman times (an initial tree-ring date of 1096 has been obtained from Nottingham University). So another project had to be rapidly mounted and funded, this time thanks to English Heritage. Most of the timbers came from two diamond-shaped pier bases or caissons made from four massive oak beams. These were well built, and were held together by cross-braces secured into the bed of the river by upright posts before being filled with stone rubble. Many of the constructional forms and joints were hitherto unknown, which is not altogether surprising, as this is the only eleventh-century timber bridge spanning a major river yet found in Britain.

Gus Milne took part in the project, with his great experience of large-scale carpentry, and he became very excited for two reasons.

---

* The term ashlar refers to square-finished or square-hewn masonry with fine joints and an even surface.

First, the Norman bridge combined the two techniques of construction that we have already come across in both domestic buildings and the waterfront. Saxon buildings were built around posts driven into the ground. In Norman and later times this earthfast technique was replaced by timber frames, but at Hemingford we see both techniques being used, which would suggest that the widespread changes that affected so many different spheres of construction were the result of people gradually adopting an improved technology, simply because it worked and made practical sense.

The second thing that sparked Milne's interest concerned the details of construction, which included joints that had never been recognised previously in Britain. A team of specialists are now examining the timbers under ideal conditions in a store, and Milne's initial enthusiasm has proved more than justified. Not only is the carpentry innovative and so far unique, but its preservation is first rate. This applies particularly to those timbers whose surfaces were not worn down by the river. Here evidence has been found of the original carpenters' marking-out lines around several of the joints. It has also become apparent that much of the carpentry was done *in situ*, and by eye, as some of the joints are not absolutely square, but yet they fit well – which would suggest that the craftsmen accommodated the unevenness of the larger timbers by shaping the joints appropriately. Perhaps most extraordinary of all – and this is something I would have loved to have discovered myself on a prehistoric timber site – they found a scratched graffito working drawing on one of the timbers, which clearly showed how the box-frame caisson structure was to be assembled. As one of the team remarked, it was just as well that medieval craftsmen didn't have cigarette packs to draw on, because then the sketch would never have survived.

Apparently Gus Milne jokingly remarked to the team on site that as they had an eleventh- and a thirteenth-century bridge, they ought to find a twelfth-century one between them – which is almost what happened next, except that the final bridge they found was early-thirteenth-century; but even so it spanned the chronological gap between the other two. This was an altogether less ambitious structure, comprising a double row of posts that ran across the river for some fifty-six metres. The roadway would have been supported on cross-pieces above bearer beams that ran along the two rows. However, the Trent can be a fast-flowing and unforgiving river, and all three bridges eventually washed away. In fact the archaeologists were almost washed away when they were about to lift the timbers. They had hired a crane for the job, and the day before they were due to start working the river burst its banks and flooded the quarry. It took four weeks for very large pumps to remove the water before work could resume.

So far we have concentrated on what has survived from below the waterline. But lying above one of the caissons of the Norman bridge the excavators found a large, trestle-like arrangement of beams that probably formed part of a bridge superstructure. This glimpse of what may have stood high above the water clearly shows that these medieval bridges involved heavy-duty engineering, and is further proof that roads, transport and travel in the Middle Ages were matters that were taken very seriously. These were not the kind of people who would have been content to battle their way through ill-maintained quagmires.

I want now to turn my attention briefly to industrial archaeology, a topic that we usually tend to associate with the Industrial Revolution of the eighteenth and nineteenth centuries. As many readers of my books will be aware, I tend to take a long view of the past and am very distrustful of terms like 'revolution', whether they be applied to the Neolithic or the nineteenth century. Of course, nobody could possibly deny that there was a rapid population increase during the so-called Industrial Revolution, and that many of the great cities of northern Britain expanded rapidly too. But terms like 'the Industrial Revolution' disguise general trends and overemphasise those periods when change became particularly rapid. They also imply that it was one specific aspect of society that changed or was the instrument of change, whereas in reality the situation was invariably far more complex than that. Recently industrial archaeologists such as Professor Marilyn Palmer have stressed the importance of placing industry within its landscape and social setting.[33] It was part of something much more broad. Industry does not work in a vacuum; it can only exist to serve the needs of people.

In the past two or three decades there has been a huge expansion of our knowledge of medieval industry. Certain areas, such as the Wealden ironworks in Kent and East Sussex, have been known about for some time. Others have been suspected, but not proved until recently. A good example of the latter was the exposure of fifteenth-century deep mining in a modern opencast coal pit at Coleorton in Leicestershire, where pit props from so-called pillar and stall mines (a system of parallel galleries where the walls of the galleries helped to support the roof) gave tree-ring dates between 1450 and 1463.[34] We also know that woollen cloth, for example, was important in the Manchester area long before cotton entered the scene there and huge new mills transformed the industrial landscape. Similarly, ironworking was happening around places like Huddersfield well before the Victorian ironmasters took hold of the trade and exploited it for all it was worth.

A recent research project carried out through Bradford University and the local Huddersfield Archaeological Society has demonstrated that medieval ironworks were far more substantial and industrial in scale than I, for one, had ever realised. The site in question is on land within a campus of Huddersfield University at a place known as Myers Wood, about 5.5 kilometres outside the city. It was found by members of the Archaeological Society who were actually looking for signs of prehistoric settlement. But instead of the Bronze Age barrows they had expected they came across large mounds of iron-smelting slag, near a stream in the depths of the wood. The Society had the good sense to realise that this was outside their experience, so they called on Dr Gerry McDonnell from the Department of Archaeological Sciences at Bradford University to help them out. With McDonnell's assistance they put together funding for excavations, and the results have been truly eye-opening.[35] It was originally believed that the slag mound, or mounds, was confined to one place, but after three seasons of excavations and detailed geophysical survey (something that Bradford University has always done superbly) it became clear that the workings covered the entire wood, which was declared a site of national importance by English Heritage.

I can only hope to give an impression of size and scale here, otherwise we will enter the strange world of tap slags, hammer-scale and other daunting terms which are probably best left for another time and a different book. However, the excavations did provide clear evidence that the ironworks mostly dated to the twelfth, thirteenth and fourteenth centuries. After the Black Death the original site was abandoned, and there are indications that activity shifted to elsewhere in the wood, probably down towards a stream which could have been used for water power. As I said earlier, the scale of the ironworking prior to the plague was indeed industrial.

The site was being used to smelt iron from ore. Survey and excavation revealed some six hundred tonnes of slag in six main heaps, which would indicate that about 2,200 tonnes of ore had been roasted to produce 1,100 tonnes of metal. So far the remains of five furnaces have been recovered, but it is very likely that a large number of other furnaces would have been located uphill of the slagheaps that went with the five furnaces. In addition the team found signs of a smithing hearth built into the natural slope of a bank – which would indicate that this was indeed a true ironworks, and not just a metal-producing plant. There was also evidence in this remarkably well-preserved site for the other ancillary activities one would associate with ironworking, such as ore extraction and charcoal-making.

Finally, who were the ironmakers of Myers Wood? Here our story acquires a uniquely medieval twist. For some time academics at Bradford had been looking into Cistercian methods of ironmaking, as practised at the Yorkshire abbeys of Byland and Rievaulx. A monastic grange (a farm attached to a monastery) is known to have existed at a place known as 'Tymberwood', less than a mile south of Myers Wood. This grange was linked to the Cistercian abbey at Roche, near Rotherham. So everything suggests that Myers Wood was a Cistercian enterprise. I find that an extraordinary thought. One normally associates monks with mead, rather than industrial muscle.

CHAPTER EIGHT

The End of the Middle Ages?

WE SAW IN THE INTRODUCTION that different scholars take a variety of dates to mark the end of the Middle Ages: some prefer the Battle of Bosworth (1485), others the Dissolution of the Monasteries (1538), while most archaeologists usually opt for 1550, possibly because it's a nice round number. Not surprisingly, my sympathies lie with the medieval archaeologists, if only because it is a date that is sufficiently vague to be largely irrelevant. People certainly did not wake up, stretch their limbs and stare out of the window with wide-eyed wonder, conscious that today, 1 January 1551, was the dawn of a new epoch, any more than they were aware that in AD 44 southern Britain was now a part of the Roman Empire. For most ordinary people in the days before instant communication, the events of history were merely ripples on the surface of time, only of relevance to subsequent scholarship.

I tend to take the view that often the great turning points in history happen quite slowly, and during times of relative stability when nothing much seems to be happening. It's only later, when circumstances change – and maybe change quite slightly – that the underlying changes that started much earlier become evident, and then the entire process speeds up. In British prehistory I think we can see this happening in the Middle Bronze Age, sometime between 1500 and 1200 BC, when changes in religion and ritual marked a gradual shift in emphasis from a way of life that had its deepest roots in the New Stone Age to a different, and more hierarchical, set of societies that would later (and mistakenly) be dubbed 'Celtic'. That way of life, like the wonderful Celtic Art it engendered, was to have influences that would extend through Roman times and into the Saxon period. Perhaps I should add here that the changes I believe happened in Bronze

Age Britain were also happening across most of northern and western Europe too.

I have long had an instinctive feeling that the major change of the past two millennia did not happen around 1550, whatever subsequent scholars of the Enlightenment might have us believe. The more I look into the past 2,000 years, the more convinced I become that Britain and north-western Europe reinvented themselves in the centuries after the fall of the western Roman Empire – those inappropriately named Dark Ages. The latter years of the Roman Empire and the dawn of medieval Europe have been termed by some scholars Late Antiquity, and it was then, when the ideals of Greece and Rome met the cultures of northern Europe, in a world where intellectual discourse was facilitated by education, and indeed by the Church, that great changes happened. The result was what some have seen as the first European Economic Community, when long-distance trade and communication flourished, and Carolingian Europe was stimulated by new ideas from the emerging Islamic Empire. This, as we saw in Chapter 1, was the truly formative epoch that Michael McCormick writes about with such erudition and insight. This period set changes afoot that would last right through the Middle Ages and into our own time.

To put it bluntly, I do not believe that, at a fundamental level, the Middle Ages ever did come to an end. Yes, there were very significant changes in the fifteenth and sixteenth centuries, but whether these were as critical as, say, the long-term impact of the Black Death, is very much open to question. With those thoughts in mind, let us examine the end-that-wasn't of the Middle Ages.

From the outset I have regarded this book as a personal exploration of a fascinating period that I wanted to share with my readers. I have not attempted to write a balanced textbook that does justice to all the principal topics – and I have said so more than once. I am aware that I will be criticised by some academic reviewers for not saying more about Scotland or Wales in the Middle Ages, but I would say in my defence that both these areas were on the periphery of the 'engine room' of change. We saw from our brief examination of north-western England that even peripheral areas had their own dynamics, but they were responding to change, rather than causing it. And in a book of this length I cannot afford the time and space to stray away from the central story – especially when that story has seen so many recent major revisions.

I am also aware that I have been unable to tackle certain key topics simply because they have been so well researched that I cannot do them justice in the space allowed me without misleading oversimplification. I have already alluded to castles, and monasteries are the other case in point. From time to time I have mentioned them, for example at the close of the last chapter and in our discussions of Shapwick, but I am not sure that they are of the same central importance to our story as, say, the development of London or the impact of the Black Death.

I have felt obliged to write that brief apologia because the Dissolution of the Monasteries by Henry VIII is seen as one of the key events contributing to the end of the Middle Ages, and so far I have only mentioned monasteries in passing. The Dissolution is always regarded as a defining moment in history, which indeed it was. But if one steps back and takes a longer view, it was also one of those historical waves on the surface that arose as the result of deeper seismic movements – movements that had probably been afoot since the aftermath of the Black Death in the mid-fourteenth century. But certainly, as historical one-off events went, it had a huge impact: assets caught up in land and buildings were realised, the Exchequer benefited, and new money was channelled in fresh directions.

One local example springs to mind. The Earls of Bedford acquired the estates of several abbeys in the Dissolution, including Woburn Abbey (hence the name of their grand country house in Bedfordshire) and others in the Fens, which could be allied with their pre-existing late medieval estates in the area. In 1630 Francis, the fourth Earl of Bedford,* following a request to him by landowners in the region, set about draining his Fenland estates and huge tracts of land all around them, organising his own agents and groups of local landowners to contribute to drainage schemes – a move that was to have a profound effect on people living within and around a very large area of eastern England.[1] One wonders whether this would have happened as early as the beginning of the seventeenth century had Henry VIII not done what he did so controversially in 1538.

---

* His son William, also a keen drainer of the Fens, was the fifth Earl and first Duke.

So what was the role of monasteries in the Middle Ages? It would be a mistake to make simple blanket statements. As we saw in urban archaeology, some were successful, others less so. Many were rural, but many too were attracted to towns, and in the case of London they clustered there like bees around a honeypot. Many acted as landlords of granges, or of farms or estates in which they had a significant interest. Most ordinary village people would have communicated with the monasteries by way of their local agents. There were also huge disparities of wealth. Glastonbury Abbey, always a successful establishment with large estates, plus the pilgrim/tourist revenue that followed the 'discovery' of King Arthur's tomb there in 1191, had an income of over £3,000 in 1536, two years prior to the Dissolution.[2] By contrast, in the same year the poor nuns of Wilberfoss Priory in the Vale of York had to subsist on just £40.[3] But was the entire system so corrupt that it needed complete abolition in 1538? The answer has to be a qualified no. That having been said, there is abundant evidence that all was not well with the system long before Henry VIII decided on such drastic measures.

I shall return to the Dissolution shortly, but now I want briefly to think about monastic archaeology, because it illustrates well the problems that many archaeologists are having to face in a world where 'pure' research is no longer held in such high regard. I do not wish to be unduly cynical, but I remain to be convinced that this is an entirely bad thing, because at least some of the supposedly 'pure' research of the recent past was merely a means to establish an academic reputation. Whether or not the new knowledge mattered, or had any actual relevance, was another issue.

There has been a wealth of literature about the archaeology of monasteries, their estates and their surviving buildings. At the most general or popular level, I can recommend books by Mick Aston and Glyn Coppack, and at a slightly more specialised level, a first-rate overview by Colin Platt which is still relevant, although written over twenty years ago.[4] If, however, one wants to learn about recent trends in monastic archaeology, the best book by some way is *Monastic Archaeology: Papers on the Study of Medieval Monasteries*, assembled by Graham Keevill, Mick Aston and Teresa Hall.[5] Only time will tell, but I think this book signals that monastic archaeology is now heading into new territories, some of which promise to be quite challenging.

Monastic archaeology can claim to be well established within scholarly circles. Whereas medieval archaeology arose in the 1950s and is a relatively new arrival, monastic archaeology has roots which extend back to the antiquarianism of the nineteenth century. As a rule it's unusual to come across Victorian papers cited in the bibliographies of modern scholarship. In fact it's quite rare to find papers that predate the last war. But a glance through the references of *Monastic Archaeology* reveals papers that appeared in the 1870s and 1890s – and yet this is a book which focuses its attention on modern developments in the subject. The fact is that if a good piece of work was carried out a century ago, there is no harm in citing it today. Monasteries were the archetypical 'romantic ruins', and they appealed to people, especially the Victorians, who wanted to sift the grains of truth from the chaff of legends.

Recent changes of direction have not taken place too soon. In the past monastic archaeology was a specialised subject, where huge emphasis was placed on details of the plans or layouts of monastic sites. It was a subject that the unwary entered at their peril, unless they had spent years of study not just of the copious ancient literature, but of equally copious modern maps and plans. Bolstered by this vast body of data, it is probably fair to say that the subject stagnated. It seemed that we knew so much already that all we had to do was flesh out a few interesting details. But we are now beginning to realise that there was something fundamentally unreliable about much of the archaeological work on maps, plans and layouts.

I remember coming across my first example of old-fashioned 'predictive' archaeology in action. This school of archaeology believed that literary and other sources had given us sufficient clues to be able to recognise different types of sites with one or two well-placed trenches that would come down on what were believed to be diagnostic features. When these had been found (as they usually were), the site had been sorted out. Archaeology had confirmed what was already known, or strongly suspected. In this particular instance I had yet to direct an excavation of my own, and had decided to visit projects that were being run by established authorities in the hope of picking up some useful tips. A graduate student friend had suggested that I should visit Professor X's Roman military site, which would be starting later that week.

I arrived on site a few days after work had begun, and was greeted by the great man with wonderful kindness and courtesy, which was all the more remarkable given that I am sure he didn't know who on earth I was, nor why I was visiting his site – which, in fairness to him, I didn't altogether know myself. After a few words of scene-setting and introduction over a mug of tea in the site hut, we went outside. It was quite unlike any dig I had ever visited. We were in a large green field – twenty-five to thirty acres, I would guess – and I could just spot little groups of people away in the distance. In the foreground was a long, thin trench that had been cleared with a machine. In it, the great man pointed out three or four post-holes which seemed to be in a straight line, although of course in a long, thin trench almost every-thing has to be more or less in line. I was told that these posts formed part of one of the garrison's four granaries. To prove this the great man took about twenty large paces to the north, where he had positioned a tiny hand-dug trench, about a metre square, in which there was another post-hole. With the eye of faith it was on line with the first group, but to my surprise the professor confidently told me it was the granary's corner post. I must have looked a little surprised that he was able to tell so much from a single post-hole, because he then gave me a short lecture on the predictability of early Roman military layouts. I remember thinking, although I kept my mouth shut, that he was certainly adding to that predictability.

Today, nobody in their right mind would open 'keyhole' trenches of that sort in an attempt to answer such specific questions, for the obvious reason that one post-hole does not make a building. Also there was no evidence to suggest that all the posts were strictly contem-porary, and because the trenches were so small we had no idea of the general archaeological 'noise' around them: if there were hundreds of other post-holes in the area, I would certainly not accept the professor's interpretation; but if there were none, then just possibly I might. The main point to make here is that modern archaeologists try to take nothing as given. If one wants to discover the layout of a place, one uses excavation, surveying or geophysics, or best, combinations of all three, to work out a feasible plan, which one then interprets in the light of what one knows about such sites from other work. The information on the ground comes first, and the detailed interpretation second.

When I was a student I came across endless detailed surveys of British monastic sites in learned archaeological journals. In those days geophysics was in its infancy and most of the work was done from surface surveys of humps and bumps, usually, but not always, combined with aerial photography. A few key trenches would then confirm what the survey had revealed. It was a sensible way of working in a subject where we did actually know a great deal about monastic layouts, not just from detailed documentary evidence but from real, surviving monasteries in countries like France that had been spared the heavy, avaricious hand of Henry VIII.

In fairness to the archaeologists who carried out these detailed and in most cases excellent surveys, I don't see how else they could have done them, given the technological and financial constraints of the time. Even so, we now realise that there was more than a little 'predictive' archaeology happening here. And of course the main problem with such an approach is that it tends to identify similarities and consistent patterns. It is less good at identifying idiosyncrasies and individuality, which are the two aspects of ancient life that inform us about the way people actually lived their lives and adapted to particular circumstances. Put another way, people are not clones: by and large they do not follow recipe books to the letter, and the way they depart from the expected is what makes them so interesting. Take that individuality away and you remove much of their humanity.

In some respects the dilemma currently confronting monastic archaeology is the same one that confronts the subject in general. Ultimately it springs from the modern realisation that all knowledge is relative – and that therefore some new information is relatively unimportant. The truths implicit in many of the early monastic surveys have been shown to be partially true, if not actually half-truths. By the same token it has not been a simple business to invent research objectives that seem relevant to current concerns within the broader church of archaeology. Reading between the lines of many of the papers collected in *Monastic Archaeology*, I detected uncertainties and doubts. In some respects their authors seemed to lack a degree of confidence.

But is that necessarily a bad thing? Personally I doubt it. In fact I would go further, because I think it is healthy to question why and how one should move forward. There are indeed huge problems to be confronted within monastic archaeology, and there will be no simple answers; but if we do not address these problems from time to time, we will return to those days of stability and stasis when nobody questioned why they were being paid to examine something as seemingly obscure as water management around the outbuildings of a medieval monastery. Today we question these things, and sometimes we conclude that time – everyone's time – is being wasted.

The doubts and challenges that are currently assailing the world of monastic archaeology should be set against the broader background of the rapidly changing world of archaeology in the past two decades. If anything, the pace of change is increasing. All archaeological planning legislation is about to be reviewed, and with London staging the Olympic Games in 2012, we can kiss goodbye to future lottery funding for the heritage sector. We have already seen how the introduction of developer-funded contract work has led to a marked diminution of centrally funded or grant-based projects. Sadly, much of the research into monastic archaeology took place on sites that were protected by law, and large-scale commercial development was therefore impossible. The result has been that there are fewer and fewer research projects carried out for purely academic reasons. Grant funding for such work is becoming harder and harder to find. This has meant that most people who want to do academic research must somehow shoehorn their interests into some other type of project. This may sometimes call for the very creative design of research projects, if not for actual creative accounting later. But it can be done, and when it's successful everyone gains – even the accountants.

One example will suffice. As I have just noted, much archaeological research on abbey sites is severely constrained by the fact that they are protected under law. So most work has to be geared towards conservation or preservation for the future, and the need to display something comprehensible to the public. If you add these limitations to the sort of budgetary constraints that apply everywhere today, there is a real possibility that the results revealed by archaeology will be more Mickey Mouse than magisterial. But these problems can be overcome.

Glyn Coppack, who was our Inspector for many years when we worked on sites in the Welland Valley, is a very sceptical person. When he visited our work he would never take anything I said at face value. He always wanted to know the reasons behind every statement I made. This could sometimes be irritating, as he was constantly cutting in and breaking the flow of my argument. But with hindsight he was dead right to do so, given his role as guardian of the taxpayer's purse. So I wasn't surprised that it was Glyn who mounted a serious challenge to the way that the archaeology of abbeys has traditionally been approached in the field, and who set about the time-consuming business of getting it right. His work was based at the stunningly beautiful and important site at Fountains Abbey in Yorkshire.[6]

Fountains was one of the great Cistercian abbeys of Europe, and today it is visited by about 300,000 people a year. This single fact has had a major impact on the way that archaeology has been carried out there. But it has not always been a happy story. Glyn Coppack tells of past scandals, such as the decision in 1968 to install floodlighting, which was taken by the Minister of Public Works against professional advice. This work involved the digging of narrow trenches a metre deep all over the site, and an unfortunate fellow prehistorian was then sent to the site to try to work out what they had revealed in order to 'mitigate damage'! If anyone had asked me to look down a series of slot trenches on such a horrendously complex site, I think I would have cut my throat.

Slowly Coppack impressed on the authorities the fact that archaeology was not an unnecessary expense, to be borne by unfortunate administrators. He showed that if academic research is integrated within the general programme of care and maintenance, although expensive, it can be made to pay for itself. Thanks to this work, Fountains is now possibly the best-understood major monastery in Europe, and as a result it has attracted World Heritage Site status and major grants from bodies in Britain and abroad. It may seem galling to be obliged to justify something which is self-evidently necessary, but as today everyone else has to, I cannot see why academic research should be considered above such things.

As monastic research in the real world has been facing all sorts of challenges, the heart of the subject itself has also been going through crises of identity. The early studies, being rooted in antiquarianism, placed much emphasis on the churches, at the expense perhaps of more domestic buildings. After the war, doubtless influenced by the growing new field of medieval archaeology, the trend was in the opposite direction. Today the study of monasteries has become well integrated within archaeology as a whole. Like other archaeological projects, monastic studies now make full use of geophysics, environmental science and other specialist expertise, such as the study of human bones and diseases. There is also a realisation that just as monasteries cannot be separated from their immediate surroundings, they also belonged to different orders, and need to be studied side by side. So collaborative projects are becoming more popular.

While acid rain, the pressures of tourism and other potentially harmful challenges, such as development, are threatening the sites that have survived, the relevance of long-dead religious houses can be questioned by a younger generation that may not share a belief in Christianity, or indeed in religion at all. As Patrick Green, a contributor to *Monastic Archaeology*, puts it: 'A sense of urgency is generated by the knowledge that the standing monastic sites are vulnerable to increasingly intensive land use. The need to interpret monasticism to a public interested in the past, yet often with little contact with religious observance, is particularly challenging.'[7] The best comfort I can draw from this is that the people involved in monastic archaeology are aware that a problem exists, and are clearly determined to do something about it.

One does not have to be a specialist in monastic archaeology to be aware that all was not well within the world of monks and nuns for many years before 1538. For example, anyone even slightly familiar with Chaucer (1343–1400) will be aware of his wonderful stories, which often have a sharp and very modern ironic edge to them. In *The Canterbury Tales* he writes about a friar named Huberd (Hubert):

> For ther he was nat lyk a cloysterer
> With a thredbare cope, as in a povre scoler,
> But he was lyk a maister or a pope.
> Of double worstede was his semycope,
> That rounded as a belle out of the presse.
> Somwhat he lipsed, for his wantownesse,
> To make his Englissh sweete upon his tonge.[8]

Chaucer's English may at first be hard to grasp, but he paints a memorably clear picture of the Friar, who was anything but 'a poor scholar', in his fine, carefully pressed, top-quality double-worsted clothes and with his horrible affected lisp. He is just the sort of person I would change seats to avoid in a train.

I selected the Friar – I could equally well have chosen the Pardoner, the Franklin or the Prioress – because he belonged to one of the supposedly mendicant orders that had arrived in Britain relatively recently. We saw in Chapter 5 how friaries were being established in London from just before the middle of the thirteenth century. They began with good intentions, but even mendicant friars were human beings, and in something over a century a proportion of them were doing quite well for themselves.

I find the history of the Dissolution a story with modern parallels. Rather like British Leyland or British Rail, the monasteries were institutions that had failed to move with the times, in which the staff had grown used to a secure and comfortable life. That is not to say that they were wholly bad. There was some petty corruption, but it was not necessarily flagrant or large-scale. Prior to the Dissolution there were more than eight hundred abbeys and priories in England, with a combined income of over £160,000 – a vast sum for the day. But as we saw earlier, this money was far from evenly distributed. In some instances monasteries became fat and corrupt, requiring the intervention of a bishop. In others discipline was above reproach.

The general decline in numbers of the fourteenth and fifteenth centuries meant that many monasteries were quite lightly populated. In these cases resources were not overstretched, and there was more than enough to go around. There was also a significant PR problem, as there was in the two modern cases I mentioned, but instead of bloody-minded shop stewards the image was of a fat friar. As Glyn Coppack observed, in a time of growing secularisation, monastic seclusion and rumoured good living off landed estates led to a rift between the common man and the cloistered religious.[9]

The actual Dissolution was not quite as sudden or as brutal as it is sometimes portrayed. There were genuine attempts at reform, starting in 1536 with an Act to suppress small religious communities where there was 'manifest sin, vicious, carnal and abominable living'. In the process of closing these places many non-corrupt establishments were also shut down, which led to the protest from the north, known as the Pilgrimage of Grace, in October 1536, and with it the Lincolnshire Rising.[10] But these protests failed, and the Dissolution began in earnest when it was ratified by Act of Parliament in 1538. The last surviving house, at Waltham Abbey in Essex, was suppressed in March 1540.

One might suppose that something like the Reformation would be extremely difficult to study from an archaeological perspective. It was, after all, essentially a change in both theology and religious attitudes, which are not the sort of things one can dig from the ground or probe with geophysics. That is indeed true, but sometimes it is better to tackle such problems indirectly. An oblique approach may sometimes throw direct light. For many years archaeologists have been studying the physical effects of the Reformation, not just in church and chapel architecture, but in studies, for example, of pottery and religious trinkets, graveyards and funerary practices. People often betray their true beliefs after they have died.

I began this book with some thoughts about the origins of modern medieval archaeology and the learned societies that have helped to give it direction, purpose and guidance. As I approach the conclusion I would like to draw briefly upon a series of studies that arose from a conference on 'The Archaeology of the Reformation 1480–1580', which was the third joint meeting of the Societies for Medieval and Post-Medieval Archaeology. The papers given at that conference have been assembled into a rich collection, edited by David Gaimster and Roberta Gilchrist.[11] This large volume shows that archaeology can make very original – even disturbing – contributions to what at first glance would appear to be a historical subject, pure and simple. From my current perspective, the papers assembled there show beyond any doubt that the Middle Ages did not come to a grinding halt either in 1536–38, 1550 or indeed 1480–1580. Like the Dissolution which formed a part of it, the Reformation was the expression of beliefs and attitudes that had been changing for some time – and would, moreover, continue to change.

Gaimster and Gilchrist describe the usually accepted historical view of the Reformation, when the Protestant Churches parted company with the Roman Catholic Church, thus: 'Traditionally, historians in western and northern Europe have viewed the political, social and economic turmoil surrounding "the splintering of the cross" as largely responsible for the rupture of the medieval order and the foundation of modern society, in giving rise to individualism, capitalism, imperialism and democracy.[12] They describe the archaeological approach to the Reformation as being essentially 'history from below'. Archaeology, or below-ground history, employs a variety of approaches to show that the ideas of the Reformation were by no means adopted by everyone at the same time. In some areas there was considerable resistance and older beliefs persisted. In others the sort of ordinary domestic artefacts one finds in towns actually changed quite fast – suggesting the opposite. But neither is there any indication to suggest that Protestantism was adopted wholesale by the entire population. And even the Protestantism that was adopted often included traditional Catholic elements. The change, in other words, was neither as complete nor as revolutionary as it is usually portrayed as having been.

Perhaps it is no more than common sense, but as I have already noted, the archaeology of graves and burial is one of the best ways to discover what people really believed in their lifetimes. Roberta Gilchrist has shown that while there were indeed innovations, certain medieval beliefs, patterns of religion, or 'resonances' as she terms them, continued to be observed after the Reformation, especially in northern and western Britain.[13] For example, graveyards from within suppressed monasteries continued to be used even though the monastery had gone. But there were important changes too, especially in the larger cities, where new burial grounds were established and there was a new tendency to treat dead adults and children equally. Medieval cemeteries generally include about 30 per cent children; after the Reformation the figure rises to 50 per cent. This probably reflects a change in social and religious attitudes towards children and young people, who were often buried in separate areas in the Middle Ages. Even the Smithfield Black Death cemetery in London included a discrete area that was reserved for children.

The other significant change apparent in the archaeological record of post-Reformation burial practices is the common occurrence of coffins and burial in vaults, which Gilchrist links with the discomfort of Puritans with the body and its physical processes of decay. She considers that the most important aspect of pre-Reformation belief to have survived into the post-medieval world had to do with the memory, or commemoration, of the dead, which was achieved in some cases through actual physical intercession, with bones being removed from graves and placed in charnel houses. The re-use of old monastic burial grounds could also be part of this process. The Reformation placed great emphasis on the survival of the soul and its separation from the body, which led to an increase in memorials that took the form of tablets or inscriptions. Despite such innovations, the need to perpetuate what Gilchrist calls 'the future memory' of the dead persisted from the Middle Ages, right through the Reformation, into post-medieval and indeed modern times.

I have already spent possibly more time than I ought in discussing urban archaeology, which has done so much to transform our understanding of the Middle Ages, and which has left me in no doubt that they were indeed modern in all significant respects. So what does urban archaeology tell us about the end of the Middle Ages in York and London, the two cities we have examined most closely? We have already seen that the situation in York was complicated by the fact that a long-term, gradual decline had begun in the final century of the Middle Ages. From 1450 trade shifted to other towns such as Wakefield, and then Leeds joined Hull, which had already captured many of York's import and export markets. As a result the population of the city declined. Even so, use of land at Coppergate seems to become ever more intensive, so that towards the end of the medieval period the long garden plots had become completely covered over with cobbled paths and yards.[14] There was also a decrease in the dumping of waste, which, with the decline of the gardens, may have been an attempt to avoid contaminating the drinking water, to decrease the chances of spreading the plague.

While the rest of the city may have been in gradual decline, the population in the area around Coppergate was increasing. Larger buildings, like the two that have survived from the fifteenth century at numbers 28–32, occupied much of the site. Some were reserved for rich merchants, but it is quite possible that others may have housed large numbers of tenants in relatively small rooms, as has been found at contemporary sites in London and Norwich. After all, land in late medieval times was cheap, and there were many decaying large houses that landlords felt were ripe for conversion to 'multi-occupancy', as it would be called today. It could also be called speculation to make a few quick pounds.

In their book on medieval urbanism in Coppergate, Hall and Hunter-Mann do not believe that the Reformation marked a sudden and abrupt change between the feudal, ecclesiastical medieval and the capitalist, secular post-medieval worlds. As they put it, the usefulness of such historical constructs is increasingly being questioned. They, like myself and the many people actively working in urban archaeology, opt for a prolonged transitional period of change extending back to the Black Death crisis of the mid-fourteenth century, or even earlier. That also fits with what we have been seeing in the rural landscape, where Open Field systems started to be enclosed and the processes of regional specialisation had begun. It is then just a matter of how you choose to label the periods at either end of the two-century-long transitional period. You could call it either 'early modern' or 'later medieval', depending on personal preference, because the strong and transparent link provided by the period of change shows that the two were intimately related.

At the conclusion of their discussion of the late medieval period (c.1400–c.1550), Hall and Hunter-Mann describe the situation that archaeology had revealed in stark and simple terms: 'At Coppergate, there is no clear evidence of a fundamental distinction between medieval and post-medieval; the medieval buildings remain in use into the seventeenth century, as do other forms of land use.'[15] That says it all.

Despite the important fact that in the post-medieval period York was a city in gradual decline whereas London was quite the opposite, there are broad coincidences which indicate that the long-term social, economic and cultural forces that lay behind the changes observed in the archaeological record were similar. We saw in Chapter 5 that by the end of the thirteenth century London and its population had grown enormously, and the City was now subdivided into a maze of small lanes and alleys. The wealth of some was accompanied by poverty for many. Disease was rife; there was, for example, a large leper hospital in Southwark, which was also notorious in the late medieval period for its stews (brothels). The average height for a man was 1.67 metres (just under 5 feet 6 inches), which is significantly below the modern average, and indicates that the diet was on the poor side for most people.

Of course the Black Death was a disaster for London, but even so, its economy recovered rapidly and then continued to grow, thanks to its wide trading links and a steady supply of new blood from quite a large area of the south-east. Christopher Thomas notes that in common with other English towns, London became a more secular place in the two hundred years that followed the crisis of the mid-fourteenth century. Its many monasteries began to resemble small towns, with areas devoted to housing, workshops and small traders.[16] The Reformation marked an important change in official attitudes, and demonstrated the power of English monarchs and their state over the Church. This political event is best seen as official recognition of processes that had been under way throughout the previous extended transitional period. After the Reformation the growth of London and the economy under the Tudors and Stuarts was, to use Thomas's term, 'meteoric', but he notes that the stage had been set through the previous four hundred years. Again we are seeing processes of change that are taking place against a background of cultural continuity. There are changes of forward gear, and in the mid-fourteenth century the brakes were applied, but at no point is momentum lost while society at large searches for new directions.

There I must leave it. But before I stop, I would request the minor self-indulgence of making a general point relevant to the world we all inhabit in the twenty-first century. I do this because I hold that history and archaeology must contribute to the modern scene if they are to survive in the future. I also believe that knowledge of the past must inform the present, because nothing else can. Far too many politicians seriously believe that a week is a long time in politics – a view which has played a large part in creating some of the global tensions that characterise our times. History and archaeology surely teach us that human culture is a long-term phenomenon that is best treated both with respect and an eye on what might be happening in fifty or a hundred years' time – not in four to five years, the duration of most democratic governments.

I have tried to make it clear that I do not think that the Middle Ages ended at all, and that we are still living in a Europe that was fashioned in early medieval times. We are also living in a world where tensions are rising between the West and the Muslim world. Ultimately the causes of the recent friction have to do with oil, exploitation and a lack of empowerment, all factors made much worse by insensitive and ignorant politicians and clerics. I do not see this situation as another Crusade, and I certainly do not share the view that the often-quoted 'clash of civilisations' exists at all. I would, however, acknowledge that there are significant cultural differences, but these can be a source of inspiration as much as tension. If human history is about anything, it is surely about accommodating such cultural diversity.

We saw in Chapter 1 that the early Muslim world contributed much by way of trade, scholarship and learning to medieval Europe, and it seems both unnecessary and unjustifiable to suggest that the two cultures are irreconcilably different. There are simply too many links that unite the two: cultural, scientific, historical, linguistic and religious. For example, Muslims, Jews and Christians share a common respect for, and belief in, the truths of the Old Testament. One of my favourite medieval buildings is the vast Moorish cathedral in Seville. If the 'clash of civilisations' was as bad as it has been painted, surely neither Seville Cathedral, nor the grand mosque that was originally the Christian Basilica of Haghia Sophia in Constantinople, would still be standing? Both are stupendous architectural creations, and both successfully switched identities – but in opposite directions. People in medieval times were too pragmatic to allow sentiment always to overrule practicality; indeed, attitudes in the past were far less rigid than some of us sometimes suppose – or would like to think.

If the jingoistic 'clash of civilisations' school of politics is to be believed, then one day Islam will be defeated, or forever separated from Christianity and the Western secular world. But by the same token, logic would dictate that the same should also apply to the even more ancient cultural traditions of Judaism. Plainly that would be absurd, destructive and impractical. In reality, Christians, Jews and Muslims lived and traded together with considerable mutual benefit throughout the medieval period, even if it was punctuated by a number of disgraceful incidents.* If history and archaeology have a lesson to teach us today, it is that we should beware of erecting facile barriers which may seem credible in a soundbite, but which are both culturally and historically irrelevant – and of course potentially very dangerous indeed.

---

* Apart from a massacre of 150 Jews at York in 1189, and serious problems later in London, Lincoln and Norwich, one thinks of the banishment of all Jews from England by Edward I in 1290, when they were given just three months to leave.

NOTES

INTRODUCTION — *Archaeology and the Medieval Period*

1 The only textbook covering all periods of British archaeology is John Hunter and Ian Ralston (eds), *The Archaeology of Britain: An Introduction from the Upper Palaeolithic to the Industrial Revolution* (Routledge, London, 1999)
2 The best account of archaeology in all its various forms is Colin Renfrew and Paul Bahn, *Archaeology: Theories, Methods and Practice*, fourth edition (Thames and Hudson, London, 2004)
3 Paul Stamper, 'Landscapes of the Middle Ages: Rural Settlement and Manors', in Hunter and Ralston, op. cit., p.295
4 Jacques Le Goff (trans. Janet Lloyd), *The Birth of Europe* (Blackwell, Oxford, 2005)
5 Brian Hope-Taylor, *Yeavering: An Anglo-British Centre of Early Northumbria*, Department of the Environment Archaeological Reports No. 7 (HMSO, London, 1977)
6 Simon Mays, 'Wharram Percy: The Skeletons', *Current Archaeology*, No. 193, 2004, pp.45–9
7 The English National Monuments Record can be visited online via *www.english-heritage.org.uk*. For Scotland see *www.rcahms.gov.uk* and for Wales *www.rcahmw.org.uk*
8 Claire Phipps, 'Less Hitler Please', *BBC History*, September 2004, pp.86–7

CHAPTER ONE — *The North/South Divide of the Middle Saxon Period*

1 Bede (ed. B. Colgrave and R.A.B. Mynors), *Ecclesiastical History of the English People* (Oxford University Press, 1969), p.288
2 J.R. Maddicott, 'Plague in Seventh-Century England', *Past and Present*, 156, 1997, pp.7–54
3 Francis Pryor, *Britain AD* (HarperCollins, London, 2004), pp.220–34
4 Sir Frank Francis (ed.), *Treasures of the British Museum* (Thames and Hudson, London, 1971), p.10
5 I have drawn extensively on Leslie Alcock's Rhind Lectures of 1988–89: *Kings and Warriors, Craftsmen and Priests in Northern Britain AD 550–850* (Society of Antiquaries of Scotland, Edinburgh, 2003). For illuminated manuscripts see pp.336–61
6 *Britain AD*, p.224
7 My well-thumbed version is that edited by Françoise Henry (Thames and Hudson, London, 1974)
8 Alcock, op cit.
9 Ibid., p.244
10 C. O'Brien and R. Miket, 'The Early Medieval Settlement at Thirlings, Northumberland', *Durham Archaeological Journal*, Vol. 7, 1991, pp.57–91. The most accessible account of South Cadbury is Leslie Alcock, *'By South Cadbury is that Camelot . . .': Excavations at Cadbury Castle 1966–70* (Thames and Hudson, London, 1972)
11 P.H. Hill, *Whithorn and St Ninian: The Excavation of a Monastic Town, 1984–91* (Whithorn Trust/Sutton Publishing, Stroud, 1997)
12 See *Britain AD*, pp.178–82
13 Carolyn Dallas, *Excavations in Thetford by B.K. Davison Between 1964 and 1970*, East Anglian Archaeology Report No. 62 (Dereham, 1993)
14 Michael McCormick, *Origins of the*

European Economy: Communications and Commerce A D 300–900 (Cambridge University Press, 2001)

15 Hugh Kennedy, 'The True Caliph of the Arabian Nights', *History Today*, September 2004, pp.31–6

16 Alastair Northedge, 'Remarks on Samarra and the Archaeology of Large Cities', *Antiquity*, 79, 2005, pp.119–29

17 McCormick, op. cit., p.776

18 Ibid., p.797

19 The Portable Antiquities Scheme website is at *www.finds.org.uk*

20 My discussion of productive sites will draw heavily on papers given at a conference at Worcester College, Oxford, in December 2000. They have been edited by Tim Pestell and Katharina Ulmschneider: *Markets in Early Medieval Europe: Trading and 'Productive' Sites, 650–850* (Windgather Press, Macclesfield, 2003)

21 For an excellent review of current research into *emporia* and *burhs* see Dominic Perring, *Town and Country in England: Frameworks for Archaeological Research*, Council for British Archaeology Research Report No. 134 (York, 2002)

22 Papers by Tummuscheit and Le Maho in Pestell and Ulmschneider, op. cit.

23 J.D. Richards in Pestell and Ulmschneider, op. cit., pp.155–67

24 Ben Palmer, 'The Hinterlands of Three Southern English *Emporia*: Some Common Themes', in Pestell and Ulmschneider, op. cit., pp.48–60

25 R. Foley, 'Off-Site Archaeology: An Alternative Approach for the Short-Sited', in I. Hodder, G. Issac and N. Hammond (eds), *Pattern of the Past* (Cambridge University Press, 1981), pp.157–83

26 Le Goff, op. cit., p.13

27 Richard Hodges, *Dark Age Economics: The Origins of Towns and Trade*, A D 600–1000, second edition (Duckworth, London, 1989). He includes a full list of *wics* and *emporia*, complete with many plans, in chapters 3 and 4 (pp. 47–86)

28 My favourite introduction to anthropology is Edmund Leach, *Social Anthropology*, Fontana Masterguides series (Fontana Paperbacks, Glasgow, 1982)

29 Peter Wade-Martins, *Excavations in North Elmham Park, 1967–1972*, 2 vols, East Anglian Archaeology Report No. 9 (Norwich, 1980)

30 Note by Richard Hodges in Keith Wade, 'The Pottery', in ibid., p.477

31 Stanley West, *West Stow: The Anglo-Saxon Village*, 2 vols, East Anglian Archaeology Report No. 24 (Ipswich, 1985)

32 West Stow is open daily, all year, 10 a.m.– 5 p.m. Tel. 01284 728718

33 R.J. Silvester, *The Fenland Project Number 3: Marshland and the Nar Valley, Norfolk*, East Anglian Archaeology No. 45 (Gressenhall, Norfolk, 1988)

34 M. Leah, 'The Fenland Management Project: Excavations at Three Middle Saxon Marshland Sites at West Walton, Walpole St Andrew and Hay Green', *Fenland Research* No. 7, pp.49–59

35 See the middle photograph facing p.69

36 Gill Hey, *Yarnton: Saxon and Medieval Settlement and Landscape*, Thames Valley Landscapes Monograph No. 20 (Oxford Archaeological Unit, 2004)

37 Paul Blinkhorn, 'Early and Middle Saxon Pottery', in Gill Hey, op. cit., pp.267–73

38 Gill Hey, op. cit., p.45

39 See *Britain A D*, pp.207–8

40 J.G. Evans, 'Habitat Change on the Calcareous Soils of Britain: The Impact of Neolithic Man', in D.D.A. Simpson (ed.), *Economy and Settlement in Neolithic and Early Bronze Age Britain and Europe* (Leicester University Press, 1971), p.47

CHAPTER TWO — *Enter the Vikings*

1 Barry Cunliffe, *Iron Age Communities in Britain*, third edition (Routledge, London, 1991), p.480

2 Julian Richards' beautifully illustrated

book of his television series is a good place to start: Julian Richards, *Blood of the Vikings* (Hodder and Stoughton, London, 2001). See also J.D. Richards (not the same person), *Viking Age England* (Batsford/English Heritage, London, 1991), also his chapter (11) in Hunter and Ralston, op. cit.; and Anna Ritchie, *Viking Scotland* (Batsford/ Historic Scotland, London, 1993). Although somewhat outdated, David Wilson's *The Vikings and Their Origins: Scandinavia in the First Millennium* (Thames and Hudson, London, 1970) has excellent illustrations of Viking objects from Scandinavia.

3 Julian Richards, op. cit., pp.7–8

4 Edwin and Joyce Gifford, 'The Use of Half-Scale Model Ships in Archaeological Research with Particular Reference to the Graveney, Sutton Hoo and Ferriby Ships', in Peter Clark (ed.), *The Dover Bronze Age Boat in Context* (Oxbow Books, Oxford, 2004), pp.67–81

5 E. and J. Gifford, 'Fit for a King', *British Archaeology*, January/February 2005, pp.20–3

6 A late Viking smith/carpenter's toolchest with a complete set of tools was found in Gotland, Sweden, in 1936. This astonishing discovery shows the sophistication of Viking craftsmen. It is published in English and is fully illustrated: G. Arwidsson and G. Berg, *The Mästermyr Find. A Viking Age Tool Chest from Gotland* (Stockholm, 1983) ISBN 91 7402 129 X

7 Sir Cyril Fox, *Offa's Dyke* (British Academy, London, 1955)

8 David Hill, 'Offa Versus the Welsh', *British Archaeology*, December 2000, pp.18–23. See also David Hill and Margaret Worthington, *Offa's Dyke: History and Guide* (Tempus Books, Stroud, 2003)

9 The two translations of the *Chronicles* are by G.N. Garmonsway (Dent, London, 1953) and Dorothy Whitelock (Eyre and Spottiswoode, London, 1961). See also the beautifully illustrated edition by Anne Savage (Heinemann, London, 1982)

10 Julian Richards, op. cit., p.18

11 Barbara Yorke, 'The Most Perfect Man in History?', *History Today*, Vol. 49, October 1999, pp.8–14

12 Dawn Hadley, 'Invisible Vikings', *British Archaeology*, April 2002, pp.16–21

13 A.D. Mills, *A Dictionary of English Place-Names* (Oxford University Press, 1991), p.350

14 Anna Ritchie, op. cit.

15 James Graham-Campbell (ed.), *Viking Treasure from the North-West: The Cuerdale Hoard in its Context*, National Museums and Galleries of Merseyside Occasional Papers No. 5 (Liverpool, 1992)

16 McCormick, op. cit., p.821

17 Patrick Ashmore, *Maes Howe: World Heritage Site* (Historic Scotland, Edinburgh, 2000)

18 Philip Rahtz and Lorna Watts, 'Kirkdale Anglo-Saxon Minster', *Current Archaeology*, No. 155, 1997, pp.419–22

19 His life of Leonard Cheshire is a masterpiece: *Cheshire: The Biography of Leonard Cheshire VC, OM* (Penguin Books, Harmondsworth, 2001)

20 Julian D. Richards, 'Excavations at the Viking Barrow Cemetery at Heath Wood, Ingleby, Derby', *Antiquaries Journal*, Vol. 84, 2004, pp.23–116

21 Martin Biddle and Birthe Kjølbye-Biddle, 'Repton and the Vikings', *Antiquity*, Vol. 66, 1992, pp.36–51

22 Julian D. Richards, 2004, op. cit., p.97. This total does not include the recently discovered cemetery at Cumwhitton, Cumbria

23 Ibid., p.105

24 M. Pitts, 'Cumbrian Heritage', *British Archaeology*, November 2004, pp.28–31

25 Kevin Leahy, 'Detecting the Vikings in Lincolnshire', *Current Archaeology*, No. 190, 2004, pp.462–8

26 *Britain AD*, p.54

27 J.D. Hill, 'The End of One Kind of Body and the Beginning of Another Kind of Body? Toilet Instruments and "Romanization" in Southern England During the First Century AD', in Adam Gwilt and Colin Haselgrove (eds),

Reconstructing Iron Age Societies: New Approaches to the British Iron Age Oxbow Monograph No. 71 (Oxford, 1997), pp.96–107

28 Francis Pryor, *Excavation at Fengate, Peterborough, England: The Fourth Report*, Northants Archaeological Society Monograph No. 2, Royal Ontario Museum Archaeological Monograph No. 7, pp.168–74 (Leicester and Toronto, 1984)

29 *Salon*, No. 114, 25 April 2005

30 *British Archaeology*, January 2004, p.7

31 Mark Rednap, 'Great Sites: Balladoole', *British Archaeology*, June 2001, pp.24–6

32 A. Selkirk, 'Scar: A Viking Boat Burial', *Current Archaeology*, No. 131, 1992, pp.475–7

33 *British Archaeology*, May 2004, p.8

34 Quoted from J.D. Richards in Hunter and Ralston, op. cit., p.194

35 Royal Commission on Historical Monuments (England), *The Town of Stamford* (HMSO, London, 1977)

36 R.A. Hall, 'The Five Boroughs of the Danelaw: A Review of Present Knowledge', *Anglo-Saxon England*, Vol. 18, 1989, pp.149–206

37 J.D. Richards, 1991, op. cit., p.57

38 Ibid.

39 Richard Hodges, 'Goodbye to the Vikings?', *History Today*, September 2004, pp.29–30

40 Duckworth, London, 1989

41 *Britain AD*, pp.159–90

42 McCormick, op. cit.

43 Richard Hodges, 'The Shaping of Medieval North-West Europe', *Antiquity*, Vol. 78, September 2004, pp.723–7

CHAPTER THREE — *Rural Life in Late Saxon Times*

1 Andrew Reynolds, *Later Anglo-Saxon England: Life and Landscape* (Tempus Books, Stroud, 1999), p.65

2 Ibid., pp.65–110

3 Ibid., pp.69–72

4 M. Aston and R.T. Rowley (eds), *Landscape Archaeology* (David and Charles, Newton Abbot, 1974)

5 For a good introduction to geophysical prospection techniques see Anthony Clark, *Seeing Beneath the Soil: Prospecting Methods in Archaeology*, revised edition (Routledge, London, 1996)

6 M. Aston and C. Gerrard, '"Unique, Traditional and Charming": The Shapwick Project, Somerset', *Antiquaries Journal*, Vol. 79, 1999, pp.1–58. See also A. Selkirk, 'The Shapwick Project', *Current Archaeology*, No. 151, 1997, pp.244–54

7 N. Corcos, *Shapwick: The Enclosure of a Somerset Parish, 1515–1839*

8 Aston and Gerrard, op. cit., p.29

9 D. Southerland and D. Parsons, 'The Petrological Contribution to the Survey of All Saints Church, Brixworth, Northamptonshire: An Interim Study', *Journal of the British Archaeological Association*, No. 137, 1984, pp.47–64

10 Stamper, op. cit., p.260

11 David Hall, *The Open Fields of Northamptonshire*, Northamptonshire Records Society (Northampton, 1995)

12 Paul Martin, 'A Review of 25 Years Fieldwalking with David Hall', in Tom Lane and John Coles (eds), *Through Wet and Dry: Essays in Honour of David Hall*, Lincolnshire Archaeology and Heritage Reports No. 5 (Heckington, Sleaford, 2002)

13 David Hall, *Medieval Fields* (Shire Publications, Princes Risborough, 1982)

14 First published by Longmans, Green and Co., London, 1883

15 Mills, op. cit.

16 Martin Tingle, 'Archaeology in Northamptonshire', in M. Tingle (ed.), *The Archaeology of Northamptonshire* (Northamptonshire Archaeological Society, Northampton, 2004), p.11

17 Tony Brown and Glen Foard, 'The Anglo-Saxon Period', in Tingle, *The Archaeology of Northamptonshire*, op. cit., pp.78–101

18 Brian Dix (ed.), 'The Raunds Area Project: Second Interim Report', *Northamptonshire Archaeology*, Vol. 21, 1986–7, pp.3–30

19 C. Lewis, P. Mitchell-Fox and C. Dyer, *Village, Hamlet and Field: Changing Medieval Settlements in Central England* (Windgather Press, Macclesfield, 2001)

20 Michael Baillie, 'Dendrochronology – the Irish view', *Current Archaeology*, No. 73, 1980, pp.61–3

21 Philip Rahtz and Ken Sheridan, 'Tamworth', *Current Archaeology*, No. 29, 1979, pp.164–8

22 'Ebbsfleet Saxon mill', *Current Archaeology*, No. 183, 2002, p.93

23 Colleen Batey, 'Earls' Bu', *Current Archaeology*, No. 127, 1991, pp.303–4

CHAPTER FOUR — *Urban Life in Late Saxon Times*

1 Peter Yeoman, *Medieval Scotland* (Historic Scotland/Batsford, London, 1995), pp.53–85

2 Reynolds, op. cit., p.87

3 Philip Crummy, *City of Victory: The Story of Colchester – Britain's First Roman Town* (Colchester Archaeological Trust, 1997)

4 Philip Crummy, *Aspects of Anglo-Saxon and Norman Colchester*, Colchester Archaeological Trust Report No. 1 (Colchester, 1981), pp.1–4

5 Martin Biddle, 'Excavations at Winchester, 1971: Tenth and Final Interim Report: Part I', *Antiquaries Journal*, No. 55, 1975, pp.96–126

6 Martin Biddle, 'Excavations at Winchester, 1962–63: Second Interim Report', *Antiquaries Journal*, No. 44, 1964, pp.188–219

7 Ibid., p.217

8 Martin Biddle and David Hill, 'Late Saxon Planned Towns', *Antiquaries Journal*, No. 51, 1971, pp.70–85

9 Martin Biddle, Daphne Hudson and Carolyn Heighway, *The Future of London's Past*, Rescue Publication No. 4 (Worcester, 1973)

10 Since the publication logjam was broken, a welcome series of overview articles has appeared in *Current Archaeology*, in issues 124 (1991), 158 (1998) and 162 (1999)

11 Taryn Nixon et al., *The Archaeology of Greater London: An Assessment of Archaeological Evidence for Human Presence in the Area now Covered by Greater London*, Museum of London Archaeology Service Monograph (not numbered) (London, 2000)

12 Alan Vince, 'The Aldwych: Mid-Saxon London Discovered?', *Current Archaeology*, No. 93, 1984, pp. 310–12

13 Gordon Malcolm, David Bowsher and Robert Cowie, *Middle Saxon London: Excavations at the Royal Opera House 1989–99*, MoLAS Monograph 15 (Museum of London, 2003)

14 The report on Lawrence Lane is expected shortly, but for an interim statement see Christopher Thomas, *The Archaeology of Medieval London* (Sutton Publishing, Stroud, 2002), pp.7–9

15 From the Foreword by Richard Hall to R.A. Hall et al., *Aspects of Anglo-Scandinavian York*, Archaeology of York, Vol. 8/4 (Council for British Archaeology, York, 2004)

16 For a clear introduction to cognitive archaeology see Renfrew and Bahn, op. cit., pp.393–428

17 R.A. Hall, 'Afterword', in Hall et al., 2004, op. cit., pp.498–502

18 Allan Hall and Harry Kenward, 'Setting People in the Environment: Plant and Animal Remains from Anglo-Scandinavian York', in ibid., pp.372–426

19 J.D. Richards, 1991, op. cit., p.48

CHAPTER FIVE — *Urban Life in the Middle Ages*

1 For an excellent summary of Malthus and the importance of population as a factor in the explanation of social change see Renfrew and Bahn, op. cit., p.485

2 Colin Platt, *King Death: The Black Death and its Aftermath in Late-Medieval England* (University of Toronto Press, 1997), p.17

3 Graham Hutton, *English Parish Churches* (Thames and Hudson, London, 1976), p.78

4 M.M. Postan, *The Medieval Economy and Society* (Weidenfeld and Nicolson, London, 1972); Platt, op. cit., p.14

5 Platt, op. cit., pp.19–31

6 Nikolaus Pevsner and John Harris, *The Buildings of England: Lincolnshire*, second edition (Penguin Books, Harmondsworth, 1989)

7 Renfrew and Bahn, op. cit., p.469, with references

8 John Schofield, 'Landscapes of the Middle Ages: Towns 1050–1500', in Hunter and Ralston, op. cit., p.226

9 Platt, op. cit., pp.22–3

10 R.A. Hall and K. Hunter-Mann, *Medieval Urbanism in Coppergate: Refining a Township*, The Archaeology of York, Vol. 10/6 (Council for British Archaeology, York, 2002)

11 *Britain AD*, pp.172–3

12 Nicholas Orme, *Medieval Children* (Yale University Press, New Haven, 2001)

13 L.F. Salzman, *Building in England Down to 1540: A Documentary History* (Clarendon Press, Oxford, 1952)

14 Ibid., p.325

15 Warwick Rodwell, *The Archaeology of Wells Cathedral: Excavations and Structural Studies 1978–93* (English Heritage, London, 2000)

16 Warwick Rodwell, *Church Archaeology* (B.T. Batsford/English Heritage, London, 1989), pp.123–4

17 The discussion of medieval building trades is based on ibid., pp 125–8

18 J.H. Williams, *St Peter's Street, Northampton, Excavations 1973–1976*, Archaeological Monograph No. 2 (Northampton Development Corporation, Northampton, 1979), pp.118–33

19 Thomas, op. cit., pp.4, 21, 67, 117

20 Eleven burials, possibly battle victims, were found on the foreshore of the River Fleet. See ibid., p.12

21 Southwark has been the subject of extensive archaeological research. See Heather Knight, *Aspects of Medieval and Later Southwark: Archaeological Excavations (1991–98) for the London Underground Limited Jubilee Line Extension Project*, Museum of London Archaeology Service Monograph No. 13 (London, 2002)

22 Bruce Watson, Trevor Brigham and Tony Dyson, *London Bridge: 2000 Years of a River Crossing*, Museum of London Archaeology Service Monograph No. 8 (London, 2001)

23 R.W. Brunskill, *Timber Building in England* (Victor Gollancz, London, 1985), p.71

24 Thomas, op. cit., pp.62–5

25 D. Keene, 'Medieval London and its Region', *London Journal*, Vol. 14, 1989, pp.99–111

26 John Schofield, *Medieval London Houses* (Yale University Press, New Haven and London, 1995); Anthony Quiney, *Town Houses of Medieval Britain* (Yale University Press, New Haven and London, 2003)

27 Schofield, 1995, op. cit., p.143

28 Mark Girouard, *Hardwick Hall* (The National Trust, London, 1989)

29 Christopher Thomas, Barney Sloane and Christopher Phillpotts, *Excavations at the Priory and Hospital of St Mary Spital, London*, Museum of London Archaeology Service Monograph No. 1 (London, 1997)

30 A. Selkirk, 'No. 1 Poultry', *Current Archaeology*, No. 158, 1998, pp.50–6

31 Thomas, op. cit., p.116

32 Hedley Swain et al., 'Shakespeare's Theatres', *Current Archaeology*, No. 124, 1991, pp.185–9

33 Thomas, op. cit., pp.122–5

CHAPTER SIX — *Rural Life in the Middle Ages*

1 Revised edition (Sutton Publishing, Stroud, 1989), p.66

2 Brian K. Roberts and Stuart Wrathmell, *An Atlas of Rural Settlement in England* (English Heritage, London, 2000), p.15

3 Lewis, Mitchell-Fox and Dyer, op. cit.

4 C. Phythian-Adams, *Re-Thinking English Local History* (Leicester University Press, 1987)

5 Perring, op. cit., p.28

6 The quotation is from the cover of Ann Williams and G.H. Martin (eds), *Domesday Book: A Complete Translation* (Penguin Books, Harmondsworth, 1992)

7 Ibid., p.1,436

8 Perring, op. cit., p.29

9 Platt, op. cit., pp.9–19

10 Ibid., p.10

11 Bellcotes are a feature of Norman churches in the area, and are also found at Peakirk and Werrington. See J.M. Steane, *The Northamptonshire Landscape* (Hodder and Stoughton, London, 1974), p.125

12 Stamper, op. cit., p.247

13 Maurice Beresford, *The Lost Villages of England*, revised edition with an Introduction by Christopher Dyer (Sutton Publishing, Stroud, 1998)

14 Maurice Beresford and John Hurst, *Wharram Percy Deserted Medieval Village* (English Heritage and B.T. Batsford Books, London, 1990)

15 Fiona Cooper, *The Black Poplar: Ecology, History and Conservation* (Windgather Press, Macclesfield, 2005)

16 Stamper, op. cit, p.256

17 Chris Dyer, 'Whittlewood: Revealing a Medieval Landscape', *Current Archaeology*, No. 182, 2002, pp.59–63

18 Ibid., p.63

19 Aston and Gerrard, op. cit., p.34

20 Tom Williamson, *Shaping Medieval Landscapes: Settlement, Society, Environment* (Windgather Press, Macclesfield, 2003)

21 N.J. Higham, *A Frontier Landscape: The North-West in the Middle Ages* (Windgather Press, Macclesfield, 2004)

22 Ibid., p.236

23 Ibid., p.241. John Leland was the first and only man to hold the position of King's Antiquary, to which he was appointed in 1533. He is principally remembered for a series of journeys he made to the regions of England and Wales, during which he noted local antiquities and made other perceptive observations, such as those noted here by Higham. For more on the history of archaeology see Glyn Daniel, *150 Years of Archaeology* (Duckworth, London, 1975); for a recent account of the earliest modern scholars see Rosemary Sweet, *Antiquaries: The Discovery of the Past in Eighteenth-Century Britain* (Hambledon and London, London, 2004)

CHAPTER SEVEN — *Trade, Industry and Security*

1 Bryony Coles (ed.), *The Wetland Revolution in Prehistory* (The Prehistoric Society, Exeter, 1992)

2 Gustav Milne and Brian Hobley, *Waterfront Archaeology in Britain and Northern Europe*, Council for British Archaeology Research Report No. 41 (London, 1981)

3 Colin Platt and Richard Coleman-Smith, *Excavations in Medieval Southampton 1953–1969*, two vols (Leicester University Press, 1975)

4 Platt in ibid., Vol. 1, p.35

5 Colin Platt, Richard Coleman-Smith and J.G. Hurst, Introduction to ibid., Vol. 2, pp.16–32

6 See *Britain AD*, pp.181–3

7 The Archaeology of York, Fascicule 17/13 (Council for British Archaeology, York, 2000)

8 For an excellent exception to this general rule see G.L. Good, R.H. Jones and M.W. Ponsford (eds), *Waterfront Archaeology: Proceedings of the Third International Conference, Bristol, 1988*, Council for British Archaeology Research Report No. 74 (London, 1991)

9 I discuss this site in *Britain BC* (HarperCollins, London, 2003), pp.149–50 and p.282; and see two colour plates between pp.272 and 273

10 In the discussion that follows I shall draw upon several of Gustav Milne's works, including 'London's Medieval Waterfront', *British Archaeology*, No. 68, 2002, pp.20–3; with Chrissie Milne, *Medieval Waterfront Development at Trig Lane, London*, London and Middlesex Archaeological Society Special Paper No. 5 (London, 1982); *Timber Building*

Technique in London c. 900–1400, London and Middlesex Archaeological Society Special Paper No. 15 (London, 1992)

11 Milne, 2002, op. cit., p.20

12 Milne and Milne, 1982, op. cit.

13 *Archaeological Journal*, Vol. 134, 1977, pp.287–96; *Vernacular Architecture*, Vol. 4, 1973, pp.18–21

14 Cecil Hewitt, *English Historic Carpentry* (Phillimore, London, 1980)

15 Ibid., p.161

16 Milne, 1992, op. cit.

17 P.V. Glob, *The Mound People: Danish Bronze Age Man Preserved* (Faber and Faber, London, 1974)

18 Francis Grew and Margrethe de Neergaard, *Shoes and Pattens* (Museum of London, 1988)

19 Milne, 2002, op. cit., p.23

20 Robert Liddiard, *Castles in Context: Power, Symbolism and Landscape 1066 to 1500* (Windgather Press, Macclesfield, 2005)

21 Ibid., p.84

22 Ibid., pp.133–4

23 A very useful book that draws together the historical and archaeological aspects of British medieval town walls has recently been published: Oliver Creighton and Robert Higham, *Medieval Town Walls: An Archaeology and Social History of Urban Defence* (Tempus Books, Stroud, 2005)

24 Ibid., p.99

25 Creighton and Higham, op. cit.

26 Elizabeth Ewan, *Townlife in Fourteenth-Century Scotland* (Edinburgh University Press, 1990), map 1

27 The argument is detailed in Creighton and Higham, op. cit., pp.217–18

28 I discuss the various issues surrounding hillforts in *Britain BC*, pp.353–67

29 Stamper, op. cit., p.261

30 Pevsner and Harris, op. cit., p.241

31 For a good example of a Romano-British timber bridge see D.A. Jackson and T.M. Ambrose, 'A Roman Timber Bridge at Aldwincle, Northamptonshire', *Britannia*, Vol. 7, 1976, pp.39–72

32 Lynden Cooper, Susan Ripper and Patrick Clay, 'The Hemington Bridges', *Current Archaeology*, No. 140, 1994, pp.316–21

33 Marilyn Palmer and Peter Neaverson, *Industry in the Landscape, 1700–1900* (Routledge, London, 1994)

34 Stamper, op. cit., p.248

35 For an excellent summary of recent work see Granville Clay, Gerry McDonnell, Bonwell Spence and Robert Vernon (eds), *The Iron Makers of Myers Wood – a Medieval Enterprise in Kirkburton Huddersfield: An Archaeological Summary* (Huddersfield and District Archaeological Society, 2004)

CHAPTER EIGHT — *The End of the Middle Ages?*

1 The standard account of Fenland drainage is still that by the late Professor H.C. Darby, *The Draining of the Fens* (Cambridge University Press, 1940)

2 I discuss the 'discovery' of Arthur's tomb in *Britain AD*, pp.35–6

3 Glyn Coppack, *Abbeys and Priories* (Batsford/English Heritage, London, 1990), p.129

4 Mick Aston, *Monasteries in the Landscape* (Tempus Books, Stroud, 2000); Coppack, op. cit.; Colin Platt, *The Abbeys and Priories of Medieval England* (originally published 1984, republished 1995 by Chancellor Press, London)

5 Graham Keevill, Mick Aston and Teresa Hall (eds), *Monastic Archaeology: Papers on the Study of Medieval Monasteries* (Oxbow Books, Oxford, 2001)

6 Glyn Coppack, 'Fountains Abbey: Archaeological Research Directed by Conservation and Preservation', in ibid., pp.175–82

7 J. Patrick Greene, 'Strategies for Future Research and Site Investigation', in ibid., p.7

8 Lines 259–65 of the General Prologue to the *Canterbury Tales*. From F.N. Robinson (ed.), *The Works of Geoffrey Chaucer* (Oxford University Press, 1957)

9 Coppack, 1990, op. cit., pp.129–33

10 Anne Ward, *The Lincolnshire Rising 1536* (Louth Naturalists', Antiquarian and Literary Society, 1996)

11 David Gaimster and Roberta Gilchrist (eds), *The Archaeology of the Reformation 1480–1580* (Maney, Leeds, 2003)

12 Gaimster and Gilchrist, 'Introduction. History from Below: The Archaeology of the English Reformation 1480–1580', in ibid., p.1

13 Roberta Gilchrist, '"Dust to Dust": Revealing the Reformation Dead', in ibid., pp.399–414

14 Hall and Hunter-Mann, op. cit., pp.864–5

15 Ibid., p.865

16 Thomas, op. cit., pp.167–71

INDEX

(Figures in italic refer to illustrations)